CLIMBING
SCHOOL

CLIMBING
SCHOOL

JOHN BARRY AND ROGER MEAR

CONTRIBUTORS

A QUANTUM BOOK

Published by
Quantum Publishing Ltd
6 Blundell Street
London N7 9BH

Copyright © MCMLXXXVIII
Quarto Publishing plc

This edition printed 2003

ISBN 1-86160-497-1

QUMCLS

Printed in Singapore
by Star Standard Industries Pte Ltd

KIM CARRIGAN Has been at the forefront of Australian climbing for several years, helping to popularize one of the sport's least well-known arenas.

DAVID CHEESMOND In May 1987 David Cheesmond died on Mt Logan's Hummingbird Ridge, which had been climbed successfully only once before. He had made ascents of Everest and K2 the previous year, and climbed the east ridge of Alaska's Mt Deborah with John Barry, Roger Mear and Rob Collister in 1983.

ROB COLLISTER An expert on the peaks of the Himalayas, his first visit was to Swat Kohistan in 1968. Since then Rob Collister has climbed and travelled in Chitral, Gilgit, Kishtware, Kulu, Zanskar, Nepal and Tibet. His skills have also taken him to Antarctica, Greenland, Alaska, Argentina and Kenya, as well as all over Britain and the Alps. After eight years at Plas-y-Brenin, Wales, National Centre for Mountain Activities, Rob Collister is now a freelance mountain guide.

PETE GOMERSHALL Has tackled most of the major European ranges, gaining special expertise in Italian, French and German climbing.

BRIAN HALL Highly respected by his peers for his climbing exploits all over the world, he has made South America his favourite venue.

JOHN HARLIN III Author of the three-volume *Climber's Guide to North America*, John Harlin has been climbing for 25 years. His main area of expertise is in North America; and he has made many first cross-country ski-descents. Dividing his time between climbing, writing, teaching and guiding, Harlin is Associate Editor of *Backpackers* and Executive Editor of *Ski XC*.

STEVE LONG A life-long interest in Scandinavia has made Steve Long an acknowledged authority on the peaks of Sweden and Norway.

DES MARSHALL Brought up in the Lake District in the UK, Des Marshall has been climbing since the age of 15, concentrating on Scottish, Welsh and Irish peaks.

NIGEL SHEPHERD One of Britain's most experienced mountaineers who has travelled widely in pursuit of his vocation as guide and instructor. He is a member of the International Association of Mountain Guides and was for a time the Training Officer to the Association of British Mountain Guides. For many years associated with the National Mountaineering Centre in north Wales and now runs his own business specializing in worldwide adventure programmes.

STEPHEN VENABLES Upheld by other climbers as one of the leading mountaineers of our generation, Stephen Venables describes himself as a 'writer, photographer, mountaineer'. He is the author of *Painted Mountains,* which won the 1986 Boardman and Tasker prize (award for best mountaineering literature). His wide-ranging climbing experience includes Xixia Pangma, highest peak in China, and Everest in 1988.

Contents

INTRODUCTION

The term 'mountaineering' embraces 'games' as diverse as scrambling, bouldering and alpinism. No matter that the scramble is along a breeze-brushed ridge of no great height or steepness; or that the boulder is only 3m (10ft) high and drenched in sun; or, at the other end of the scale, that the 'alp' is in the Himalayas, rises to 6,000m (20,000ft) and the route is 2,000 vertical metres (6,500ft) of stone-swept, north-facing ice and rock; by some thread, spiritual and physical, all these games (and many more) together comprise a greater game – a sport, maybe – that we call mountaineering.

We will begin with hill walking. That is perhaps the place where most embark. And just how far you journey along the mountaineering game's chain depends largely on inclination. There are no rules. One of the delights of mountaineering is that within its broad and ill-defined boundaries, you can wander at your own pace, in any company, anywhere, and in any direction.

You don't even have to begin with hill walking. There are those who have started in the Alps and worked towards hill walking – because age, perhaps, drew in their furthest horizons (though it doesn't necessarily have to). There are those who began in the Alps and went straight away to the Himalayas, where they have played their game ever since. And there are those who have done it all differently, as well as those who have done *none* of these things yet still play a mountaineering game with fervour. Some who have done *all* these things nevertheless consider themselves to be dilettantes and try hard not to try too hard!

The aim of this book is to supply sufficient knowledge for you to begin safely. A book, any book, can teach only so much: the greater teacher is experience. We hope this book will be useful as well as entertaining, but the *required reading*, the absolutely essential reading, will not be found in its pages – nor in those of any other manual: it is to be found only out on hill or rock. You write it yourself through your own experience and adventure.

Knowledge gleaned from within these covers should better prepare you to make the most of that experience, better equip you to reap reward from the adventure. True satisfaction is not to be found in courting unknown dangers for which you are ill prepared, but in matching your own skill and experience against danger and difficulties of which you are aware.

Read this book, or any of its sections, a dozen times, and you will still not be master of the game; but you will be master of the first step. After that, your guides must be a judicious mixture, for which there is no fixed recipe, of ambition, ability and experience – though you can always return to the book to refresh your memory, relearn things you may have forgotten, or just read on.

Sun, rock, snow, summits — the essence of mountaineering.

Edward Whymper once wrote: 'Climb if you will, but remember that courage and strength are naught without prudence, and that momentary negligence may destroy the happiness of a lifetime. Do nothing in haste, look well to each step, and from the beginning think what may be the end.'

The prudence, the looking well to each step, of which Whymper wrote can begin in earnest among these next pages. Here you may learn enough about those skills and equipment that you will need to run riot through the hills, walking, camping, scrambling, climbing; that will lead you to the mountains and then bring you home again; and that will allow you to enjoy all of these things, bringing indeed the happiness of a lifetime.

'Look well to each step' – but with no more than a pocketful of simply acquired skills you can be afforded a lifetime's adventure.

Above British hills can be transformed by snow any time from October to May, although even in midwinter the snow can disappear just as dramatically. A dusting of snow low down means a depth of snow higher up, so you should carry ice axe and crampons. **Left** A flower-filled meadow — one of the joys of alpine walking.

WALKING SKILLS

Scree running can be fun – but also dangerous to yourself and others. Never run so fast that you get out of control; if in a group, descend diagonally to avoid kicking stones down onto each other. Good scree runs are today something of a rarity in all the popular regions – all the stones have already been tumbled to the bottom!

Walking comes naturally to us all – usually at between 9 and 18 months old – and fortunately there is not much more to walking in the hills than doing what comes naturally. The only overall advice worth offering is to go slowly at the beginning of the day – you can always speed up at the end of it if you have the need, energy or inclination. Go rhythmically, too, in a sustained and steady plod, rather than in spurts, which are far more tiring and over the course of a full day take you no further than a steadily maintained pace would have done.

As far as possible, walk as if you are out shopping or on a stroll to the pub – perhaps not that fast! Loose, easy – lazy, almost. Try to avoid conscious effort. On steep ground shorten the step, slow the rhythm (but try to maintain one) and place your feet flat wherever possible – walking up-hill on your toes is exhausting on the calves after more than a few metres. Try to put your feet down in areas of local flatness, even if they are less than the full size of your foot, rather than on places which are at a slope: rocks, stones and tufts of grass may provide such areas of flatness. If the slope is very steep it is probably best to zigzag. Strike a good rhythm and set your feet well and you will walk all day with ease.

Take it steady in descent too. It is easy to jar a foot through taking an overlong bound, or to stub a toe on a rock. You can use the downhill as a rest period if you wish or run if you prefer. Scree running is great fun: arms wide for balance, and away you go. Unfortunately it is bad for boots and bottoms if you slip. Be thoughtful of those beneath you on the scree and beware those above: a tumbling stone can make a dent in more than morale. Small gravel-sized scree gives runs that are tremendous sport; larger stones are harder, more painful work. Experiment. You will soon learn which screes 'run' and which do not. If you are descending a convex slope it is advisable to consult the map to check that no crags or other obstacles are hidden in the convexity.

CHOOSING GROUND

Selecting the best line calls for judgement, which comes from experience. Some tips are:
● Paths usually take the easiest line; short-cutting them is often pointless, but they may be difficult to follow across bogs, under snow or in thick mist.
● Loose rock and big scree can be unpleasant – even dangerous. Slow down, move together and move carefully. Do not throw loose stones – there may be other people below. If a stone is inadvertently dislodged, shout 'Below!' to warn anyone who may be beneath.
● Steep grass and rock slabs can be treacherous when wet or covered in snow. Be careful: it is sometimes hard to stop, especially in poor footwear or when wearing waterproofs, which slide with alarming ease on wet surfaces.
● Zigzag up steep slopes, and avoid climbing straight up on the toes. Keep heels down and place feet flat if possible.
● Keep an eye on the weather and make your decisions before the weather makes them for you. A day in the rain can be a most satisfying experience for a properly equipped walker, but a disaster for the ill-equipped and unwary. Wet, cold weather increases the risk of exposure, the causes, symptoms and treatment of which are dealt with on page 32.

USING A ROPE

Unless you already have some experience of rock climbing – or you want to go scrambling (page 39) – try to choose walks that avoid ground that is 'ropeworthy'. There are few areas where fine walks cannot be completed entirely without the use of a rope and fewer where, should a rope become necessary, an alternative way cannot be found. Indeed it might be said that if a rope becomes necessary then a poor route has been chosen – though that is scant consolation at the time. The section on scrambling has a lot more to say on the subject. If you choose to carry a rope for safety then 25m (80ft) of 9mm should suffice.

11

RIVER CROSSING

Heavy rain may turn a friendly stream into a dangerous torrent. River crossing should not be undertaken lightly; rivers are powerful forces. When in doubt, look for a bridge, go upstream in search of an easier crossing, or wait. If you must cross, prepare as follows:

● Remove trousers to reduce drag and so that they will still be dry when you reach the other side.
● Keep boots on. Socks may be removed to keep them dry.

● Release the hip belt of your rucksack and ensure that you can off-load it quickly if necessary.
● Use a branch or pole as a third leg, or go arm in arm with a companion.
● Face upstream.
● It is usually safest to cross between bends – not on them.
● The water is usually shallower and the flow slower where the river widens. Safe places are often where the river splits into channels.
● Remember, after crossing your team may be cold and dispirited.

Left This river is not deep but it is fast-flowing and its current is powerful, so the task of crossing it must be treated with some respect. *Below* Some methods of crossing fast-flowing rivers. Groups of two and three are much safer than a single person. Green arrows indicate direction of travel, black arrows direction of flow.

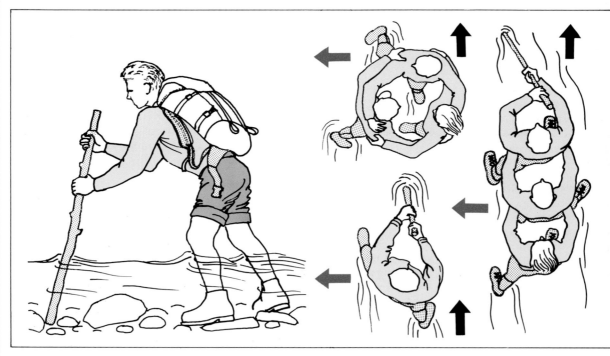

CLOTHING

Clothing for hill walking must do two things: it must provide protection from rain, snow and wind, and it must provide warmth by way of *insulation* from the cold, by retaining body-warmed air close to the skin and around the body. Clothes should at the same time be strong and light, and allow unrestricted movement. In ideal circumstances the waterproof/windproof shell should 'breathe', so as to allow the body's water vapour to escape and thus avoid condensation. So many requirements of one set of clothing pose a tall order to manufacturers. Sometimes compromises have to be struck, as between, for example, lightness and durability, or between waterproofness and breathability. Cost comes into it, too. There is no perfect solution, no ideal clothing range, but an understanding of the principles of keeping warm and dry, and the characteristics of the materials that do those things, will help you find a personally acceptable combination.

UNDERWEAR LAYER

This provides some insulation, but its main job is to lessen the chilling effect of moisture on the surface of the skin, the unavoidable product of activity. (Insulation is provided by the next series of layers.)

In hot weather, loose, absorbent material is preferred by most. Air flows freely between skin and cloth, cooling and drying, while excess sweat is absorbed into the material. Cotton is a good material for wear in hot weather; silk too.

However, in cool weather a different set of rules apply. The under-layer should be snug, so that no air flows freely between it and the skin, and all the moisture (given off as water vapour even before you begin sweating) is absorbed or conducted by your underwear.

People have strong feelings about the best material for underwear. In fact, there is probably no such thing as the ideal underwear. It is largely a matter of preference—and some prejudice. There are two broad categories: natural fibres and man-made fibres. Natural fibres like silk or wool absorb moisture, retain their loft and therefore their thermal properties when wet, and even when wet can feel friendly to bare skin (unlike wet cotton). Synthetics, like polypropylene, on the other hand work by repelling water. Therefore, to function properly, polypropylene must be thin and tightish on the skin—a second skin—so that sweat can be physically transported through it in a 'wicking' action. The more you perspire, the more effective is this transport of moisture.

Underwear should be kept clean—not merely for social reasons but because clean underwear is warmer than dirty. Dirt lessens the effectiveness of natural fibres by clogging and matting them, thereby reducing their capacity to hold air. Similarly, dirt and body salts interfere with the 'wicking' properties of such fabrics as polypropylene so that you get damper than you need—and colder. Cleanliness may or may not be next to godliness, but it's certainly close to warmth.

INSULATING LAYERS

As a general rule, thickness is warmth. Nylon fleece, polyester silk and fibres, goose-down and wool all have much the same insulation efficiency if they are of identical thickness and if they are dry. (Some high-density forms and synthetics like Thinsulate are an exception to the thickness = warmth rule, and give roughly twice as much insulation per centimetre of thickness.) But all of them have pros and cons, which may be summarized as follows:

Down
Weight for warmth, the lightest. Weight for weight, the warmest. Easily compressed. Expensive. Almost useless when wet. Long time drying. Long-lasting – a lifetime if cared for.

Synthetic Fibres (Hollofil, Qualofil, Isodry, etc.)
Heavier than down for equal warmth. Less expensive. Dry relatively easily. Cheaper than down. Bulkier than down. Life expectancy of 3 or 4 years.

You can see that it is largely a matter of 'you pays your money and you takes your choice'. If you live in a very cold climate, you might opt for down; if you take your recreation in the British hills, with their wet and their cold, you ought to consider a synthetic filling.

The traditional material for body insulation is wool. Woollen shirts, trousers, socks, sweaters, mittens and hats are commonly available and still make good hill clothing. Wool holds air within its fibres: air is a good insulator; therefore, wool is warm. Any material that holds air—fibre pile, the down in down jackets—will give warmth.

It is an advantage if your insulating layers are designed and worn in such a way that you can regulate the temperature. This is most easily done by opening or closing fastenings at neck, waist and wrist – and sometimes underarm – or by the removal of an article of clothing, a pullover perhaps. And herein lies an important principle, that of layering the insulation. For example, two thin pullovers worn together are both warmer and more useful than a single thick one because they incorporate three layers of air, two within the pullovers and one between, and because a single pullover can be only on or off: two levels of heat regulation. Two pullovers, on the other hand, offer three permutations.

A host of modern materials made from artificial fibres have to some extent superseded wool, if not in pure efficiency then certainly as far as cost and convenience are concerned. Such fabrics as fibre pile, Polarplus and fleece are usually lighter than wool, quicker drying and cheaper.

At the last, however, it is personal preference, allied to some initial experience, that makes the selection. Some general principles are:

● Several thin layers are warmer and more versatile than one thick.

● Cover the whole body if need be, including legs, hands and head. Legs represent about a half of total average body surface area. You can't afford to ignore them. And as much as 20 per cent of body heat can be lost through the head. When *overheating* this might be a desirable thing – a good way to ventilate. Treat the head as a thermos flask, to be capped or uncapped according to temperature!

● Hats should be generous enough to pull over the ears and, preferably, over the neck too. A Balaclava is ideal.

● Mittens are warmer than gloves – in them fingers store a 'commingling heat'.

● Jeans are generally too tight and inflexible for comfortable hill walking. Furthermore, they are made of cotton, which gives no warmth when wet. Nor are they windproof.

● Insulating clothing should be snug, but not too tight (tightness restricts movement and, in some cases, the blood supply) nor too loose, lest the clothing flaps or bellows and spills out precious warm air.

Salopettes and jacket made of fibre pile. The mittens have a Gore-Tex outer layer and a fibre-pile inner.

PROTECTIVE LAYER

Your insulation needs to be protected from the wind and from the rain (and snow). In still air a shell adds something to the total warmth of any system of clothing: in windy weather a wind shell will contribute as much as 10C° to the general warmth.

Three basic kinds of fabric are used in the construction of shell garments:

1. Cloth that is windproof but not waterproof, and which allows water vapour (from the body) to evaporate through the material; e.g., uncoated nylon, cotton or blends of these fabrics.
2. Cloth that is both windproof and waterproof, and which does not allow water vapour to pass through; e.g., urethene-coated nylons.
3. Cloth that is windproof and waterproof, but transmits water vapour from the inside to the outside. Fabrics such as Gore-Tex and Entrant achieve this by 'breathing' through micropores which allow water vapour to pass out but which do not let water in. The same effect is achieved by an entirely different process in fabrics such as Sympatex which work on a hydrophilic principle.

Above A *waterproof, insulated jacket.* *Below* Down *jackets provide little insulation when wet.*

If no rain is expected you can save money and weight by opting for a comfortable, breathable, non-waterproof windshell – cotton or ventile perhaps. In wet conditions you will want something from category **2** or **3**. Garments in category **2** will protect you from the rain, but you will get damp from condensation during heavy work or when walking hard – which is still probably preferable to a soak in the rain. Garments in category **3** are not the panacea they seem, nor as their accompanying blurb will claim: they are very expensive and work well only when not coated in a film of water – as they will be when it is raining – the very time that you want them to work! There is no perfect waterproof – yet.

Waterproof tops – anoraks – of any material should be roomy enough to pull over bulky warm clothing. The longer the garment, the greater the protection afforded. Other desirable factors to bear in mind when making your choice are: an ample hood, windproof cuffs, taped seams (especially on Gore-Tex or one of its relatives), and perhaps a zipped map pocket – though zips often allow water in as well as hands.

Legs need a shell too, so a pair of windproof or waterproof trousers will be required. It is worth checking that you can bend your legs in them – and, ideally, pull them on over boots. To this end, a zip in the lower leg is probably the answer.

Sensible clothing might be:

Socks
Clean, thick wool. One pair should be enough.

Trousers
Thick in winter, light in summer. Loose fitting, giving the legs freedom. Old flannels or tracksuit trousers (perhaps backed up by longjohns of polypropylene or light wool) are good. Or breeches, less than fashionable these days, but practical nevertheless.

Underclothes
Longjohns in wool or polyester or polypropylene, plus vest of the same.

Sweaters
Wool or pile and as many as the day demands. (These days shirts and sweaters are virtually indistinguishable and usually interchangeable.)

Gloves/Mittens
Wool or pile.

Hat/Cap/Balaclava
Wool or pile or fleece.

Windproof/Waterproof Jacket
Windproof/Waterproof Pants

15

EQUIPMENT

Even on the easiest of walks a party bound for rough country should consider carrying among them – or, better still, individually – the various articles referred to in the checklist on page 38.

DAY SACKS

A small day sack is a useful item on all but the shortest of walks. A simple single-compartment sack, with perhaps a pocket in the lid for easy access to those things most likely to be needed – chocolate, plasters, knife, gloves – and a back padded and stiffened with a closed-cell mat such as a Karrimat, is sufficient. (For longer walks, or planned camps, a bigger and better sack is desirable; for more on these, see page 37.)

If you are not wearing your anorak and overtrousers, it is a good idea to keep them near the top of the sack where they can be easily withdrawn without disturbing the remainder of the contents.

A typical day sack. Note the adjustable straps on the back for holding ice axes and the side-straps for carrying ice axes, a shovel or skis.

BOOTS

Good boots need to be neither expensive nor heavy, but should have a composition-rubber sole designed for the mountains. Boots have undergone something of a revolution in recent years and a dazzling, even confusing, selection is available. Most good mountain-equipment shops will offer sound advice.

When choosing a pair, spend some time in ensuring a good fit; too small will cramp, too large will blister. Boots are best fitted with thick, soft hill socks on. As a general rule, choose the lightest pair of boots that will do the job. For very easy walks, good training shoes are fine.

Some kinds of modern boots need little or no 'breaking in', but if you select a traditional pair of leather boots, then break them in slowly by wearing them for a few hours each day. *Never* attempt a full day's walk in brand new, stiff boots.

After getting wet, boots should not be dried rapidly close to a fire or by artificial heat; instead, leave them in a draught or place them in the sun. If possible, hasten drying and keep them in shape by stuffing them with newspapers.

If hill walking is your immediate aim, it is not necessary to wear a pair of stiff-soled heavy boots of the type designed for mountaineering, which are able to accommodate crampons when needed. Choose instead a supple-soled pair. You will have to choose between leather or plastic and perhaps synthetics. Lightweight leather boots are still probably the best bet for hill walking. Some features that are worth looking for are a comfortable, padded ankle, a cleated sole, D-ring or hook lacing, and a broad fit.

A NOTE ON FEET

Feet need maintaining and looking after too. Wear your boots, even old ones, for a day or two around the house or at work before going on a long walk, especially if it is some time since you were last out in them. Feet and boots need to be reintroduced after absences. Treat your feet to clean socks. They are warmer and much more comfortable. Ensure that socks, whether you prefer one or two pairs, are smooth about the feet. A fold or rough edge leads all too readily to blisters. Keep the toenails short. They do not do anything useful inside a boot and long ones are easily (and painfully) bruised, and can also cause cuts in adjacent toes which, in turn, may lead to infection.

If, despite all precautions, your boots rub during an outing, *stop at once* and apply a large plaster smoothly over the rubbed area before it becomes a blister. Make certain, when you replace your sock, that the edges of the plaster are not turned and that it lies smooth and flat underneath. Areas of foot that have been troublesome one day may be worth taping the next day before you set out. A blister is best treated by piercing carefully with a needle sterilized

Below *A good-quality hill-walking boot. Note the well padded ankle.*

Right *Food for a camping trip. Everything is packed in polythene bags or plastic containers.*

by holding it in the flame of a match for a few seconds. Improvise a ring plaster from chiropody felt and sticking plaster in order to keep pressure off the blister. If the blister has been torn, cut away the surplus skin with a sterilized razor or sharp knife before applying the ring plaster.

FOOD AND DRINK

Have a hearty breakfast before you set out and take something rich in carbohydrates for lunch – sandwiches, biscuits, jam, chocolate, nuts, raisins, cake, etc. Eating between meals may be discouraged at home but it is commendable on the hill, gradually replacing a little of the energy you are expending. Another good habit is to carry some emergency food which, like your first aid kit, should live in the top of your rucksack. This might be chocolate, sweets, glucose tablets, dried fruit – anything that will provide quick energy.

Morale boosters can be provided by a hot drink from a thermos. Try sweet tea, coffee, soup or orange juice. In summer, take plenty of liquid to ward off dehydration, drinking little but often.

Here is a list of foods that make good meals in the hills. They are nutritious, robust, compact and simple to prepare. Experiment to taste. The list is not exhaustive:

Food for main meals on camp Bacon, sausages, small tins of meat or fish, continental boiling sausage, egg (fresh or dried), quick packet soup, tomato purée, salt, pepper, herbs, dried milk, cheese, pasta, cous-cous, bulgar wheat, dehydrated potato, quick cook rice, porridge, muesli, granola, dried custard mix, fruit pudding, Christmas pudding.

There is also a variety of dehydrated meals available in supermarkets and camping shops. For occasional meals, they are satisfactory, though not appetizing or nutritious enough to serve as a staple diet. If used, they can be improved with fresh onion, garlic, green pepper, etc.

Food for lunches and snacks Cheese, cream cheese, sardines, etc., pork pie, salami and other cooked or dried sausages, margarine/butter, bread, honey, ham, peanut butter, oatcakes, flapjacks, fruitcake, shortbread, dried fruit (raisins, apricots, bananas, pears, etc.), fruit and nut mixes, 'trail mix', muesli bars, condensed milk, sweets and chocolate.

Remove all unnecessary packaging before carrying the food into the hills. Food in glass jars is best repacked into plastic containers, which are softer and lighter. Bring all litter out from the hills. Litter is a public nuisance, and spoils the enjoyment of all climbers.

ROUTE FINDING AND NAVIGATION

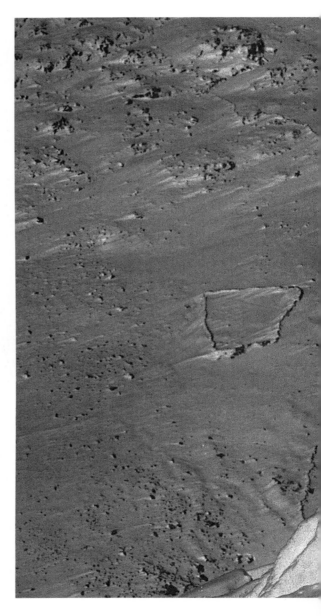

Good navigation is an essential hill skill; being lost is not much fun for very long. The key to good navigation is the ability to read a map, for properly interpreted a map will tell you where you are and where to go – and it will tell you much about the way too. The sections that follow are concerned with the wherewithal of navigation – map reading, maps, the compass and the coordination of map and compass – but all of that will not on its own teach you how to navigate. To reading you must add practice and experience before you can learn to navigate – and navigate well. Some hints on navigation are:

● Keep your map handy – either actually in your hand or in an easily accessible pocket. A map will tell you nothing from the depths of a rucksack.

● Refer to the map frequently, and certainly during rests or at natural breaks such as on the crossing of a feature – a stream, wall, or path. If you are unsure of your position, stop and work it out. Don't rush. You shouldn't be far off your planned route if you have been using the map often enough. Try to decide where it was that you were last certain of your position and then, recalling the ground you have recently covered since that point, try to match it to the map (not the other way around). Feed time and distance into your calculations too and try to work out where it is you must be now. Then you might decide to:

1. Retrace your steps to your last certain point and begin again.

2. Look for a safe way down.

3. If completely lost, aim for a feature that runs laterally across your likely path on the map – a wall, stream, road or railway. Once you reach this you should soon be able to establish your position once more.

If, when aiming for this lateral feature, a secondary aim is to arrive at a precise spot along it – e.g., a junction or a house – then it is better to deliberately 'aim off', so that on gaining the lateral feature you know whether to turn left or right to walk to your chosen spot (see page 29).

Don't rely on a sense of direction. Humans have a natural tendency to walk in a circle and a so-called 'sense of direction' is more wishful thinking than natural fact. When you move off from your last spot, keep a careful eye on the compass bearing and count paces so that, in the event of your becoming lost again, you can at least safely retrace your steps to that spot.

Getting lost is time consuming and it can be a nerve-racking business, so it is better to work hard at map reading and navigation along the way.

● Get into the habit of doing your own navigation even if those about you seem to be more adept. It's hard to improve when others are doing the work.

● Another good habit is to orientate your map before consulting it – that is, to line it up with features on the ground so that they and their representations on the map correspond.

You can practise at home, too. Try:

● Making a game of studying the maps of a recently completed walk and comparing your version of the experience with the tale told by the map.

● Studying the map in preparation for a coming trip.

Where are the paths, the streams, the steep bits? Are there dangerous cliffs or obstacles of any sort?

● Comparing the same outing on two maps of different scales.

● Studying the information shown in the map's margins — scales, contour intervals, conventional signs, grid references, grid, true and magnetic norths and so on. Each is a piece that helps to transform the jigsaw from puzzle to picture.

Walkers pick their way down a broken slope in winter. On this sort of terrain good route finding is of the utmost importance. Think ahead, take care, and be prepared to retrace your steps if necessary.

MAPS

Maps are pictures; but formalized, two-dimensional pictures of three-dimensional subjects. They hold hundreds of thousands of bits of information – but not all the information that every interested party might wish for: that would be impossible. Indeed most maps in general use are compromises between the often conflicting needs of various groups of users: motorists, canoeists, hill walkers, picnickers, ramblers, farmers – and all the rest. They all want precise, but different, things of a map. Maps are not made for the exclusive use of hill walkers and mountaineers – although many hill walkers and most mountaineers think either that they are or, at the very least, that they should be.

Because there is often more information that ideally should be included than there is room for, cartographers have developed a representative code, a sort of shorthand, that reduces common features – a church or a crag, for example – to symbols. It is worth getting to know these symbols well – they are standard for any given series – because some of the symbols are unavoidably similar and it is not difficult when tired, or in a hurry, or in the rain, to confuse symbols such as those for a footpath and a parish boundary. The result of such an error could be very inconvenient.

POPULAR SCALES

Scale	Meaning	Use
1:10,000	1cm = 100m	Orienteering
1:25,000	1cm = 250m	Ideal for walking, but you may require more than one map to cover your area
1:50,000	1cm = 500m	The most popular map for walking
1:63,360	1in = 1 mile	Now replaced by 1:50,000 maps
1:100,000	1cm = 1,000m	Cycling, hostelling, holidaying route selection
1:250,000	1cm = 2,500m	Cycling, motoring, etc.
1:1,000,000	1cm = 10km	Map of UK

CARE OF YOUR MAP

Some Ordnance Survey maps of the Leisure Series are now produced with a protective skin. Usually, though, you will have to protect your map, either by covering it with a transparent adhesive film such as 'transeal' or, more simply, by keeping it in a polythene bag or clear plastic envelope, having first folded the map in such a way that the day's route is exposed.

WHICH MAP?

Maps come in many scales and many sizes. The most popular and useful scales for hill walking and mountaineering in the British Isles are 1:50,000 (2cm = 1km), such as the Ordnance Survey Landranger Series, which cover a relatively larger area fairly cheaply, and the 1:25,000 (4cm = 1km) of which there are several series in Britain – the Outdoor Leisure and the Pathfinder series being designed with hill walkers and mountaineers in mind. Clearly the second and larger scale shows greater detail than the first – though only a quarter of the ground area on the same-sized map.

THE NATIONAL GRID

Most maps are overprinted with a grid of lines, most countries have their own grid system, and most systems operate identically – or very nearly so. On Ordnance Survey maps the grid lines are 1km apart. It is therefore possible to give every spot in the country (with an area not less than 100m square) a unique reference number.

The diagram opposite shows how Britain is divided into large squares 100km × 100km (100km = 62 miles). Each of these is subdivided into smaller squares, 1km × 1km (1km = 5/8 mile). The grid is based on two main axes which are in fact a convenient line of latitude – 49°N – for the horizontal axis, and a convenient line of longitude – 20°W – for the vertical axis. Grid lines are rectilinear and therefore differ from lines of latitude and longitude, the difference increasing with the distance from the axes. There is only one grid line which points to true north; the one which coincides with the 20°W line of longitude. All remaining vertical grid lines vary slightly from true north. This difference is shown in the map margin. It is never more than about 3°, though as we shall see shortly the difference between grid north and true north is, for the purpose of map reading and navigation, purely academic. Because grid lines are individually numbered it is possible to identify a particular 1km square by giving the number allocated to the two lines which bound it to west and to south.

The vertical lines, called 'eastings' because they are numbered eastwards, are always given first, followed by the horizontal lines, called 'northings' because they are numbered northwards. By another subdivision, coordinates for 100m squares can be given. A grid reference therefore refers to an area 100m × 100m and not to a point on the ground.

SETTING A MAP TO THE GROUND

Because a map is a plan picture of a particular piece of ground it is possible to align it in such a way that, with yourself as the pivotal point, features on the map and ground correspond. This is called setting or orientating the

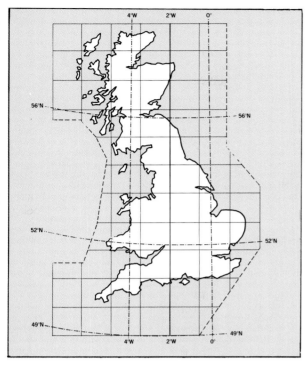

IN PLAN

Metres

Sea level
IN SECTION

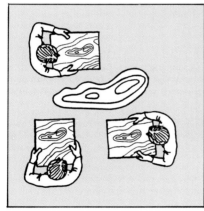

Above The
National Grid.
Right Walking
with a map set
on a natural
feature. **Far
right** Lliewedd,
on Snowdon.
Top right How
contours relate
to the landscape:
Lliewedd,
assuming 10m
contour intervals.

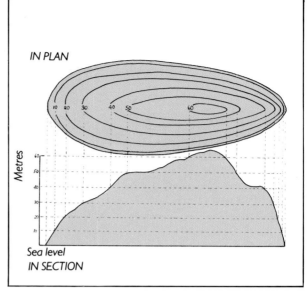

map, and it is fundamental to map reading. (The same result can be achieved, perhaps more speedily, with a compass – see page 24.) Map and ground will now combine in eye and mind to give you a vivid picture of what lies immediately ahead – and well beyond.

If you are walking along a linear feature – say a stream or path – it may be unnecessary to spend time in identifying surrounding features in order to set the map. Instead, turn the map until the real path or stream line up with the path or stream on the map. When on the move always set the map before consulting it. That is the way in which a map should be read – even though it might take some getting used to because, as you look at the map, place names will often be upside down. But they are far less important than the terrain, knowledge of which can be gained from the map only once it has been set.

RELIEF
The height, slope and steepness of ground is brought into relief on a map by means of lines known as contours. Imagine an incoming tide leaving a 'tidemark' at every metre of height gained. This is what contours are to dry ground, except that the height between 'tidemarks', or the 'contour interval' as it is called, varies according to the type and scale of map. In Britain this interval is soon to be standardized at 10m with a thickened contour every 50m. The contour interval will always be advertised in the margin of the map. When looking at a map you should be able to build up a three-dimensional picture of the slope of the ground by studying the contours. To help you, the peak shown above is illustrated in plan and in section.

As you will appreciate from these diagrams, the closer the contour lines, the steeper the slope – and vice versa. On very steep ground the contours will get so close as to be nearly indistinguishable. Steeper than that and the space is so constricted that contours are left out. Shapes characteristic of mountains – ridges, crests, cols, convex and concave slopes – will soon leap from the page and into the mind's eye. Then you will be map reading.

THE COMPASS

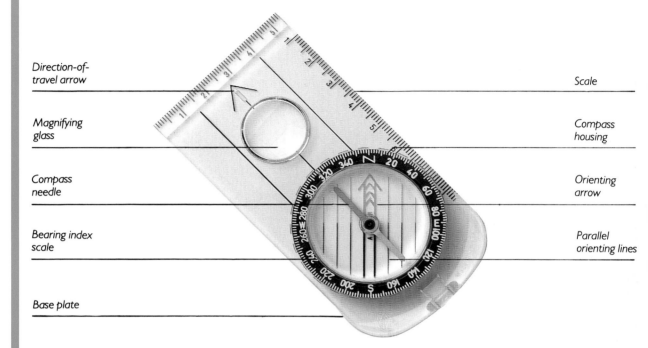

Direction-of-travel arrow

Magnifying glass

Compass needle

Bearing index scale

Base plate

Scale

Compass housing

Orienting arrow

Parallel orienting lines

The Vikings navigated the Atlantic by suspending a magnetized bar on a string. This showed them where north lay. Things have not changed greatly. Even today the most modern compasses are little more than magnetized bars suspended in the earth's magnetic field. In poor visibility or on the move at night, a hill walker or mountaineer cannot afford to be without a compass. Even on a clear day they are an indispensable aid to accurate navigation.

For our purposes, the compass need be only a fairly simple affair: light and compact, yet robust enough to shrug off bumps and knocks. The most common compasses for hill use are probably those of the Silva range – though there are other manufacturers whose compasses are equally good: Sunto is one such.

The best type of compass is the one in which the movements of the needle are dampened through the fact that it is floating in oil. It settles more quickly that way, and remains steadier on its bearing when you are walking by compass. Other desirable features are a scale marked in millimetres and centimetres for measuring distance; a built-in protractor for measuring angles (the Silva and Sunto compass both have this facility) and a clear sighting line or arrow to follow when walking on a bearing. Some compasses boast a number of other gadgets, but none are essential and all add to the cost. Many compasses are adorned with luminous dots, particularly on the north end of the needle, the orienteering arrow and the direction

arrow, but few are nightworthy without a torch. It is always safer to assume that you will need to illuminate your compass at night in order to use it. Despite its apparent simplicity, your compass is a precision instrument: treat it with care It is worth investing in a case to carry it in, though a sock or length of tubular bandage will serve as well.

At home, keep it away from other compasses and electrical appliances such as radios, TV sets and video recorders; they are all likely to disturb a compass's polarity.

DEVIATION
The compass needle is a magnet, and so it will be affected by magnetic fields other than the earth's. Objects containing ferrous metal, large enough or close enough to the compass, will cause the needle to deviate from its desired orientation – that of magnetic north. So keep your compass clear of metal when you are using it to navigate – and that includes small objects like knives or the frames of some older rucksacks.

TRUE NORTH
True north and true south are at the geographical poles, imaginary points where the earth's axis of rotation intersects with the surface. In the northern hemisphere the direction of true north is indicated with acceptable accuracy by the pole star, Polaris. Two bright stars, the 'Pointers', in the Plough or Dipper (part of the constellation called the Great Bear, Ursa Major) can be used to locate

the pole star in the night sky. Of course, sometimes the Plough may be obscured by cloud. If so, first find the square of Pegasus. Follow a line from its brightest star, Alpheratz, down through the nearest star to it in the prominent 'W' of the constellation of Cassiopeia. This line will eventually lead your eye to Polaris. A further method is to look for the constellation Ursa Minor (the Little Bear), which resembles the Plough, but in miniature. Polaris is the star at the end of the 'handle' of this 'little dipper'.

In the southern hemisphere there is only a very faint star to be found at the celestial pole. This can be located by following the line indicated by the two stars forming the longer 'arm' of the Southern Cross (Crux).

It is also possible to find north by using a watch – provided that you can see the sun. Hold the watch horizontally with the hour hand pointing in the direction of the sun. Then bisect the angle between the hour hand and 12 o'clock. This line points south in the northern hemisphere, north in the southern hemisphere. In Britain between April and October (British Summer Time) you should direct the angle between the hour hand and 1 o' clock. If your watch is digital then take the time from it, sketch a conventional clockface on a piece of paper and use that in place of a watch.

GRID NORTH

As has been explained on page 20, maps are drawn using grid north as a reference. In Britain this will always vary slightly from true north except at longitude 2°W, the longitude on which our national grid is based.

MAGNETIC NORTH

The earth has a powerful magnetic field. Within this field a suspended magnetized needle will consistently align itself in a constant direction. Fortunately this direction is almost that of north, though, less fortunately, seldom exactly so. In fact, the magnetic pole currently lies in Canada, just to the north of Hudson Bay, which, from Britain, is some way west of the geographical pole. Less fortunate still, magnetic north is not a fixed point but one which varies by a number of minutes (a minute is 1/60th of a degree) each year. This change is, however, predictable, and your map will show you what to allow when making your calculation.

The magnetic variation in Britain is currently about 5½°W of the geographical pole, reducing by about ½° every five years. Magnetic variation varies according to which part of the world you are operating in. For example in the Alps the magnetic variation is currently 2°W – so small as to be hardly worth allowing for. In other parts of the world magnetic north is east of true north.

The importance of the variation to the navigator is this: since maps are nearly always married to a national grid then an angle or direction of desired travel taken from a map will have to be adjusted when converting to a compass bearing – an angle based on magnetic north – and vice versa.

Since from Britain magnetic north is always to the west of grid north, the compass or magnetic bearing is always greater than the grid bearing.

Comparison of the three norths – true, magnetic and grid. The magnetic variation, 'x', decreases as you move west. (Note: the poles are, of course, much further from the British Isles than shown here.)

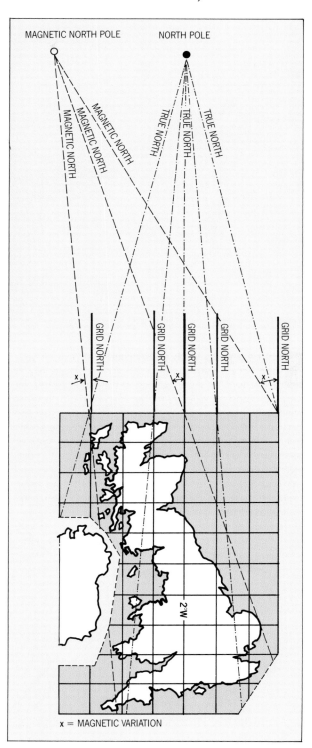

x = MAGNETIC VARIATION

MAP AND COMPASS WORK

Setting off on a bearing in moorland, where a compass is as important a tool as in the mountains. The walker holds the compass at waist-level so that he can see when the needle and the orienting arrow are aligned. Then, facing the direction of travel, he may sight a prominent landmark and use that as a target.

Setting a map with a compass We have already seen how a map is set to the ground (page 20). A quicker way of aligning a map to the ground is to set it with the compass, orientating the map so that it corresponds with the ground. Lay the compass on the map and turn both until the red end of the compass needle points north on the map. If your situation demands greater precision, you can set the magnetic variation on the dial, align the edge of the compass with the N-S grid lines and turn map and compass together until the needle lies inside the orienting arrow. Try to get into the habit of casing and reading your map from a 'set' position.

Far left Setting a map roughly: turn both map and compass until their 'norths' align. **Below** Setting a map accurately, using the dial to allow for the magnetic variation.

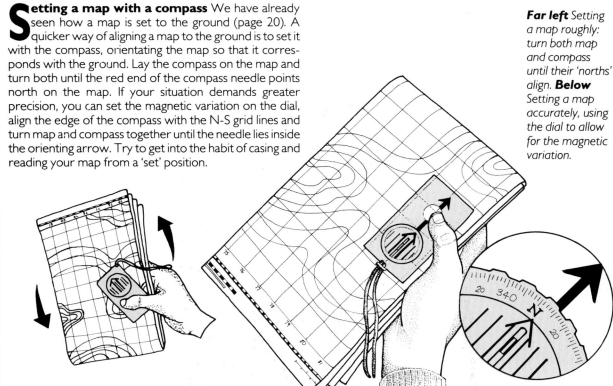

Taking a compass bearing from the map to follow on the ground There will be times when you wish to take a bearing of the map in order to follow it on the ground. Such occasions might be when your vision is obscured by trees, fog or darkness – or any other time when you can't see your destination from your present position.

The first thing to do is to measure the angle between grid north (on your map) and your desired direction of travel. Any protractor can be used for this, though if you have a Silva- or Sunto-type compass you can use the compass itself as a protractor. The degrees between grid north and your selected line of travel are shown on the rim of the compass housing against the direction arrow (see page 22). This is your 'bearing'. Double check in case you are 180° out – not as daft as it sounds and a common error with beginners or even among tired veterans.

Now you need to know where this direction or bearing lies on the ground – *but* the compass needle points not to grid north, but to the magnetic north pole. You must, therefore, allow for this in order to navigate with any accuracy, especially if the difference between the line at that time and in your area is greater than two or three degrees. (Anything less than that can usually be ignored – compass and map are precision instruments: people are not!)

In Britain magnetic north is left (or west) of grid north and bearings are read in a clockwise direction; therefore the angle between a given direction of travel and magnetic north will always be greater than that between the direction of travel and grid north by the number of degrees that magnetic north is to the west (left) of grid north – the magnetic variation.

Rhymes, such as 'add for mag, get rid for grid', 'mag to grid, get rid' and 'grid to mag, add!', may be helpful reminders, but it is much better to understand the differences in the first place. In any case the rhymes work only in those parts of the world where magnetic north is west of grid north – which is by no means the case for the entire globe.

Following a bearing set on the compass Once you have calculated the magnetic variation and applied it to the compass you will want to use your compass to follow in the direction of that bearing. Simply hold the compass in front of you with the direction-of-travel arrow pointing straight ahead of you (see left). Holding the compass steady, rotate until the compass needle lies exactly within the arrow outline drawn on the floor of the compass housing – the orienting arrow. The red end of the compass needle should lie on the orienting arrow head.

Now walk along the direction indicated by the travel arrow. Refer to the diagram of a compass on page 22 so that you are clear which arrow is which. If you have a

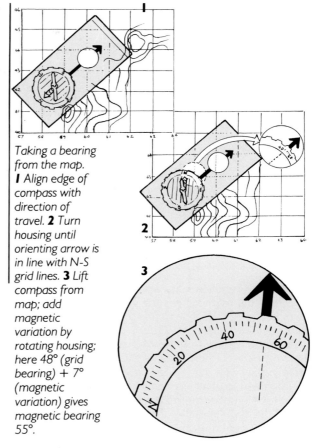

Taking a bearing from the map. **1** *Align edge of compass with direction of travel.* **2** *Turn housing until orienting arrow is in line with N-S grid lines.* **3** *Lift compass from map; add magnetic variation by rotating housing; here 48° (grid bearing) + 7° (magnetic variation) gives magnetic bearing 55°.*

compass in your hand at the time it will soon be clear. It's a simple process and not so complicated in practice as it may read on paper.

Compass and map There will be times when you need to take a bearing with a compass and then apply it to the map, perhaps in order to identify a hill that you can see or in order to help you to calculate your own position by taking a bearing to some feature which you have already identified on the map. Again it is a simple business: point the direction-of-travel arrow at the feature; hold the compass steady in that position and turn the housing until the orienting arrow lies exactly underneath the compass needle with the red end of that needle corresponding to the top of the orienting arrow. The figure shown where the direction-of-travel arrow and housing intersect is the angle between the line to the feature and magnetic north – the magnetic bearing of that feature from yourself.

Now, in order to arrive at the grid bearing, subtract from the magnetic bearing the magnetic variation – and then set this figure on the compass housing. For example,

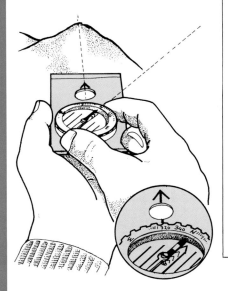

Below *Compass to map: taking a bearing to a distant hill.* **Right** *Transferring the compass to the map having first accounted for the magnetic variation.*

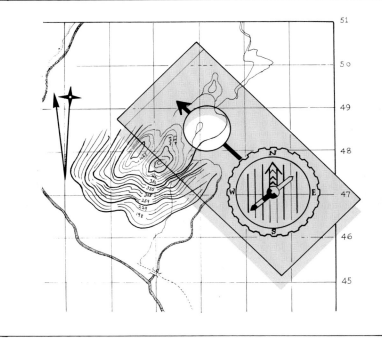

the magnetic variation in Snowdonia, Britain, in 1987 was 5½°W. If the magnetic bearing you had recorded had been 237°, your equation to find the grid bearing would have been 237° − 5½° = 231½°.

Place the compass on the map so that the orienting arrow is parallel (there may be other orienting lines to assist in this) with the N-S grid lines. Then, holding the housing steady so that the orienting arrow remains parallel with the N-S grid lines, turn the base of the compass so that one of the long edges runs through either the feature or your own position – whichever is known to you. When you do this, ensure that the direction-of-travel arrow is pointing away from your position and towards the feature. Now you know that the feature in question is somewhere along the edge of the compass, or along an extension of the edge. It won't tell you the distance, but you should now have enough information to be able to identify the feature and to work out the distance. Similarly, if you are trying to define your own position, you will now know that you are somewhere along that edge.

MEASURING DISTANCES

Most walking and mountaineering maps are covered by a grid system of 1km squares. Estimating distance against such a grid pattern should be fairly easy and usually accurate enough for most walking purposes. Practise at home, matching your eye and estimated distance to the same distance measured with a ruler. Your compass too is likely to have a measuring scale along some of its edges, though it may not be long enough to measure longish distances at one sighting.

Measuring distances on Ordnance Survey maps can be done using the grid lines, which are 1km apart. The diagonal across a square is just over 1.4km.

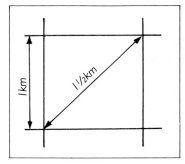

KEEPING ON COURSE

In good visibility, simply pick out a prominent feature that lies along your path of travel and walk to it – or as far towards it as you need to go. Once you have selected an 'aiming work', you will hardly need your compass and, as long as you keep an eye on the aiming work, you can wander off the exact line as whim or obstacle persuades, choosing the best path and yet keeping on course.

In poor visibility, you will need to refer to your compass often – very often, if the visibility is really poor. In fact in the worst conditions you are likely to be following your compass all the time and perhaps even getting your companion to walk beyond you on the bearing until near the limit of visibility, while you give instructions, such as 'go left', or 'go right'. Once he has halted on course, you can walk to him and repeat the procedure.

HEIGHT DIFFERENCE ESTIMATION

If you wish to calculate the height you will gain or lose on a given section of your route, first count all the contour lines

Cairns are sometimes (not always) marked on the map, giving you a check on your position.

you will cross in *ascent* and multiply by the contour interval. In a separate calculation, count all the contour lines you will cross in *descent* and again multiply by the contour interval. Then simply subtract the lesser total from the greater one. Assuming a 10m contour interval (check in the margin of your map), your sum might look like this:

Ascent:	11 contours × 10 =	110m
Descent:	3 contours × 10 =	30m
Ascent:	4 contours × 10 =	40m
Net height gain:		120m

HOW FAST OR HOW FAR?

Way back in 1892 a Scottish climber called Naismith worked out a formula for gauging how far the average party would walk in a given time – or, variously applied, how long a given distance would take to cover. His rule allowed an average speed of 5kph *plus* half an hour for every 300m of ascent (3mph *plus* an additional half hour for every 1,000ft of ascent). While Naismith's is a surprisingly accurate generalization there are obviously a number of factors which may be particular to a day that need to be taken into account:

Going down Most of us go faster down gentle slopes up to about 12°, after which we tend to slow again because of the steepness and the care that that demands of us. On an average day we discount descent as far as these sums are concerned, but if the amount of downhill is significant, you could adjust by deducting 10min for every 300m (1,000ft) of descent on gentle slopes, and by adding 10min per 300m of descent on steep slopes. In practice, this is hardly ever worth the extra mathematics.

Load and fitness Both these are factors that, in any extreme, will clearly affect Naismith's generalization. A

heavy pack could reduce your overall speed by as much as 50 per cent. The easiest way to allow for it is by reducing the estimate of your average speed to 3kph (2mph) or even, under very heavy loads, 2kph (1 ¼mph).

Terrain Uphill scree will slow you (and tire you) considerably, as will bogs, very thick woods, boulder fields and deep snow.

Weather Common sense suggests that some allowance must be made for foul weather. Wind, rain or snow – and sometimes very hot weather too – all are enemies of speed. With all these variables you could be forgiven for concluding that it is a waste of time to try to estimate your time from point to point. The fact is, however, that with only a little experience, you will be able to calculate times with surprising accuracy – and anything within 10 per cent of the actual figure is a very useful guide and might help to

avoid missing the train!

To navigate accurately in bad visibility over short distances, it is useful to know how many paces you average to 100m, or for that matter 100yd, on various kinds of surface. Use a normal stride and count every time the right foot comes down. Try it; practise.

ROUTE PLANNING

It is nearly always a good thing to study your proposed route on the map at home – or at least in comfort – before embarking on it. Don't be too ambitious at first – there's plenty of time for feats of endurance later – and try to anticipate all contingencies: weather, obstacles, loads, fitness, etc. Many hill walkers enjoy formalizing this planning process in the form of a route card, an example of which is shown at the top right of the opposite page.

Left *On rocky hills it is difficult, and sometimes impossible, to walk on a compass bearing, and even in good weather you will take longer to get from A to B than you might expect.*

Right *An example of a typical route card.*

	Dusk at					
	Bearing	Distance	Height Gain/Loss	Time	Description	ETA–ATA
	Map	Grid				
A to B (Description & Grid Reference)						
B to C						
C to ... etc.						
Totals						

ETA = Estimated Time of Arrival; ATA = Actual Time of Arrival

Possible escape route:

Below *Aiming off. The party's target is the stream junction. They have deliberately aimed off to the south.*

Below right *Assuming a walking speed of 5kph, route B would take two hours. Route A would take 78 minutes (48 minutes plus 30 minutes for the height gain/loss).*

You may care to leave a copy of your route card with someone connected with your group – a parent perhaps – or displayed on the windscreen of your car.

AIMING OFF

It may be that you are aiming for a particular spot on a road, a junction perhaps, or maybe the junction of a stream and path. The chances of you hitting exactly the right point in poor visibility over a distance much greater than 2-3km (1-2 miles) are slight. A greater likelihood is that you will miss the junction and gain the road to one side of it. But which side are you on? Much better to deliberately aim off, to west say, or to east, so that on gaining the road you will know whether to turn to left or right.

CONTOURING

A straight line may be the shortest distance between two points, but it may or may not be the quickest. Take the situation illustrated here:

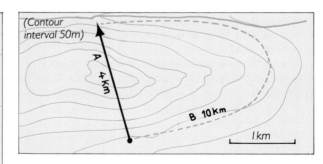

(Contour interval 50m)

A 4 km

B 10 km

1 km

There are no hard and fast rules, but if you have a completely free choice about which way you go, a comparison of the two distances, the height gain and the application of Naismith's Rule with allowances for terrain, surface, wind and weather – which may be significantly worse on high ground – should make it plain which route is the quicker. Even then, you may prefer a flat, streamlined walk, or again the view from a hill. At least, having studied it, you will know what you are in for.

WEATHER

Left *Clouds like these look innocent from a distance, but beware: it could be raining or snowing, and the wind will probably be stronger.* **Below** *Wind chill: the stronger the wind the colder it feels, with the greatest discernible effect being in winds of 4-15mph (6.5-24kph).*

We all know how weather affects our daily lives. Its role is even more significant in hills and mountains. It is not so much that bad weather should be avoided – though perhaps very bad weather should – but more that it is helpful to know what to expect and what, therefore, to prepare for. Wild days on hills and mountains can be great fun given some preparation and the right equipment.

• Try to learn a bit about weather.
• Solicit a weather forecast before going out. They are available from radio, TV, newspapers, telephone services, recorded forecasts, mountain climbing centres and in some areas the local meteorological office (listed in the telephone directory).

The first four sources give general weather predictions only and are not specific to the hills: they must be adapted – which generally means exaggerated – for mountain use.

GENERAL RULES

Temperature normally decreases as height is gained by between 2°C and 3°C per 300m (about 2-3°F per 500ft). This is called the lapse rate. Warm valleys therefore do not necessarily indicate warm summits: the average July temperature on the top of Ben Nevis, for example, is only 5°C (41°F).

Wind speed increases as height is gained; it can be three times as strong on mountains as on low-lying ground. Besides the buffeting a strong wind delivers, there is also the wind-chill factor to consider.

Walking in a strong wind is tiring. Try to take a sheltered route and to avoid ridges and ledges, wear windproof

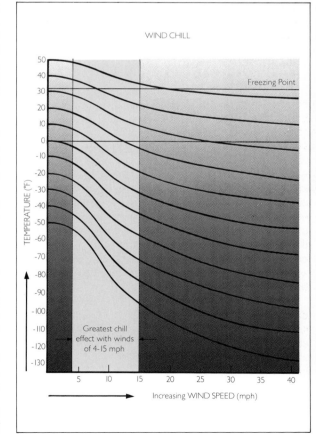

WIND CHILL

Freezing Point

TEMPERATURE (°F)

Greatest chill effect with winds of 4-15 mph

Increasing WIND SPEED (mph)

clothing, and camp low. Even for adults a wind speed in excess of 50kph (30mph; force 6-7) makes walking difficult. In winds above 80kph (50mph; force 10) progress of any sort is a trial.

Rain and cloud occur more often in mountainous regions than in lowlands. For example Snowdon's summit is washed by 500cm (200in) of rain a year compared with 100cm (40in) on a coast only 15km (10 miles) distant. Wet, cold rain is unpleasant: be prepared. Clouds reduce visibility and make greater demands on your navigation. Be the equal of those demands – and allow time for it all.

WINTER WALKING

For the hill walker or mountaineer there are few finer sights than mountains ruffled with snow and hung with ice, and few of us can resist the greater excitements, the bigger challenges and the deeper satisfactions that winter conditions offer. But if the allure is greater, then the potential hazards are too. Some of the reasons are obvious, others are less so. At any rate they are all worth a look.

Snow itself is a complex and unpredictable beauty. It may be soft and fluffy at one time, wet and soggy only a few hours later, and sheet ice not long after that. Driven by ferocious winds it may accumulate in lethal deposits of windslab at the backs of corries and cwms, or in cornices, as dangerous as they are attractive. Snow needs to be learned about and this takes time and experience.

The presence of snow and ice requires that some extra equipment is carried: crampons and an ice axe, two items that, combined with a knowledge of how to use them and some practice, make friendly places of wintry mountainsides. Snow and ice are great stuff as long as you know how to use them. The section on snow and ice climbing deals with the essential information. Winter conditions may also influence your clothing and footwear. You will almost certainly need more insulation to deal with colder weather, while a pair of gaiters to keep the snow out of the tops of boots is considered essential by most. The boots themselves will be sturdier than the lightweight walking boots of summer, mainly because they must be able to accommodate crampons, something that lightweight boots don't always do well.

Winter hills are enormous fun and the rewards of winter days are rich; but go gently at first, practising the skills itemized in the snow and ice section in safe places and on easy ground.

Dangerous electrical storms might sound an unusual hazard to the average hill walker but they are not uncommon in bigger mountains such as the European Alps. If you are caught in one, don't shelter under overhangs or in cracks or chimneys in a rock face, or by the side of outstanding boulders. Forsake peaks and ridges –

The slope on the left is a straightforward scree slope in summer but in winter, covered in snow, could present a less-than-straightforward problem to the unwary or ill equipped hill walker.

they attract lightning – and sit out in the open. There is no need to throw away any metal equipment (such as an ice axe); metal objects do not attract lightning any more than you do – and you may need that equipment later.

EFFECTS OF WIND

The wind, as everyone will have noticed, makes a warm day cool, a cool day cold, and a cold day miserable. A windproof shell will prevent the wind from penetrating your insulating layers and robbing them of body-warmed air. It is difficult to gauge exactly how much colder a wind makes the day feel – it has no effect on the actual temperature, but a palpable effect on the apparent temperature. This phenomenon is called 'wind chill', and its effect on the body is best shown by a chart giving approximate equivalent temperatures (see page 30).

In addition to its chilling effect, a wind can exert a force sufficient to sweep grown men off their feet. It is hard to stand in a wind greater than 80kph (50mph; force 10) and it may be necessary, if caught in such a wind, to crouch, even to crawl. Look for the shelter of a lee slope. Keep close to your companions and, if it looks necessary and you have a rope, rope-up and keep away from ridges.

FIRST AID

Every mountaineer should know the basics of first aid: not only are there many classes covering the subject in general, it is easy enough to find courses specializing in first aid on mountains. Failing that, there are numerous books on the subject. Here are a few general principles:

● Check the airway for obstructions, and thereafter check frequently to make sure it is kept clear.
● Stop any bleeding. Dress open wounds.
● Do not move the victim, unless you are quite certain there is no spinal injury.
● Treat for shock (see below).
● If need be, immobilize broken limbs to prevent further damage and to relieve pain.
● Keep it simple. Do only as much as is necessary for the comfort of the patient.

Shock Shock follows most accidents: the symptoms are cold clammy skin, weak and rapid pulse, and gasping for air. Reassure the person, relieve pain and calm him/her. Make the person comfortable and insulate them – but do not overheat.

Bleeding Cut back clothing to ensure the bleeding is not dangerous. Raise the injured part, and apply firm manual pressure over a sterile dressing.

Spine injuries Symptoms are numbness in the legs and/or back pain, but spine injuries are hard to diagnose. If in doubt, do not move the patient – and certainly not until you have a stretcher and as many helpers as possible.

Broken leg As with all other fractures, immobilize the limb only if the patient is in extreme pain and/or has to be moved. Pad an ice axe or roll up a karrimat to use as a splint; pad also the knees and ankles, bind the two legs together, and elevate them.

Broken arm Pad and splint as above. Rest an injured forearm in a sling; an injured upper arm should be bandaged to the chest.

Broken collar-bone Place the hand of the injured side against the opposite collar-bone and bandage the arm to the patient's chest.

Sprained ankle Leave the boot in place (usually), but loosen the laces to allow for swelling.

Burns and scalds Cool the damaged area in water; treat for pain and shock, and use a non-adhesive dressing or a sterile polythene bag. Leave burnt clothing in place: it has been sterilized. With scalds, though, remove the surrounding clothing if it is hot and wet.

Unconsciousness Make sure the airway is unobstructed and turn the patient on his/her side into the recovery position to help drain fluids and prevent against the tongue obstructing breathing.

Heat exhaustion Move the person out of the sun and, if possible, immerse him/her in water. Increase air movement around the person by fanning. Heat exhaustion is often related to dehydration, so give plenty of fluids.

Hypothermia Mountain hypothermia, or exposure, is an extremely dangerous condition in which the body's core temperature drops below 35°C (95°F). It is nearly always related to exhaustion as well as cold, and can often be traced to a lack of fitness or a failure to eat enough at breakfast or during the day. First signs of hypothermia may be loss of coordination, slurred speech, apathy and uncharacteristic behaviour. At this stage, the situation can be remedied by finding or making shelter, warming up, and eating some sugary food. If the casualty has reached a state of collapse, it is vital that he or she not be moved any further. The procedure is to place the person in a polythene survival bag, preferably with another person inside it so as to generate more body-heat, and with plenty of extra insulation, especially beneath them. The head should be downhill and the feet raised to ensure maximum blood-supply to the core, particularly the brain. Use a stretcher to take the person off the mountainside, being as careful as possible to make the journey comfortable; this is important because the blood's viscosity is greater when it is cold and so imposes an increased strain on the heart, an effect you do not wish to exacerbate.

Frostbite Watch out for white noses and ears among your companions, and be aware of your own fingers and toes. Treatment is by warming the affected area – at the simplest level, you can put a hand in your armpit to warm your fingers. Parts once affected by frostbite should be specially protected until you get home, as they are at high risk of being stricken again. Severe frostbite is not a matter of first aid: the person should be taken to hospital as swiftly as possible. Bear in mind that it causes less tissue damage to walk on feet that are still frozen than if you thaw them out first.

The above discussion of first aid is only a very general one. On no account venture out onto high mountains without having thoroughly studied a specialist first-aid text or attended a course – preferably both.

Taking the proper precautions – which includes a working knowledge of basic first aid – will reduce the chances of injury and illness on a climb. Accidents do happen, however, which may necessitate the victim being stretchered down. It is important, if difficult in practice, to make the journey as smooth as possible in order not to aggravate existing problems.

33

MOUNTAIN CAMPING

Left *A winter camp beneath the north-facing cliffs of Ben Nevis, Scotland – one way of avoiding the long slog up to reach winter climbs.*
Below *A backpacker in California's High Sierra. The sleeping mat provides comfort on the stony ground as well as insulation from the cold beneath.*
Right *A modern mountain tent, able to withstand all but the strongest of winds yet weighing only 3-4kg (7-9lb). Note the roomy 'bell entrance' giving space to store gear and to cook.*

The use of a tent of one form or another as shelter is almost as old as the hills themselves. Even today a tent is still home for many peoples, such as the Bedouin of Arabia and desert tribes such as the Tuareg of the Sahara. For our purposes, however, the tent is a temporary home, though that does not mean it has to be an uncomfortable one or a less than thoroughly reliable shelter: good tents, properly pitched and sited, are homes from home. Indeed, there is no cosier feeling than that of lying warmly wrapped in a tent, mug of tea in hand, with the wind and rain beating against the walls. Camping in the hills is an understandably popular pastime, the perfect end to a perfect hill-day. It can be an exquisite pleasure to camp in some remote mountain area, independent of civilization, self-sufficient and free.

EQUIPMENT FOR CAMPING

Camping necessarily entails acquiring some specialist equipment – tents, sleeping bags and a rucksack are the obvious items. When you first acquire them, some of these things will be strange. Practise using them at home before attempting to deploy them on the hill. You can erect and dismantle a tent half a dozen times at home, in a room or garden (in the dark too), until you know exactly what you are doing. You will be glad of that practice if your very first night on camp is a wild one. Practise with your new stove too. Get to know its quirks, so that you become slick with it. This may save you some frustrating hours and will certainly save you fuel – which you have to carry. It may also save some meals!

TENTS

Tents perform much the same function as the outer layer of your clothing: they protect you from rain and wind. Most modern tents have two skins to make them water-proof and condensation-free. The outer, or flysheet, is a proofed (usually nylon) shell while the inner is unproofed and breathes. (Tents made from Gore-Tex are single-skinned.) A sewn-in ground sheet is advisable in all but the most agreeable of climates.

There is a wide and colourful array of tents available to the prospective camper. Some general hints will assist in your selection. Generally speaking, since you will have to carry your home on your back, the lighter the tent, the better – although not so light that quality, robustness or waterproofness are sacrificed entirely. Very good, very light tents are fairly expensive.

Designs vary enormously but can be roughly categorized as hoop, dome and ridge. Hoop and dome tents are hung from, or stretched over, a framework of alloy or fibreglass hooped poles. They offer the maximum volume for a given floor area and need few guys and pegs for supplementary support. Indeed, a dome tent can be easily lifted and shifted from one tent position to another, in its

A secluded grassy hollow in a wilderness of rock makes an idyllic camping site.

erected form, by one person. The ridge tent is an older idea, but it is still a good fundamental design – tough, stable in winds and usually cheaper because construction is simpler (and because some are still made of cotton fabric). As with clothing, buying tents is a case of paying for what you want. Other considerations are:

● *Ventilation* – by tunnel vent or by unzipping a corner or top of a door. There should be a clear space between the flysheet and the inner, too, to stop water penetrating, to allow the inner to breathe, and to allow air to circulate between the two layers so that condensation is kept to a minimum.

● *Storage Space* – is there an area at one end for the storage of boots, rucksack and other paraphernalia?

● *Cooking Area* – a well ventilated porch or bell-end is useful when the weather makes cooking alfresco an unattractive business.

● *Entrance* – has this been designed to allow the camper to enter unaccompanied by wind and weather? A tent full of blown snow is an uncomfortable and, ultimately, a damp place.

● *The Flysheet* – this should come very close to the ground, so that the weather does not find its way underneath.

CHOOSING A CAMP SITE

Select a site that is sheltered from wind and rain, where the ground is as flat as is available and as free from bumps, lumps and tussocks as possible. Look for a well drained site too – though a handy stream gives a ready water supply. Trees, walls and hillocks can offer shelter. In cold weather avoid local hollows – they collect cold air in the night and will be much cooler than surrounding areas.

The precise way in which you pitch and erect your tent will depend on its configuration. Most ridge tents with sewn-in ground sheets can be pegged out first, getting the exact shape at the first step. Pitch with the back end of the tent to the wind (or the unused door in the case of a tent with a double entrance). Set up the windward end first and peg out the main guys. Other guys should run out in line with the tent's seams. Stretch rubber guys and tension-cords so that the tent is taut and wrinkle-free. In poor weather dome and hoop tents can be more of a problem to erect than ridge tents. Threading long, very flexible poles into narrow sleeves in a gale in the dark is no easy matter – hence the importance of practising at home.

To strike a tent simply reverse the order. Make sure you have gathered up all your poles and pegs and clean any earth from the pegs – there is no point in carrying unnecessary weight. Clear away and take with you any litter too. The idea is to leave the place as you found it. When you get home, hang up your tent to dry – cotton tents will mildew if stored wet and even nylon tents may have components that are susceptible to damp. In any case you will want a dry tent next time out.

KEEPING WARM AND DRY

Sleeping bags are filled with either down or one of a variety of polyester fillings – the same as those used for insulated jackets. The same pros and cons apply. People will argue long and hard about whether down or synthetic fill is better for sleeping bags; these arguments centre on warmth for weight, compressability and durability, but perhaps the greatest consideration is the comparative warmth of synthetic fills when damp or wet. In these circumstances down is useless, heavy and extremely difficult to dry. Polyester fillings are still about 50 per cent efficient when wet, do not hold as much moisture and do not, therefore, gain so much weight. Also, they dry relatively easily. These all seem to be good arguments for polyester fillings where there is any chance of dampness affecting your bag. A Gore-Tex outer skin or a bivvy bag of the same material matched to a down bag may redress some of the balance. Even the resistance to compression, a distinct disadvantage of polyester fillings when packing a sleeping bag into a rucksack, is turned to advantage when sleeping. Because sleeping bags give warmth as a result of the air they hold as insulation, and because an occupant will expel 99 per cent of this air from the underside of the bag when lying in it, sleeping bags are vulnerable to the conduction of cold from the ground upwards; down more so than less compressible synthetic.

Whatever the filling, any bag will need to be supplemented by a sleeping mat of some sort – whether inflatable or of closed-cell construction such as a Karrimat. The same mat, which will weigh only ounces, adds softening comfort too, so it's as essential a part of your camping gear as a tent, stove or sleeping bag. Indeed mat and bag are seldom separated.

All loose sleeping bag fillings, down in particular, need to be restrained in compartments to stop them migrating to one corner of the bag, leaving the remainder without insulation. There are several ways of achieving this. Some are more efficient than others, and the 'sewn-through' construction is to be avoided unless the budget dictates – in which case it would be better to wait and save.

WARMTH AND COMFORT

After taking the tent from the rucksack – and it should be near the top, or even on the outside – replace the contents (especially clothing) and close the lid.

Before entering the tent, take off waterproofs, wet clothes and boots (they are hard on the ground sheet). Keep these wet items away from dry clothes and sleeping bags by placing them in a polythene bag. Polythene bags make useful storage for many things besides wet clothes – personal belongings, sugar, salt, potato powder, etc.

Once inside put on dry clothes and get into your sleeping bag if you are cold – having fluffed it up first to fill it with air.

Use heather, grass, spare clothes, rope or your rucksack to make the floor more comfortable and to provide extra insulation.

On rough ground it is usually more comfortable to sleep on your stomach and on sloping ground to sleep with your head uphill. Store tins, unwanted rope, wet clothes and anything that is not attractive to animals outside under the flysheet. Pots and pans thus stored should be within easy reach from the inside in case the weather turns bad.

It is seldom a good thing to try to dry wet clothing by wearing it inside your sleeping bag. You will end up with a wet bag and a greater problem. Better to dry it by using wind and sun and maybe an improvised clothes line or, if on the move, by tying the wet garments onto the outside of your rucksack. In very cold conditions, it may be necessary to take boots, gaiters, gloves and anorak into your sleeping bag to prevent them from freezing. If this is the case wrap them in a polythene bag first.

Useful camp items include: head torch, alloy fuel bottle, flat 'jiffy'-type can openers, penknife, waterproof matches or gas lighter, loo paper, bootlace-nylon, nylon pot scrubber, sponge for mopping up leaks and spills, transistor radio for weather forecasts and entertainment, anti-midge cream (May-October especially), repair spares for tents and water purifying tablets. See the checklist at the end of this section for a fuller selection.

HYGIENE AND CONSERVATION

Camping presents problems of personal hygiene, and can also inflict damage to sensitive environments. To minimize adverse effects:
● Do not pitch a tent on the same spot for more than a few days; let vegetation regrow.
● Use a small trowel to bury excrement by at least 15-20cm (6-8in) and as far as possible from open water.
● Wash hands thoroughly after defecating, and again before cooking.
● Use *hot* water to clean pots, pans and utensils.
● Do not dig rubbish pits, light fires or move large stones; the scars last for years.
● If you think there is any chance that your water supply is polluted, use sterilizing tablets or boil all water for at least five minutes.
● Leave your camp site so that no one will ever know you have been there.

CAMP FOOD AND COOKING

Sleep does not come easily to the cold or hungry. Appetites on camp can be enormous and so to eat well can bring contentment, warmth and a good night's sleep. However, any food taken with you will have to balance maximum appeal, nourishment and ease of cooking with minimum weight and bulk.

Normally, campers have two big meals a day, at breakfast and supper, with a packed lunch at midday. Obviously individual requirements and preferences will differ but it is important to have a full and varied diet at a time when your body needs energy to walk, to carry a rucksack and simply to keep warm. Great fun can be had whiling away the evening concocting gourmet dishes from a few basic ingredients, each course to be savoured before the next is prepared, and all eaten off the same plate! Some suggestions about the sort of food you might carry are given on page 17.

Cooking may need some practice; it is better to perfect your porridge production at home than to ruin it at your first attempt on a windy hillside. Caught in bad weather you may have to cook inside your tent and this needs practice too.

- Get fully acquainted with your stove at home.
- Prepare all food, collect water and organize your meal *before* lighting the stove.
- Always refuel and light stoves outside the tent to avoid leaks, fumes and flare-ups.
- Keep the stove close to the door where it can be ejected if necessary and there is a good ventilation.
- Tie back tent doors which could otherwise drop against the stove.
- Avoid stirring your food or adjusting the stove while a pan is on the heat.
- Have a rag to hand to mop up spillage.
- Don't be tempted to hurry the cooking.

WARNING
Tents burn easily! Stoves, candles and cigarettes are potentially dangerous. Also, make sure that there is adequate ventilation to prevent a build-up of carbon monoxide.

STOVES
Gas stoves are clean and easy to use, but the fuel is rather expensive. Also, for about half an hour before a cylinder is exhausted, the stove burns at a gradually reducing rate as pressure drops. This can mean a long wait for a cuppa.
Pressure stoves burn paraffin or petrol or some similar fuel (white gas, Blazo and the like, in the U.S.). Paraffin must be pre-heated with solid fuel or a splash of meths, but once in action such stoves provide plenty of cheap, regulatable heat – though with more fuss and dirtier hands than their gas counterparts. Petrol stoves do not need to be pre-heated and burn well – even a little too well on occasions! They and their fuel need to be treated with great respect.
Meths burners The most common is the Trangia system, the stove component of which burns methylated spirit. Because these stoves burn fuel that is not under pressure they have no mechanical parts to go wrong and they are free from all the ills and spills that pressurized stoves suffer.

They can include integral pans, and they work better than any other type of stove in windy conditions. Under normal windless operating conditions, however, they produce less heat than a paraffin stove and are more expensive to run. Remember that meths burns silently and nearly colourlessly – it is easy to forget that the thing is lit, as a number of campers with tender fingertips will testify!

Changing gas cylinders and filling paraffin and more especially petrol stoves should always be completed in the open air, away from candles or any other naked flame. Practise at home, especially since in wild weather you will want to be out of your tent for as short a time as possible while performing this delicate operation.

If you are cooking outside, a breeze, no matter how slight, will significantly reduce the effectiveness of most stoves. This is especially true of gas. Build a windshield from stones or turf or use your rucksack.

Store gas stoves and spare cylinders outside when you sleep. Leaking gas is dangerous, and being heavier than air accumulates in the base of a tent, where it is most likely to affect sleeping campers. The results could be fatal.

RUCKSACKS
Once you have decided to carry your home on your back and to camp, you will need to acquire a comfortable, medium-sized rucksack in which to pack and carry all your equipment. Fortunately there are dozens of very good models available – the consumer has benefited from intense commercial competition between rival manufacturers. The ubiquitous pack frames of the late 1960s have all but given way to more comfortable rucksacks with internal stiffening or padded backs or frames integral to the rucksack's construction. Some models have adjustable frames or harness systems while others come in differing back lengths. Choose with care, get the size right in the shop and buy a sack that is big enough for your needs but no bigger (or more expensive) than those needs dictate. A

basic requirement of any sack is resistance to wear and tear and to water. Since no sack is completely waterproof, it is worth keeping a 500-gauge polythene liner as a live-in part of your sack. The rucksack should sit comfortably at the hips (a padded hip belt is a good thing) and lie comfortably between hips and shoulders – and close to the back so that its weight, when loaded, is with you rather than behind you. Pockets on a rucksack are a matter for personal taste but they can be very useful. Generally, rucksacks used for climbing have no side pockets because they may catch on projecting pieces of rock. Some sacks boast detachable pockets.

PACKING

A well-packed sack can be a joy to carry, but a badly packed sack is a pain. Put at the top or in sidepockets those articles that you are likely to need during the journey, or immediately upon arrival at the camp site – snacks, first aid kits, hat, gloves and tent. Keep heavy items as high and as close to the shoulders as possible. Avoid placing corners and sharp edges against the back of the sack, where they are likely to dig into your own back. Keep stove and fuel in a polythene bag and if possible in a pocket, and in any case well away from food. Your sleeping bag is usually the thing you need last and, being light in weight, is best compressed into the bottom of the sack.

CHECKLIST

Here is a checklist of items you should give consideration to carrying when camping, as well as those that you should consider for a day trip – see pages 16-17.

Mountain walks and camps make enormously varying demands – every trip is unique – and the kit you carry will vary according to length of camp, climate, season, numbers in the party and so on.

Modern lightweight camping equipment can give backpackers freedom to roam, as here on the west coast of Scotland. Such equipment may seem prohibitively expensive, but try to buy the best you can possibly afford. The fact that you have saved a little money will give you no consolation should your equipment fail you when you most need it.

see pages 16-17.

CHECKLIST

For All-day Trips
Rucksack
Waterproof liner for rucksack
Boots
Walking clothes
A little money
Pencil and paper
Torch, spare bulbs and batteries
Watch
Spare clothes
Windproof anorak
Waterproof cagoule (suited to season)
Overtrousers
Gloves
Woollen hat or Balaclava
Maps (allow for spares)
Compass
First aid kit
Emergency plastic bivouac bag
Length of cord (many uses)
Walking rope
Thermos
Water bottle
Day food
Emergency food
Penknife
Any personal medical requirements

Additional Items for Camps
Tent
Sleeping bag
Camping mat
Stove
Fuel and priming fuel
Billycans and handles
Matches (keep dry) or lighter
Knife, fork, spoon, mug, plate
Camp food
Tin opener
Sponge or cloth (for mopping up spillages, etc.)
Toilet paper
Water-sterilizing tablets
Trowel
Pad of steel wool
Candles
Stove spares/repair kit
Small sewing kit
Waterproofing dressing for leather boots
Polythene bags (for wet clothes, etc.)
Towel
Toilet gear
Soft shoes for camp
Spare socks and underclothes

Additional Items for Winter
Gaiters
Overmitts
Spare gloves
Scarf
Ice axe
Crampons
Goggles
Extra sleeping bag or duvet

SCRAMBLING

A scramble up a steep hillside in Llanberis Pass, Snowdonia, Wales. Here the walkers have decided that the dangers of loose rock falling from above are sufficient to warrant the wearing of helmets.

No one has ever satisfactorily defined the point at which hill walking becomes scrambling and scrambling rock climbing. Nor is such a definition really necessary. Perhaps the best judge is the walker, who knows soon enough when walking has become scrambling. It is enough to say that somewhere along the path from the horizontal to the vertical you will find yourself using a hand for balance. Then, as the going gets steeper, maybe two hands; then a rockhold for one hand to pull on and perhaps later two rockholds for two hands. At the same time you are very likely searching out footholds too. By now you are certainly scrambling. And soon you will be climbing.

Scrambling is great fun and the natural next step from hill walking. It is also exciting and requires little skill beyond what comes naturally. Even the most exhilarating scrambles demand very little specialized equipment beyond what the walker will already own. Some of the finest expeditions in the British hills are extended scrambles along exposed, but technically straightforward, ridges. Two that come readily to mind are Crib Goch on Snowdon, which gives a fine airy traverse well within the scope of most competent hill walkers, and, rather airier and more serious, the Aonach Eagach ridge of Glencoe in Scotland. Both are superb; neither is quite climbing.

Most of us scramble naturally, as youngsters have done for millions of years on trees, bomb-sites, adventure playgrounds – or whatever were the historical and prehistoric equivalents. Scrambling in the mountains requires little more by way of abilities and techniques than those displayed naturally by youngsters. Some tips, if tips are necessary, would be:

● Keep your weight on your feet and use your legs more than your arms – they are always much stronger.
● Go slowly and try to establish and maintain a rhythm.
● Look at your feet and hands to see where they are going – and choose hand- and footholds carefully. Don't be haphazard.
● Beware of loose rock. Shout 'Below!' if you do dislodge rock as there may be people below. Beware if you hear 'Below!' called from above.
● If a scramble is a chosen part of your itinerary, carry as light a rucksack as possible. A heavy sack is no fun to scramble with and it makes balancing difficult.
● In descent, face outwards for as long as nerve and steepness allow. It is easier and you get a better view of what is coming next – also it is much quicker. From facing outwards, as steepness persuades, turn sideways, and at last inwards for fairly steep descents. For even steeper descents, you may consider abseiling, for which you will need a rope, some minimal equipment and a working (and practical) knowledge of the contents of pages 76-77.

ROPING-UP

As your scrambling grows more adventurous you may decide that a rope affords some comfort and security. The point at which a rope becomes necessary during a scramble is clearly a matter of individual inclination, ability and confidence. An expert rock climber would probably never feel the need of a rope when scrambling; a novice hill walker might feel it fairly soon. Moreover, it is as difficult to suggest when a rope ought to be carried as it is to say when it ought to be used. As a very rough guide, and using my two specimen scrambles, I would suggest that a rope is almost never necessary on Crib Goch and quite often handy on the Aonach Eagach.

You might wish to rope-up when:
● The exposure is such that a fall would result in injury.
● The steepness and difficulty of the route make a slip a possibility.
● You have plenty of time, and a desire for safety outweighs the need to be speedy.
● You are frightened and feel that a rope will add both to security, real or perceived, and to enjoyment.

A rope must be of an approved construction and material – see page 46. A 30m (100ft) length of 9mm kernmantel or hawser-laid rope will do very well in most scrambling circumstances. But a rope is useless without the knowledge of how to use it. If you are already a rock climber, or if you have ambitions to be one, you will find these more advanced techniques explained in the next chapter. However, if scrambling is your objective, then the same principles can be applied, but somewhat simplified.

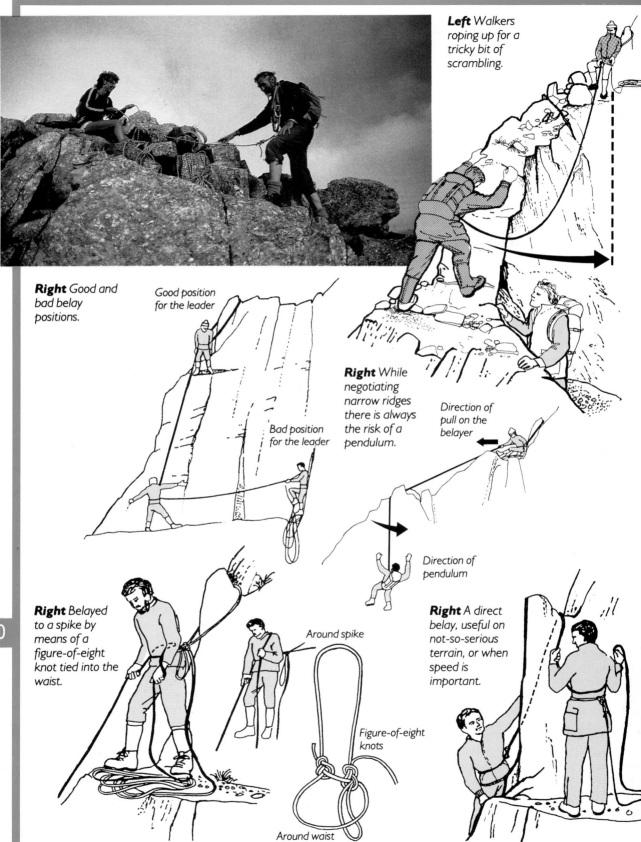

Left Walkers roping up for a tricky bit of scrambling.

Right Good and bad belay positions.

Good position for the leader

Bad position for the leader

Right While negotiating narrow ridges there is always the risk of a pendulum.

Direction of pull on the belayer

Direction of pendulum

Right Belayed to a spike by means of a figure-of-eight knot tied into the waist.

Around spike

Figure-of-eight knots

Around waist

Right A direct belay, useful on not-so-serious terrain, or when speed is important.

1 *The rope is passed around the waist; a loop is made on the 'live' end such that the 'live' rope is the lower one.*

2 *The end of the rope is passed up through the loop under the 'live' rope, and then back down through the loop.*

3 *Tying a bowline is sometimes likened to a rabbit leaving its burrow, running around a tree, and diving back into its burrow again.*

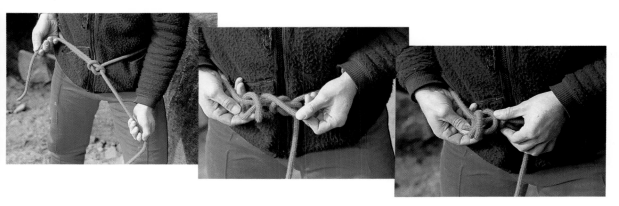

4 *The rope must be snug around the waist, and the knot tightened as shown.*

5 *The bowline is a quick knot to tie and to adjust, but left to itself it can work loose. Back it up with a 'stopper' knot.*

6 *The best 'stopper' knot is the double hitch, as shown here. Note that the second turn should be inside the first.*

7 *The completed bowline secured with a double-hitch 'stopper' knot.*

TYING-ON AND BELAYING

Rock climbers tie-on to the rope via a harness. Scramblers will usually, and perfectly satisfactorily, tie-on direct to the rope. There are many ways of tying the rope directly around the waist but the two commonest and most practical are by a bowline or by a double figure-of-eight knot.

When tied-on direct to the rope, the simplest technique is to tie into a belay anchor. The belayer does an important job. He takes in the rope or pays it out as required, ensuring that there is never more slack between partners than is necessary – and that the rope is never too tight either.

If you elect to carry a sling or two for additional security, then these should always be joined with a tape knot. Slings are very useful items which add little to the weight or cost of your expedition – and you can use them in any or all the ways of a rock climber.

Tying-on and belaying are discussed in more detail on pages 64-70.

41

ROCK CLIMBING

Left Steep free climbing at Arapiles, Australia, one of the world's best free-climbing playgrounds. Weather that is almost always good and rock of the very best quality combine to enable modern rock athletes on Olympic-style training schedules to push climbing standards ever higher. A dangling chalk bag and shorts are considered de rigueur on the sun-kissed rock. **Far right** Artificial climbing is a slower and heavier business. Here pitons and étriers are being used to surmount a roof. While aid is still required for a pitch like this one, free climbing is advancing so fast that this obstacle may soon fall to a shorts-clad athlete with a bag of chalk!

DEFINITIONS

There is no mystique to the art of climbing rock. At its most basic level the activity is an intuitive pastime – it is as natural as running. Children have no need of instruction in its art, nor of rules to give the game form, and equipment would only be an encumbrance. You only have to watch a child clambering over barnacled rocks at the seaside to realize this: the fingers reach and grasp each rough flake of rock in succession, one leading to the next as if they had been placed by design. The movements are fluid and effortless, for the child remains innocent of any risk, climbing with uninhibited grace. Some years later the same hands, dusted with chalk, can be found reaching around the lip of a great overhang, searching for an edge, a rugosity upon which to pull.

Rock climbing has often been likened to a gymnastic game of chess, with the player engaged in silent battle between himself and gravity; or to a dance performed upon a vertical stage. For every participant the game is different. Who can say whether the rock athlete, living only to climb, stretching his sinews as he hangs from tiny holds, spending hours, even days, trying to solve the problem posed by a few short metres of limestone, is enjoying climbing *more* than the child clambering about on seaside rocks?

The sport of rock climbing is unfettered by formal rules. Its precepts are established by consensus, and the individual can choose whether or not to conform according to his or her own will. This is the greatest freedom of the climber: to be able to define what the game is and how it will be played. Unfortunately, the spread of organized climbing competitions threatens this freedom, for competition demands conformity between competitors, with rule breakers being disqualified.

FREE CLIMBING

Free climbing, as it has become universally known, is the basis of the sport. It is practised differently in various parts of the world, but it can be broadly defined as climbing during which all the paraphernalia of rock climbing – the ropes, pitons, nuts and karabiners – are used only for safety, while progress upward is achieved by the climber's own unaided efforts. (See page 54.)

ARTIFICIAL (OR AID) CLIMBING

Artificial climbing entails the direct use of equipment (aids) to assist the climber's progress up the rock. Generally, such techniques are employed only when free climbing becomes impossible. It may be a question merely of gaining a moment's rest by hanging from a sling or a nut on a strenuous free climb, or, at the other extreme, it may be the multi-day ascent of a massive rock wall where almost every metre is gained by artificial means.

BOULDERING

Bouldering is the art of climbing short but generally very difficult climbs on isolated rocks or at the base of larger crags. The art is climbing in its simplest and purest form. It offers freedom from the encumbrance of rope and equipment. With a pair of climbing shoes and perhaps a chalk bag as the only tools, the climber tackles the rock unaided, and success is determined by the strength of muscle, the suppleness of limb and the mastery of technique. Ideally, problems never occur so high up as to make falling off inadvisable and the ground beneath should be soft enough to make for relatively safe landings.

The activity can be intense and very demanding, for it gives you the opportunity to attempt the impossible without risking life and limb. It can be a highly sociable – even competitive – event, as when a group of friends are each spurred to greater endeavours by the example of others; yet it can also be a private affair, a spontaneous and creative activity, wandering from rock to rock, savouring the moves of favourite and familiar problems, or searching out new possibilities – seeking not just the conquest of mere difficulty but that sense of elegance that tells of perfect execution.

Bouldering is often used as training for bigger things, and it is an excellent way to improve fitness, polish technique, and attempt levels of difficulty that would never be contemplated on longer climbs. Yet the activity is significant in its own right and it has its devotees. To use an analogy from athletics, running the hundred metres is every bit as valid a sport as running the marathon.

SOLOING

The line between bouldering and climbing solo is difficult to draw, but when you realize that there is no longer any question of jumping off you have crossed it. Despite the obvious risks, many people, by seeking out easy climbs that are well within their capacity, have discovered the joy of continuous upward movement uninterrupted by the need to belay or place protection. Few are willing to undertake long and difficult climbs in such a style, and it is often assumed that those who solo without any form of roped protection have faint regard for their own lives. This is a reasonable assumption for the dangers are real. Yet soloing offers the climber the ultimate personal challenge, and it will be a sad day when the individual is prevented from accepting that challenge.

44

Left and *above* *Playing at the bouldering game — climbing in its simplest and purest form. Boulders can be used for warming up, for training to gain strength and suppleness, for follow-my-leader-type games, for competitive fun between friends, or, more recently, for deadly serious international climbing competitions of Olympic complexity, complete with television coverage and prize money. At the other end of the scale, children will boulder happy hours away without any thought beyond playing a game and having fun.* **Right** *Soloing — when there is no longer any option of jumping off! There can be little doubt that this climber has crossed the bouldering/ soloing divide.*

EQUIPMENT

The time has long passed when a single stout pair of leather boots provided all the climber might need in the way of footwear, whether he was scaling a dark Welsh crag, an icy ridge in the Rockies or an alpine peak. The modern plastic mountaineering boot, though a great improvement over its bendy, nail-shod ancestor, is still a compromise of conflicting needs. It must provide support for the ankle, insulation against the cold and a rigid sole for crampons. The rock climber needs none of these and even before the development of the specialist rock boot he would often, on difficult climbs, resort to tennis shoes, or 'rubbers' as they were called.

MODERN BOOTS
In the late 1950s the Frenchman Pierre Alain designed a boot specifically for the demanding gymnastic climbs found on the sandstone boulders of Fontainebleau, near Paris. The original 'PA', with a light leather and canvas upper and a flexible and smooth rubber sole, became the model for all the many hundreds of high-performance rock boots now available.

The latest generation of boots use a soft 'sticky' rubber sole that provides remarkably high friction, but this wears out quickly, and so a choice must be made between durability and performance. Some boots are designed for 'edging' – standing on paper-thin flakes of rock – and these tend to be stiffer across the width of the sole. Others, intended for 'smearing', are more flexible, allowing the rubber to mould itself to the rock's contours. Between these two extremes can be found compromises that are ideal for most climbs and climbers. Most important, however, are excellent fit and comfort; let those dictate the shoe you buy more than the performance characteristics claimed by the manufacturer.

HELMETS
Head injuries remain a major cause of death or serious injury to the rock climber. Despite this, the use of helmets has become increasingly unfashionable. Rhetorical excuses abound, but helmets are never as uncomfortable or restrictive as is often claimed. Rather, it is that they do not fit with the popular image of the rock athlete. Before you decide, consider whether your choice is based on an appraisal of risk or sartorial conformity. There is always a possibility of injury in a fall, and on many crags loose rock adds an extra risk. Stones are more often dislodged by other climbers than by the unassisted force of gravity. Always wear a helmet when your safety depends on the sure-footedness of others.

THE ROPE
The fundamental purpose of the rope is to safeguard the climber in the event of a fall. In this capacity, it both limits the length of the fall and absorbs the energy generated by the arrest of the fall. Secondly, it is a tool to aid descent and sometimes ascent, with abseils, tension moves, Tyrolean traverses and pendulums.

Before nylon ropes became generally available at the end of World War II, the rope most commonly used by mountaineers was made of hemp. It was heavy and horribly stiff, and because it absorbed copious amounts of water it became even heavier and almost unmanageable when wet. Worse still, it was relatively weak and inelastic, and it was sensible to mark well the dictum that 'the leader never falls' in an era when the climber could never be sure

A pair of modern rock shoes. Lightness, comfort and stickiness of sole are considerations when choosing your footwear. Some climbers favour a flexible sole for good friction (e.g., on granite); others prefer a measure of lateral stiffness for edging (e.g., on limestone).

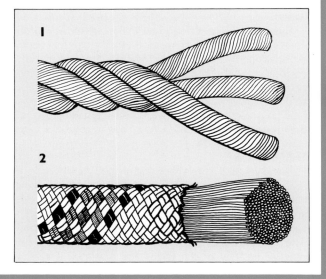

that the rope would not break. That fear at least is no longer uppermost in the mind of today's rock climber as the ground rushes up to meet him. Modern ropes are well able to withstand the force generated by the worst falls.

Like the hemp ropes they superseded, the nylon ropes used for climbing were at first of hawser-laid construction (three strands of filaments twisted together in a spiral) and classified according to their circumferences. The smallest, Nos. 1 and 2, were used primarily as slings for running belays. Single lengths of fullweight No. 4 or the No. 3 doubled were used as the main climbing ropes.

Laid ropes have poor handling characteristics. It is difficult to tighten knots in them, and they have a tendency to kink and twist; not only does this make them awkward to coil, a climber hanging in space from the end of this type of rope will spin dizzily. Nor do they lend themselves to use with abseil and belay devices such as the figure-of-eight descendeur or the belay plate. They have only one advantage: they are relatively inexpensive. For this reason their use today is largely confined to outdoor centres and to top-rope climbing on small outcrops.

The modern kernmantel rope is engineered specifically to meet the somewhat conflicting demands of the climber. The mantel is a smooth sheath of tightly braided, multi-coloured nylon fibres, fitted over a more loosely plaited core or, sometimes, a core consisting of straight nylon filaments. The performance is markedly superior to that of laid rope.

After its strength, the most important characteristic of a

*Rope manoeuvres. **Above left** A Tyrolean traverse, useful on sea traverses and for crossing rivers. **Above right** A climber using the rope to arrest a fall.*

***Below** The structure of **1** a hawser and **2** a kernmantel rope.*

1

2

climbing rope is its degree of elasticity. Ropes used for lead climbing must be dynamic, their stretch capable of absorbing the energy of a fall so as to minimize the impact on the climber, the belayer and the belay. However, climbing ropes are also required to perform in circumstances where elasticity is less desirable, such as abseiling and especially prusiking (see pages 76 and 78), when the bouncing weight of the climber will cause the rope to saw up and down on any edge over which it might pass. Good ropes, therefore, stretch little when laden with no more than bodyweight.

The majority of climbing ropes now exceed the minimum requirements laid down by the Union Internationale des Associations D'Alpinisme (UIAA), and most manufacturers publish information about their ropes that will help in making comparisons between particular brands.

Kernmantel ropes used singly have diameters ranging between 10mm and 12mm, with 11mm being the commonest (1in = 25.4mm). Those recommended for double-rope techniques are usually 9mm in diameter, but can be as thin as 8.2mm or as thick as 10mm. They are generally available in three lengths – 36m (120ft), 45m (150ft) and 50m (165ft). A typical 11mm rope has a weight of 7g per metre (about $\frac{1}{4}$oz per yard) and a tensile strength of more than 2,000kg (4,400lb).

There are a few other things to look out for. The impact load should be as low as possible, usually as low as 1,000kg (2,200lb) and never more than 1,200kg (2,650lb). If the rope is to take knots well, its flexibility, measured in millimetres, should at least equal the rope's diameter. Next, the rope's elongation, a measure of its elasticity, should be no more than 8 per cent of the rope's overall length under a load of 80kg (175lb). Finally, manufacturers sometimes quote the number of falls the rope is capable of sustaining in the standard UIAA fail test before it breaks. This could be as few as five or six, or as many as fourteen. The number gives you a rough guide as to the quality of the rope.

Also worth considering, although they cost a little more, are ropes in which either the sheath or both the sheath and the core have been treated to limit the absorption of water.

Take care of your rope and it will take care of you. Nylon fibres are easily cut, so avoid standing on the rope, especially on the rocky ground found at the base of most crags, and avoid contact with chemicals, battery acid and petrol. Ultra-violet light can also have a detrimental effect, so don't store the rope for long periods in direct sunlight. Don't buy second-hand ropes, unless you can be sure of their history – and don't use your rope to tow your car!

THE HARNESS

Suspend yourself from a rope tied around your waist for a few seconds if you wish to be convinced that a climbing harness is a necessity. Made of broad nylon tape, harnesses are designed to distribute the considerable force transmitted by the rope to the climber's body in the event of a fall. The sit harness spreads this load to the pelvis and the massive muscles of the thighs and buttocks. It is now universally favoured by climbers engaged in all aspects of the sport as the most practical, comfortable and convenient means of attaching the rope. The chest harness, still commonly sported by a few conservative continental alpinists, makes hanging belays a nightmare, and the use of descendeurs and belay plates difficult. Full body harnesses, while safer, are restrictive, take an age to fit and make you look as if you have just landed by parachute.

A good sit harness will suspend you in an upright position, though if you are wearing a heavy rucksack there may be a tendency to flip upside down, so beware of abseiling over overhangs when encumbered by weighty baggage. There is a proliferation of makes and models, some mean and rudimentary, others multicoloured with attachments for carrying equipment and padded for extra comfort. There are one-piece harnesses and others with separate and interchangeable leg loops. Many come in specific sizes; others offer adjustability, an advantage if you intend to climb in winter as well as summer or are likely to put on weight!

KARABINERS

The karabiner is a metal snap-link with a spring-loaded gate through which the rope can be easily clipped. It

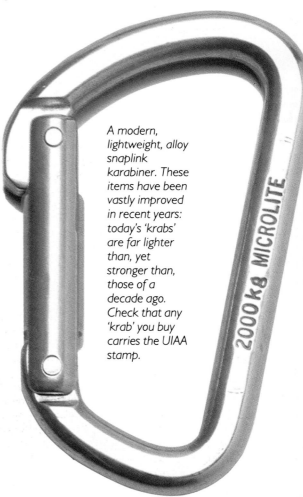

A modern, lightweight, alloy snaplink karabiner. These items have been vastly improved in recent years: today's 'krabs' are far lighter than, yet stronger than, those of a decade ago. Check that any 'krab' you buy carries the UIAA stamp.

provides a fast and efficient method of connecting the ropes to the various protection devices used by the climber, and for attaching equipment to the harness or bandolier ready for use. Karabiners are made of steel or preferably a light aluminium alloy – the climber may have to carry thirty or more. The gate is designed to lock when the karabiner is loaded heavily, but it should remain free under bodyweight.

Karabiners are available in strengths which range from 1,800kg (4,000lb) to more than 3,000kg (6,600lb). Light-weight karabiners with strengths below 2,200kg (4,850lb) should be used only in situations where they will be required to endure low forces (see page 80). They should not be used as a vital link in the main belay. With the gate open, the strength of a karabiner is drastically reduced. Screwgate karabiners can be locked manually and they should always be used in preference to the standard snap-link variety in, for example, a belay where accidental opening would result in failure of the belay, or when connecting a descendeur to the harness for abseiling. In such circumstances, twist-lock karabiners, which lock automatically, are useful for the forgetful.

TAPE SLINGS

Slings made of strong nylon webbing are useful in a variety of situations. They can be threaded around chockstones or trees, and looped over spikes of rock for belays or protection. A climber will usually carry three or four single slings of 60cm (2ft) length and one longer sling of about 120cm (4ft). These can be carried conveniently over one shoulder like a bandolier. Short slings linking two karabiners are called 'quick draws' and are used primarily to connect wired nut runners to the rope.

You can make your own slings by joining the two ends of a length of climbing webbing with a tape knot, but the neat pre-sewn joints of manufactured slings are stronger and remove the need for bulky knots, which can often be a hindrance.

Right A quick-draw sling armed with two 'krabs' and ready for action. A climber on a modern hard route may well carry more than a dozen of these.

Below Rainbows of tape slings. Check that your tapes, slings and quick draws are free from nicks and frays, and replace those that are badly worn. Very short tapes are suitable as extensions to wires on straight-up-and-down climbs. Longer tapes are useful to fit over flakes or around trees or as extensions when the route wanders or goes over a roof.

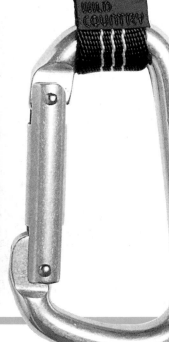

Left Karabiners: top is an offset-D screwgate and bottom is an offset-D twistlock. Both are equally good for abseiling and belaying, the screwgate variety being, arguably, the more secure but slightly slower in operation.

49

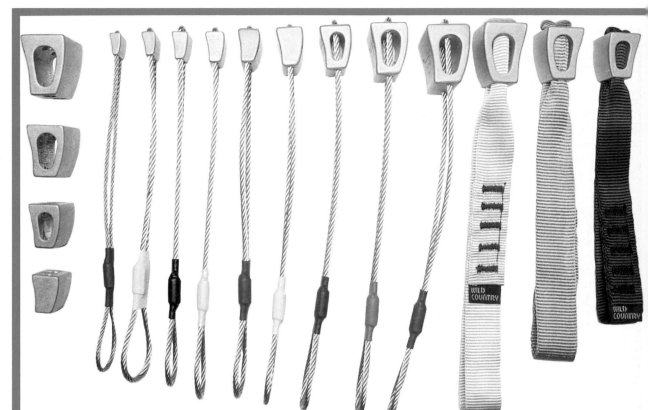

NUTS

The only means the early pioneer had of safeguarding his progress up a climb was to search out a natural feature, a spike of rock or a tree, to which he could secure himself. Sometimes, if he was lucky, he would find a fortuitously jammed rock or chockstone in a crack, behind which he could thread his rope. Later, some climbers began to carry a selection of pebbles with which to manufacture their own chockstones and by the 1950s the technique had become a fine art.

The next stage in the development of this type of artificial protection came with the substitution of hexagonal machine nuts for pebbles. Once the threads had been drilled out and the holes lovingly filed smooth, a number of 'nuts' of various sizes would be strung together like beads on a rope sling. The bewildering array of modern protection devices that have evolved from these humble beginnings enables the climber to arrange some degree of protection in a range of cracks from those as thin as a coin to some wider than the fattest fist.

The simplest type of nuts are wedge-shaped and are threaded with a loop of cord or thin steel cable, to which the climbing rope can be attached by means of a karabiner. They rely for their security on slight constrictions or irregularities in a crack. More sophisticated devices, such as 'Friends', convert the pull exerted upon them into outward pressure by means of a camming action or mechanical expansion. They enable protection to be arranged in smooth, parallel-sided, and even outward-flaring cracks and they are generally faster to place then conventional alternatives.

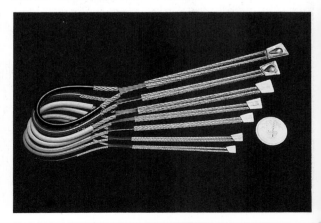

Above An armoury of nuts. *Left* A large hexcentric cammed into a parallel-sided crack. *Below* A full range of micronuts — there is something here for even the smallest of cracks.

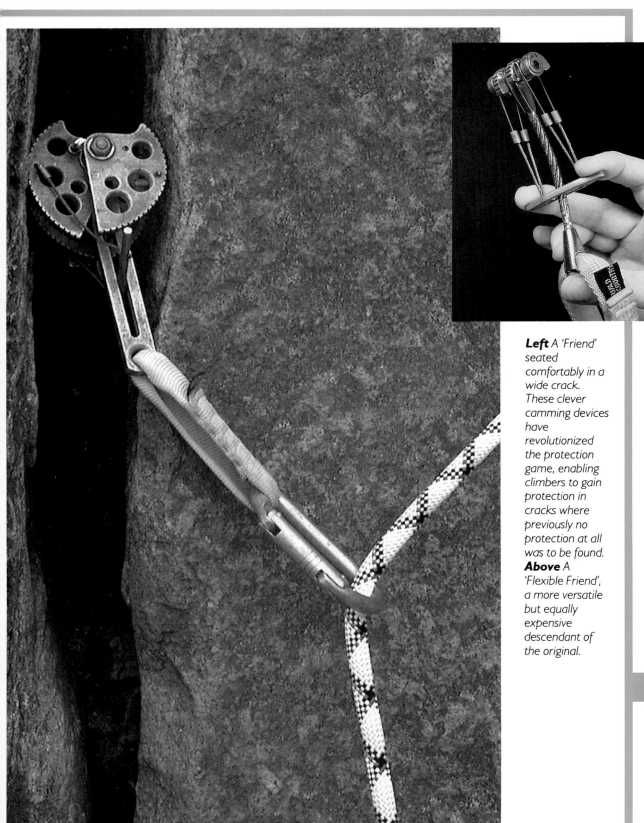

Left A 'Friend' seated comfortably in a wide crack. These clever camming devices have revolutionized the protection game, enabling climbers to gain protection in cracks where previously no protection at all was to be found.
Above A 'Flexible Friend', a more versatile but equally expensive descendant of the original.

PITONS

Pitons are steel spikes with an eye at one end into which a karabiner can be clipped. Like nuts, they provide a means by which the climber can attach himself to the rock, but they are driven into a crack with a piton hammer. They should be reserved for occasions when adequate nut placements are unavailable, for they have a tendency to damage the rock. In many areas pitons are left permanently in position on established climbs. Particularly on sea cliffs, where corrosion is rapid and not always obvious, ancient ironmongery should always be treated with suspicion.

We shall look at the subject of pitons in more detail on pages 80-81.

BOLTS

When faced with a section of rock that offers no possibility for the placement of nuts or pitons, the climber has three alternatives: he can go and climb elsewhere; he can trust to his skill and judgement and climb without protection; or he can drill a hole and place a bolt. The use of bolts is rightly controversial, for when they are placed indiscriminately they remove the sense of uncertainty that is fundamental to adventure. Every successive era has bequeathed to posterity virgin rock on which climbers have subsequently fashioned bold, epoch-making routes. The promiscuous proliferation of bolt-protected climbs denies the challenge that would be offered to future generations.

Bolts can be used creatively, however. Many of the finest climbs on the great granite walls and monolithic slabs of Yosemite Valley in California have been made possible by the frugal use of bolts, either to manufacture belays or a modicum of protection, or to link vast areas of climbable rock divided by short blank sections. When and where bolting is acceptable is a matter of consensus.

DESCENDEURS AND BELAY PLATES

Devices for belaying and abseiling have largely replaced traditional methods which use the friction generated by the rope running around the body. Their use makes these activities safer and more comfortable, greatly reducing the possibility of rope burns and making falls easier to hold, particularly when the climber is considerably heavier than the belayer. Though usually designed specifically for one purpose or the other, some, like the Sticht plate, can be successfully employed for both. It is a small metal plate with slots for either 9mm or 11mm ropes through which a bight of rope is pushed and linked to the belayer with a screw-gate karabiner. Of all abseil devices, the figure-of-eight descendeur is perhaps the most popular.

ASCENDEURS

To speed the ascent on artificial or very long, steep climbs the second will often climb the rope left by the leader. This can be done using prusik knots, but a pair of mechanical ascendeurs makes the task significantly easier. When clamped to the rope, a cam prevents downward movement, but by transferring the bodyweight alternately from one to the other, ascendeurs can each in turn be slid upwards.

52

A 'krab' being clipped into a bolt. Preplaced bolts offer probably the easiest-won protection of all. They are not, though, necessarily the safest. Their use also excites heated ethical debates in which they have been described as 'the murder of the impossible'.

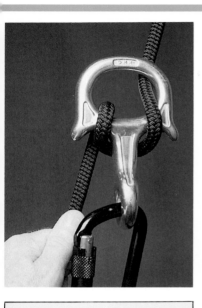

Left A descendeur – a device that makes abseiling easy, painless and safe. It is not, however, essential to carry one unless you are expecting to abseil. A Sticht plate or an Italian hitch can be used almost as effectively.
Centre left A belay plate.
Bottom left A Clog expedition ascendeur. Ascendeurs enable a rope to be climbed quickly and easily. Although not as efficient, prusik knots do the same job and are lighter and much cheaper.
Right A climber moving from the protection of one bolt to another on a steep slab. On rock such as this, bolts probably offer the only possible form of protection: without them, a daunting prospect may grow too difficult to contemplate.

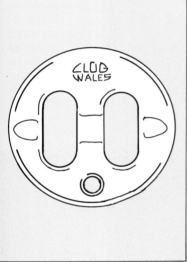

FREE CLIMBING

A climber on 'Suspense' in the Lawrence Field, Peak District, Derbyshire. He is wearing modern 'sticky' rock boots, which will 'stick' wondrously well on this rough gritstone – perhaps even well enough to enable him to reach and grab that long hold and then the thin finger crack above it. The expression on his face is a conundrum! Uncertainty, determination or quiet confidence?

The rock, the imperfections of its surface, the rugosities and cracks, its angled facets, corners, walls, overhangs and slabs provide a climber with the 'choreography' of the slow dance of ascent. The physical act of climbing is intuitive and natural, and yet it also requires skills that must be learned and practised before they can usefully be included in the climber's repertoire. Sometimes the required movements are obvious but depressingly difficult to perform; conversely, it can be that you have great difficulty in working out how you should tackle your next stage of the ascent but that, as soon as you have done so, the actual execution is elementary. Some climbs demand the repetition of a single technique, while others require complex combinations of disparate techniques and movements.

Rock climbing involves the whole body, not just the arms and legs. If you stand with your feet apart and your weight equally distributed between them, you will notice that your head is directly above a point midway between your feet. Try and lift one foot, and the position of the head and body must inevitably change if balance is to be maintained. On the ground you do this without thinking, but on the crag this natural fluidity of movement is often inhibited. Nevertheless, when climbing it is important to relax: only then will your body be given the freedom it needs to move, and relaxed muscles use far less energy than tense ones. It helps to make a conscious effort to relax. Take a few deep breaths and think *relax* before you begin a difficult section, and often you will find that the white-knuckled grip is rarely necessary.

The traditional principle that the climber should always maintain three points of contact with the rock – two hands and a foot, or two feet and a hand – can still be regarded as basically sound advice (although on some of today's more gymnastic climbs the principle might be reinterpreted as an endeavour to have at least three *fingers* in contact with the rock!). Keep as much weight on your legs as possible, and use them rather than the arms to lift the body, for they have the stronger muscles. This dictum holds good on even the steepest of climbs, where the need to conserve arm strength is at a premium.

On slab climbs keep your body well out from the rock, so that your head is poised directly above your feet: this gives the body room in which to move, increases the feet's traction on friction holds, and gives you an unhindered view of the rock in front of you. On steep-face climbs, however, keeping your weight over your feet means that you have to bring your body close to the rock. Take small steps rather than big ones if there is a choice, and try not to overreach, as this not only restricts movement but forces the muscles of the arm to work over the least efficient part of their range. As much as possible avoid holding positions where your bodyweight is supported on bent arms: you should always aim to keep your arms straight so that you are supported by bone, not muscle.

CRACK CLIMBING

Crack climbing is at once a brutal and a subtle art, born of the dank cracks that split the sombre gritstone edges of England's peaty northern moors. Over the years climbers have devised methods of jamming most of their bodily parts into cracks, inflicting pain upon themselves and leaving their hands torn and ragged.

There are three basic types of jam: those like the classic hand jam, which rely upon the expansion of muscle; those that utilize torque or the camming of appendages and limbs; and those that use the diverse available possibilities that occur for wedging relatively thicker bits of the body into fortuitous constrictions.

A jam-crack to end all jam-cracks! Such a crack would have been difficult, if not impossible, to protect before the advent of 'Friends'. Now, however, provided your body can bear the weight and your pocket the cost, this kind of parallel crack is quickly and easily protected.

55

Left Hard moves and a long neck on the crux of Void (E4 [6a]) at Tremadoc Rocks, North Wales. **Top** Finger jamming – the degree of contortion betrays the pain involved. **Above** A finger jam for both hands: this technique is about half as painful and about twice as effective as the one shown at top. Note how the thumbs, too, are being brought to bear.

FINGER CRACKS

If you examine your fingers you will notice that the bone is substantially thicker at each knuckle joint, particularly at the second knuckle. It is possible, therefore, to climb finger-width tracks by wedging the knuckles in above a constriction as if they were nut runners. This is particularly effective in very thin cracks that have been widened intermittently by the repeated placements of pitons. Vertical cracks slightly wider than the knuckles offer possibilities for finger locks. Purchase can be gained by inserting two or more fingers into the crack with the thumb pointing downwards, and then twisting the hand to rotate the fingers over one another – clockwise for the right hand, anticlockwise for the left – in a crude camming action. Another effective lock can be produced by pressing the pad of the thumb against one wall of the crack and curling the first, second and even the third fingers over it, pulling down on the fingers so that they wedge into the narrowing space between the back of the thumb and the opposite wall of the crack.

Thin cracks can be 'spragged' (a term borrowed from coal mining) by using the opposing pressure of the thumb pushing against the edge of the crack and the fingers pulling against the other. Only if the crack is faced square-on will both hands be thumbs down; if the crack is to the right of the climber's body the right hand will be thumbs up, and *vice versa*. The sprag is often used to add a degree of stability to layback moves (see page 62), and a degree of laybacking will often add security not just to a spragged hand but to jammed knuckles and torqued fingers as well. Most likely the solution will come as the result of a subtle combination of these techniques.

HALF-HAND CRACKS

There are no easy answers when you are coping with this unaccommodating size of crack. If the hand can be inserted past the third knuckle the crack is too wide for the fingers to be crammed into a secure lock; yet, if the crack is too narrow to take more than half the hand, the powerful muscle at the base of the thumb cannot be brought into play. With the fingers straight and tightly together, try forming a bridge so that the fingertips press against one wall and the knuckles on the back of the hand against the other. This is very strenuous and not very effective. With the thumb downwards, you can try camming the hand – to equally uninspiring effect. However, the two techniques used in combination might work. Another possibility is to insert the hand with the fingers pointing upwards and the thumb out, so that you can wedge the edge of the hand where it widens above the wrist. Alternatively, just muster your courage and layback.

HAND CRACKS

If the crack is wide enough to allow your entire hand to be inserted, you can use the most powerful and secure of jams. Hold your hand in front of you with the thumb fully extended, perpendicular to the fingers. Move the thumb across the palm of the hand until it is touching the base of the little finger, and watch the movement of the muscle at the thumb's base as you do this. It is this massive range of

expansion that is used to lock the hand in the crack. At the same time the fingers are flexed forwards from the third knuckle to form a solid bridge. (In slightly wider cracks the fingers would be flexed also at the second knuckle.)

Notice that the base of the hand is thicker than the wrist. In the same way as with knuckle jams in smaller cracks, constrictions can be utilized to great effect if you wedge your hand in above them.

If you are face-on to the crack, then it is likely that both your hands will be inserted with the thumbs uppermost, although this is not always the case. If the crack is a little too wide, you should try rotating your hand, something that is often more effective if you inserted your hand with the thumbs downward.

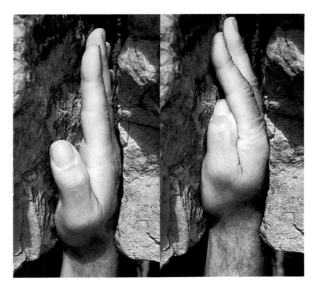

Hand jams: the secret is to arrange things so that the hand fits the crack. **Above left** A hand jam, thumb out. **Above** A hand jam with the thumb in in order to achieve a good fit. **Left** Here the hand has been made to fit the crack by including the thumb and flexing and splaying the hand. Clearly the permutations are endless.

Two ways to jam a fist. The secret is to use whichever works best – i.e., fits best.

FIST CRACKS

The fist jam is hardly an elegant device, and climbing cracks that demand fist jamming can often be a brutal business. However, often only a minimum of force is required to use a well placed fist to give you a maximum of security. Insert your open hand vertically and rotate it until it is squeezed horizontally across the crack, either palm-up or palm-down. If the crack is of the right width, closing your fingers into a fist will make a tight jam.

There are three variations. Of these, the standard fist with the thumb wrapped across the outside of the fingers is the most useful. A slightly thinner version is produced by crossing the thumb over the palm inside the fist. Third, by keeping the thumb out to the side of the fist and wrapping it over the index finger, you can gain a little extra width.

FEET

So far we have been considering various ways of jamming the hands, but what about the feet? In climbing thin cracks one often uses one's hands for fingerjams while seeking with the feet for holds on the outside wall or simply using friction, with feet flat against the rock.

The most obvious way to use the feet in a crack is to insert the foot above a constriction or a slightly wider part of the crack. Many rock boots have pointed toes with very low profiles which make insertion into thin cracks or small pockets much easier. By turning the foot on its side, so that the outside ankle points downwards, this low profile can be exploited if you then rotate the foot back towards the horizontal so that the boot is locked in the crack. This twisting of the foot gives a powerful and useful jam in cracks of any size between those that will take only the tip of the toe to those that are only a little narrower than the boot.

Purchase can be found in slightly wider cracks by dropping the heel and inserting the toe of the boot diagonally across the mouth of the crack, with one of the crack's edges running against the instep or midway across the outside of the boot.

58

Using the feet.
Above
Sometimes there are no footholds, so using the feet means finding friction. Here a climber angles his feet in opposite ways to make the best possible use of the smallest of cracks. **Right** *Good footholds can be found by angling and jamming the toes into a suitably sized crack.*

OFF-WIDTH CRACKS

Off-width cracks are seldom climbed with finesse; more often they are the scene of battle. By definition they are too wide for the fist jam and too narrow for more than an arm or a leg. Most often upward progress is possible only with tremendous effort, and sometimes even downward movement is difficult. The general sensation one feels when tackling such cracks is one of great insecurity – if not stark terror!

Over the years, many ingenious methods of jamming bits of the body into off-width cracks have been devised. Progress is caterpillar-like, with the upper body clawing upward while the lower body is locked in the crack, or *vice versa*, each half of the body taking turns in moving and locking.

For cracks that are only just bigger than fist size, it is possible to pad out the fist jam by placing the palm of the other hand flat against the wall of the crack and jamming the fist in the narrowed gap. Alternatively, both fists can be stacked side by side, the thumb of one hand held firmly in the other. Both of these rather exotic techniques suffer from the problem that you have to move both hands at the same time.

A foot can be jammed heel-to-toe across the crack unless the crack is wider than the foot is long, in which case the other foot can be stacked with the instep behind the heel of the first, so that together they form the shape of a letter T.

The muscles of the forearm can be expanded to lock in the crack by bending the arm at the elbow and then clenching the fist. Similarly, the knee can be locked in the crack by bending the leg, a technique that is sometimes very effective.

Wider cracks allow arm-bars to be employed. You insert the arm shoulder-deep into the crack, with the palm of the hand pressed flat against the forward wall and the bent elbow against the back wall. By pulling the hand in towards your body, your forearm can be forced across the crack – although not without effort. The same bar used the other way up, with the hand close in by the hip and the fingers pointing downwards, is less strenuous as it is the body's own weight that provides the force. Also useful, particularly for resting, are inverted bars, in which the arm is fully bent inside the crack with the elbow pointing up above the head and the palm of the hand, with fingers down, pressed hard against the rock beside the face. This is a very powerful bar, for any downward pull tends to lock the forearm more tightly across the crack. It can be used also in a horizontal position, with the elbow pointed into the crack.

Quite often it is the leg and arm outside the crack that provide the upward motion and the limbs locked inside it that maintain whatever position has been gained. Look for potential footholds on the outside wall or nicks in either edge of the crack that could be used to give purchase for a toe or a heel. The outside foot can be tucked back flat against the back wall of the crack, and the outside hand can grip the forward edge at waist level to provide an upward push.

Above Off-widths are the most feared cracks of all because they are difficult to protect and take their toll of clothes, energy and flesh.

Above A hands-off rest won by the judicious jamming of a knee. **Left** Arm-barring, a useful and effective technique when climbing off-widths.

59

CHIMNEYS

The borderline between an off-width crack and a chimney is essentially that a chimney can be entered by the whole body. Very narrow 'squeeze' chimneys are climbed using basically off-width techniques with a few additions. Rests may be obtained by inhaling deeply and jamming the expanded chest. If the chimney is no wider than the distance from hip to knee, then both knees can be pressed forward against the front wall, with the feet (heels up, toes down) flat against the wall behind and the back pushed against this same wall.

Wider chimneys are climbed using the classic technique of 'back and foot': the feet are pushed against one wall and the back against the other. To move the body upward, either both hands are pressed flat against the back wall at hip level or one foot is tucked back against the back wall to oppose the pressure of the forward foot: in either case, the back is released, and so it is possible to make a few centimetres of upward progress. Then, by pushing off the far wall with the hands, the body can be held while the feet are moved higher, and so on.

If the chimney is too wide to be spanned between back and feet than the technique of 'bridging' may be used. With one foot and one hand on each wall, all pressing in opposition, or even both hands on one wall and both feet on the other, one can slowly advance upwards by letting each limb move in turn.

Left A climber silhouetted in a chimney. However, although this image looks pretty, climbing chimneys is often more a matter of energy than of aesthetics. **Above** A climber bridges to the bottom of a chimney and contemplates his next move.

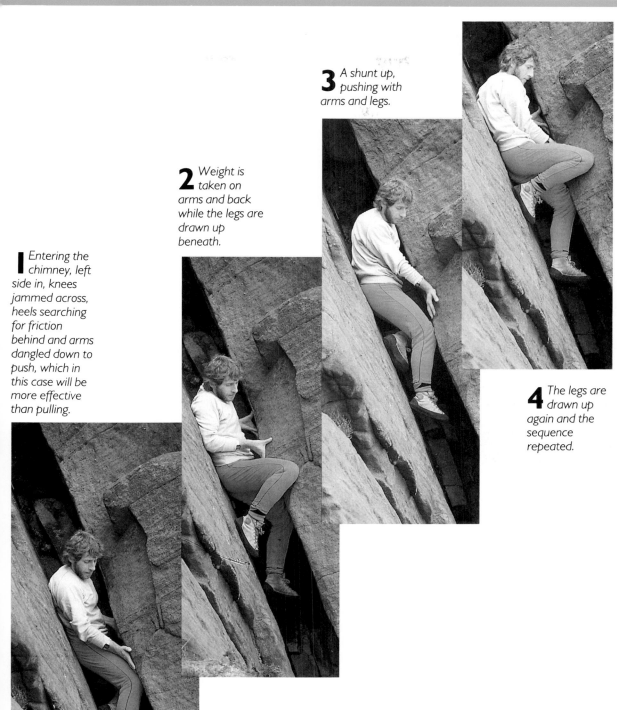

3 A shunt up, pushing with arms and legs.

2 Weight is taken on arms and back while the legs are drawn up beneath.

1 Entering the chimney, left side in, knees jammed across, heels searching for friction behind and arms dangled down to push, which in this case will be more effective than pulling.

4 The legs are drawn up again and the sequence repeated.

61

LAYBACKING

Like chimneying, the layback requires the use of opposing forces. The technique is of use when climbing arêtes, right-angled corner cracks, and cracks which cannot readily be tackled using jamming. It is often athletic, and it is nearly always strenuous.

When you are laybacking a crack, your body remains in the same plane as the rock, with a shoulder rubbing the wall to one side of the crack. You then lean back with your arms straight, grasping the crack's nearside edge in both hands, while your feet push against the crack's far edge. Sometimes you can leapfrog your hands over each other up the crack, but more often it is the hand of your inside arm which takes the lead. You must keep your hands and feet as far apart as stability will allow, for the closer they are together the more strenuous the position becomes.

A problem commonly encountered in laybacking is the tendency to pivot out of the layback like a door swinging on its hinges. 'Barndooring', as it is called, can be countered by pushing off the rock beyond the crack with the outside foot or, if you are climbing a corner crack, by keeping the foot out to one side of the corner so that you can restore the equilibrium by pushing off the far wall. Alternatively, it may be necessary to search in the opposite direction for a handhold which will halt the swing.

THE MANTELSHELF

In its most basic form, the mantelshelf is the technique anyone would naturally employ to heave themselves up in order to stand on the flat top of a brick wall. The first part of the manoeuvre is generally the most strenuous, as it requires a fair amount of impetus to raise the body to a position where its weight is balanced on straight arms, with the hands pushing down onto the hold. The second part, although it too can require a considerable amount of power, is primarily a matter of balance. The weight is moved onto one arm, making it possible for a foot to be brought up onto the hold beside the hand. You have to try to get the foot as close to the supporting hand as possible in order to make the transfer of weight from hand to foot easier. There is sometimes a temptation at this stage to use a knee instead of making the extra precarious effort to get a foot onto the hold. Using your knee is regarded as poor style, but in such circumstances style is quite often not your top priority! More important, though, is the fact that, while using a knee can be expedient, it usually makes it more difficult for you to struggle to a standing position. Before you use the mantelshelf, try to anticipate which foot you will need to raise and where it will have to be placed, for it will be difficult to move your hand on the hold once you have committed the full weight of your body to it.

Mantelshelfing.
1 *A climber reaches up and grasps the mantelshelf.*
2 *The second hand, too, grasps it, and the climber launches upward in a continuous and dynamic movement using the feet for friction, should there be nothing more substantial available.* **3** *Maintaining the upward momentum, he rises over the hands, pushing until the arms are straight.*
4—5 *Now a foot can be brought up and the mantelshelf completed.*

BELAYS AND BELAYING

It is usual for one member of the team to secure himself to the cliff and tend the rope while the other climbs. This use of the rope to safeguard the climber is called belaying. The object to which the rope is anchored, be it a spike of rock, a tree, a piton or a nut, and the means by which the rope is secured are both referred to as the belay. The term also designates the place or stance where the belay is set up, whether it is a luxurious ledge or simply a point at which the belayer hangs suspended from the rope. Longer climbs are ascended in a succession of stages called pitches. The length of a pitch is dictated by the distance between stances, the availability of suitable belays, or the length of the rope.

Start by uncoiling the rope, throwing the end to one side so that it does not become lost under the growing pile, then pay it out loop by loop into a loose heap on the ground near the base of the climb. If the coil is badly twisted, it may be worth pulling all the rope through your hands once or twice until you are sure it will run smoothly, for it will be embarrassing if, with your arms beginning to tire, you are unexpectedly halted in the middle of the crux of the climb while your second struggles to unravel the tangled rope.

Whoever is to lead the first pitch should tie-on to the end of the rope running from the top of the pile, the second tying-on to the end running from the bottom.

TYING-ON
The exact method of threading the rope through the climbing harness will vary from one type of harness to another and the manufacturer's instructions should be carefully followed.

The two knots most commonly used for tying-on to the end of the rope are the bowline and the double figure-of-eight. Because of its symmetry, the ubiquitous figure-of-eight is particularly suited for use with modern harnesses. It is strong, uncomplicated and unlikely to work itself loose. The bowline is faster to tie and is more easily undone after it has been heavily loaded, but it does have a tendency to work loose, especially if the rope is unusually stiff. It should therefore always be used in conjunction with either a full or a half hitch to secure the end.

A rock-climbing team in action. Here are belayer and belayed high and lonely on smooth, steep limestone. On this sort of terrain, bolts are often the only means of protection. With no ledges to stand on, the second has taken a hanging stance.

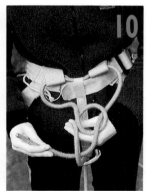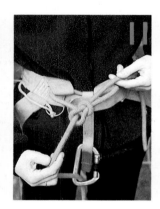

*Two methods of tying-on. **1—8** Tying-on with a figure-of-eight knot and finishing with a stopper knot. This is probably the commonest way of attaching the rope to the harness. **9—12** Tying-on using a bowline — equally satisfactory, but not as popular as the other method.*

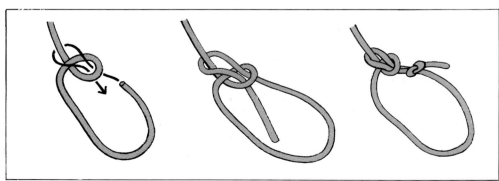

Left *When using a bowline secure the tail with a full or half hitch .*

BELAYS

Though a belay anchor may be required to withstand a force more than twenty times that of bodyweight it is rarely put to the test. When selecting an anchor ask yourself if you would, without hesitation, abseil off it. If there is the slightest doubt, then multiply that doubt by twenty and ask yourself again if it will make a safe belay anchor.

At the same time, consider what would happen if the climber you will be belaying were to fall. In which direction would you be pulled, and will the anchor sustain a force from that direction? A good thread belay is multi-directional, but a sling draped over a spike of rock is not. As a climber progresses up a pitch, the likely direction of pull on the belay will often change. If a leader falls before he has placed any protection, he will fall past the belayer, until held by the rope, and the pull will be downwards. If the climber has managed to fix protection before he falls, then the pull on the belay will be upwards. Should the protection fail, the direction of pull will change from up to down.

Let us assume that you have successfully climbed to a ledge on which you intend to belay and you find there a convenient anchor in the form of the tortured trunk of an ash tree growing from a crack (it could just as easily be a large flake of rock). Wrap a tape sling around the tree, joining the two loops with a screw-gate karabiner into which the rope is tied (with either a clove hitch or a double figure-of-eight). Bear in mind that an insufficiently long sling may cause a dangerous three-way loading of the karabiner. When using a single belay point, the anchor and the belayer should be in line with the direction of pull. Make sure that the rope between the belay and the belayer is tight, and screw up the karabiner.

Tying directly onto the belay in this way uses a minimum of rope, but if the anchor is some distance from where you intend to stand, or if you have to climb up a metre or two above the stance to reach it, then estimating exactly how long to make the belay will be more difficult. The alternative is simply to clip the rope through the belay karabiner and lower yourself back to the stance. Adjust the length and secure it by threading a bight of rope through an appropriate place on the harness (preferably the loop formed in the knot used to attach the end of the rope to the harness) and tie the bight off with a figure-of-eight or two half-hitches. If a second belay point is used the process can be repeated, or you have the choice, once again, to tie-on directly with a clove hitch or a figure-of-eight.

It is the belayer's job to adjust the amount of rope between the climber and himself, taking in or paying out as necessary. The waist belay utilizes the friction generated between the rope and the belayer's body to arrest a fall. The rope running from the belayer to the climber is known as the active or live rope, the remainder as the inactive or dead rope. The rope runs under both arms and across the lower back of the belayer, the live rope through one hand and the dead rope, wrapped once around the forearm, into the other hand, which controls the rope. In the event of a fall, friction is increased by bringing the controlling arm swiftly across the front of the body.

66

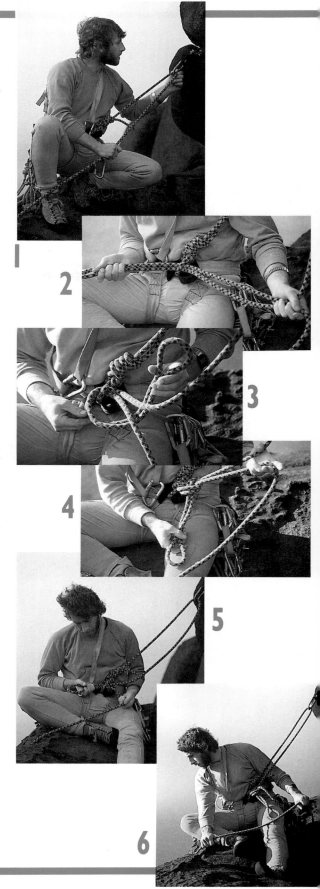

Left Belaying. **1** Select and position an anchor. Take the rope from the harness and pass it through the 'krab' clipped into the anchor. **2—5** Tie a figure-of-eight on the bight, ensuring the rope between you and the anchor is snug. **6** Now you can bring up your partner.

Above Things can go wrong. You may desire a second anchor point. **Above right** Using a figure-of-eight tied into a bight and clipped directly into the second anchor. **Right** Ensure all ropes between yourself and the anchor remain taut.

The clove hitch is another way of securing to a second anchor point. **1—5** Form a clove hitch and clip into the second anchor, as with the figure-of-eight. An advantage of the clove hitch is that it can be readily adjusted to keep the rope taut.

67

It is important to ensure that the belay is so arranged that a fall does not cause the rope to be ripped from the hands of the belayer. If the belayer turns to face out from the cliff the rope running from the belay anchor to the tie-in at the front of the harness should pass on the same side as the live rope. On a hanging belay where there is no choice but to face the cliff, the live rope should run across the front of the belayer from the side opposite the direction of pull. Alternatively, by running the live rope through a karabiner clipped into the tie-in loop at the front of the harness, the risk of having the rope torn from the belayer's grasp is alleviated.

BELAY PLATES

Belay plates such as the Sticht provide an alternative to the waist belay that is in almost all respects superior. A bight in the rope is pushed through the slot in the plate and clipped into a screw-gate karabiner which is attached to the loop in the bowline or figure-of-eight knot that has been used to tie the rope to the harness. With the active rope held in one hand and the inactive in the other, the rope can be paid in or out through the plate by bringing the hands together so that the rope runs closely parallel. Braking is applied by moving the hand holding the inactive rope through nearly 180° away from the direction of pull, forcing the plate up hard against the karabiner. It is important to ensure that the plate is set up so that the live rope emerges from it on the same side as the direction of pull, and that the movement of the braking arm cannot be impeded by the belayer's own body or the rockface.

Belay plates provide dynamic belaying. It is intended that some rope will slip through under load. There remains the possibility, therefore, that in arresting a fall the braking hand will sustain rope burns if a glove is not worn.

A better way of belaying uses a friction plate, as we see in pictures 1–3.

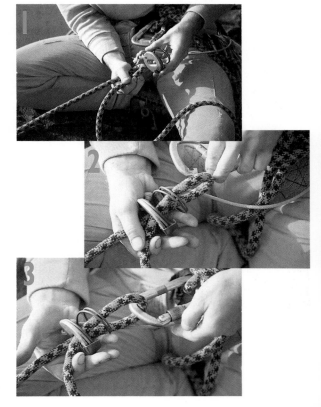

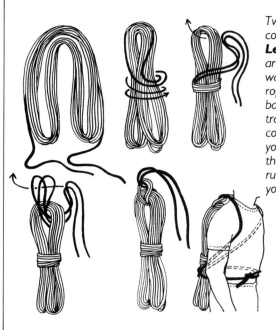

Two methods of coiling a rope. **Left** Alpine coils are useful if you want to carry the rope on your back. **Right** traditional coiling, used if you want to sling the rope on your rucksack or over your shoulder.

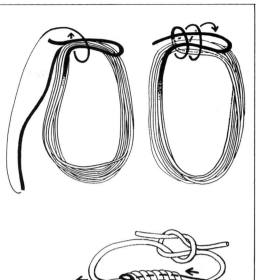

1

1—5 *Taking in the rope through a belay plate. As with the waist belay, it is important that at no stage should the controlling hand be removed completely from the rope. Study this sequence and, preferably, practise it until you are certain of every stage. Never be tempted to take shortcuts while going through the sequence of actions: a shortcut could cost a life.*

2

3

4

5

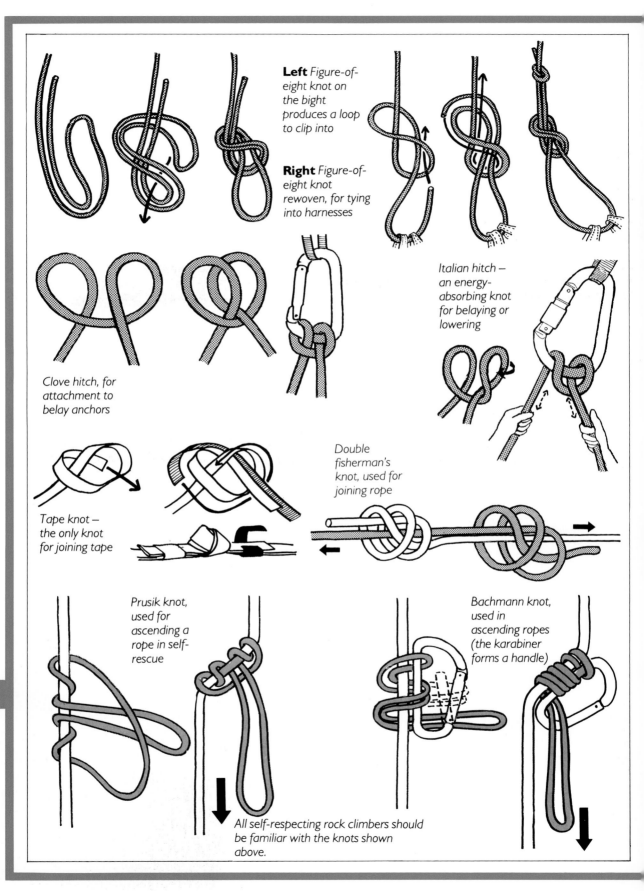

Left *Figure-of-eight knot on the bight produces a loop to clip into*

Right *Figure-of-eight knot rewoven, for tying into harnesses*

Clove hitch, for attachment to belay anchors

Italian hitch – an energy-absorbing knot for belaying or lowering

Tape knot – the only knot for joining tape

Double fisherman's knot, used for joining rope

Prusik knot, used for ascending a rope in self-rescue

Bachmann knot, used in ascending ropes (the karabiner forms a handle)

All self-respecting rock climbers should be familiar with the knots shown above.

COMMUNICATION

It is not unusual on a climb for visual contact between the leader and the second to be lost, and in windy conditions voice communication can also be difficult. In such circumstances a set of calls whose meaning is understood by both climbers will prevent misunderstanding.

'Safe!' The leader indicates that he has finished the pitch and is secured at the stance. The second can therefore relax from the task of belaying and, if a belay plate is being used, it can now be removed from the rope. However, the second should not at this stage remove his own belay.

'Taking in!' The leader informs the second that he is about to pull up all the surplus rope that remains between them. The second should continue to tend the rope while this happens, making sure that it does not snag and rises free from tangles.

'That's me!' The second tells the leader that all the surplus rope has been pulled in.

'Climb when ready!' The leader instructs the second that he is ready for him to begin climbing. It is now safe for the second to remove his belay, and when he is ready to climb he shouts:

'Climbing' Before he sets off, however, he should await confirmation from the leader, who after making a final check that all is safe calls down:

'OK!' The second can begin to climb.

As understanding develops between them, climbing partners will often forgo the strict formality of such a system. If it is anticipated that voice communication will be difficult, such as when climbing on sea cliffs with the roar of waves crashing against the rocks below, it is sensible to agree beforehand on a series of tugs on the rope that will signal the required information. Learn also to comprehend the 'informal' information that the rope can communicate on those unexpected occasions when shouts cannot be heard. The long pause while the leader searches for, or places, belay anchors and the sudden uptake of rope as he pulls up enough to tie the knots, will be followed by a slight slackening of the rope as he settles himself at the stance. Then, if the remaining rope is taken up with a steady and rhythmic pull, it is probably reasonable to assume that the climber is 'taking in', but belaying should not be dispensed with until all the rope has been paid out. The second should not untie his own belay until all the signs indicate that it is appropriate. Even then, remember it is only an *assumption* that this is a safe course of action. It would be wise to remain connected to the anchor by means of a tape sling, or simply to undo the belay knots but leave the rope running loosely through the belay karabiner as if it were a runner. If the slack rope thus generated is immediately taken up and the pull remains strongly insistent, then perhaps it is safe for the second to begin to climb.

When leaders traverse it is important they protect their seconds as well as themselves. Climbing calls may be the sole means of communication.

Other calls that may be used as the need arises are:

'Slack!' The climber requires the belayer to pay out more rope.

'Take in!' The belayer should pull up any slack rope that has accumulated. The term 'take in slack' should be avoided as it may be confused with the previous call.

'Tight!' The climber wants the rope to be taken in tightly to support some of his weight. This call is often shouted with a note of urgency which gives an indication of how tight 'Tight!' should be.

'Watch the rope', **'Watch me'**, **'Take me'**, **'I'm coming off'**, **'I'm off'** and other more colourful exclamations warn the belayer that the belay is about to be tested. On long pitches the leader will find it helpful if the second informs him of how much rope remains to be paid out, with calls of **'Six metres'**, **'Three metres'** (or **'Twenty feet'**, **'Ten feet'**) and lastly **'That's me'** when all the rope has been used.

ROPE MANAGEMENT

The lead climber can protect himself as he ascends by periodically placing running belays. 'Runners' can be manufactured with nuts or slings or any of the many devices that the climber uses to attach himself to the rock, and the rope is clipped to them so that it runs freely through the karabiner. A runner not only reduces the potential length of a fall but also its severity. If the leader places a runner at 6m (20ft) and then falls off after 7·5m (25ft), he will, as long as the runner is secure, be held by the rope after falling little more than 3m (10ft). That is double the distance he was above the runner, plus a little for the rope's stretch.

THE FALL FACTOR

The severity of a fall can be described by the 'fall factor'. This is determined not just by the distance fallen, but also by the amount of rope between climber and belayer which absorbs the energy of the fall. Thus the fall factor = length of fall divided by length of rope.

Until a runner is placed the climber will continue to face a fall of the highest possible severity – that is, double the amount of rope run out from the belay. The severity remains the same regardless of the distance fallen. Only when running belays are placed is the factor reduced; on multi-pitch climbs place a runner as soon as possible to prevent the belayer taking the load directly. The factor continues to be reduced as additional runners are placed and the ratio between the length of rope and the length of fall increases.

Above *Making good use of the rope. Modern climbing ropes are designed to bear up to five falls of Fall Factor 2. After that, they are best discarded.*

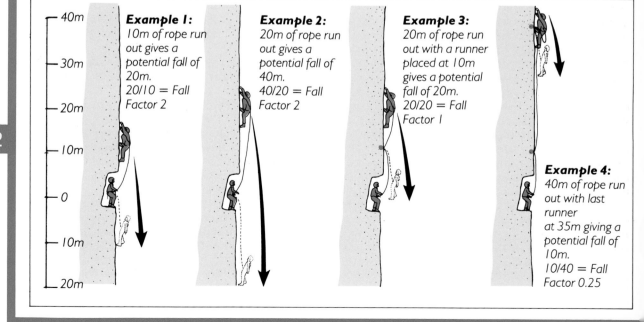

Example 1:
10m of rope run out gives a potential fall of 20m.
20/10 = Fall Factor 2

Example 2:
20m of rope run out gives a potential fall of 40m.
40/20 = Fall Factor 2

Example 3:
20m of rope run out with a runner placed at 10m gives a potential fall of 20m.
20/20 = Fall Factor 1

Example 4:
40m of rope run out with last runner at 35m giving a potential fall of 10m.
10/40 = Fall Factor 0.25

Learn to recognize when a fall could be particularly disastrous and climb accordingly. Consider if there is a chance that you might be arrested by something other than the rope: if you hit something, you get hurt! Falling into space from a hard overhanging wall is often less serious than falling on much easier, low-angle climbs. The further you fall, however, the more likely it is you will hit something, a ledge or even the ground, and the faster you will be travelling at the moment of impact.

On the first pitch it is important that the belayer is positioned close under the climb. If the belayer stands away from the base of the cliff the rope will run down from the climber to the first runner and then out to the belayer at an angle. A fall will cause the rope to straighten and pluck the lower runners from the rock in succession, leaving only the topmost runner and a gibbering climber suspended from it.

Some climbs, especially those that follow crack systems, offer abundant opportunities for the arrangement of protection. On others the possibilities are rare or nonexistent. It is this variance that decides the seriousness of a climb. Fixing nut protection efficiently is a difficult art. Training the eye and the imagination to recognize potential placements and selecting the correct type and size of nut require practice. Often it will be necessary to clip the rope into the karabiners using only one hand. Make sure that the gate faces away from the rock so that it cannot be opened accidentally by a protrusion, and that the hinge is uppermost. Grasp the rope between the thumb and index finger and, hooking the tip of the middle finger into the karabiner, pull down to hold it steady as you push the rope through the gate. By simply repeating this process the rope can also be unclipped from the karabiner.

THE RACK

The mass of ironmongery the climber takes with him up the climb is called the 'rack'. It can be carried on the gear loops of the climbing harness or on a bandolier across the shoulder. Both methods have advantages and disadvantages. On overhanging routes, the equipment on a bandolier tends to swing around behind the climber, making selection difficult, and weight carried high on the body raises the centre of gravity and thus puts more load onto the arms. Gear carried on the waist-belt of a harness can also be difficult to reach at times – for example, when the nut required is on the quarter opposite the only free hand. Also it is not so easy to hand over the rack to your partner if you are alternating leads on a multi-pitch climb.

It is a good idea to arrange the equipment into some sort of order and it helps greatly if the position of every item is known so that it comes easily to hand. Rack the equipment systematically according to category and size, group the

73

Well placed protection. With protection arranged thus the Fall Factor will never be very high and you are unlikely to come to grief. Alas, geology is not always so considerate and it may be impossible to place runners so comfortingly above the head.

Left *There are many ways of racking gear; the only real criterion is that it should be readily accessible and should not encumber the climber. Here, the longer slings might have been better around the neck since, dangling from the waist, they are likely to tangle with the climber's legs.*

quick draws together (two karabiners connected by a very short sling), and arrange the wired nuts, those threaded with cord and the 'Friends' separately in groups of ascending size. Wired nuts of a similar size can be carried on one karabiner, giving several bunches ranging upwards from the smallest micro nuts. Placements are then made by removing the appropriate bunch from the rack, and selecting and fitting the nut into the crack before unclipping the karabiner carrying the remainder. The nut should then be linked to the rope with two karabiners joined by a sling. This is necessary to prevent the nut being lifted out of its placement by the upward movement of the rope, which is likely if the wire is linked directly to the rope with one karabiner. Larger nuts are generally threaded with cord and do not suffer from this problem. They are therefore usually carried individually on a single karabiner that is then used to connect the nut directly to the rope.

ONE ROPE OR TWO?

The dilemma facing the novice climber buying his first rope is whether to opt for single- or double-rope technique. The cost of one 11mm rope is less than that of two 9mm ropes. The cheapest option is to purchase one 9mm rope and to choose a climbing partner who can provide another.

The use of a single rope has the advantage of simplicity. There is less rope to tangle and less weight for the climber to drag behind him up the climb. The belayer's job of managing the rope is simplified, and the leader, with only one rope to clip into the runners, is saved the need to perform yet another demanding intellectual task.

Single ropes are popular in areas like Yosemite Valley where climbs of uncompromising directness follow single cracks in the monolithic granite. In Britain, where climbs often take devious and wandering lines, the use of two differently coloured ropes is common. Double-rope techniques offer the climber several advantages but great potential for mismanagement.

Imagine a climb that snakes its way through angled walls of rock, moving left and right between two parallel cracks that rise a metre or two apart. With runners placed alternately in either crack, a single rope would zigzag upwards, causing unwanted friction at each turn and increasing the likelihood that the runners would be lifted out. With double ropes this problem can be alleviated by clipping one rope into all the runners on the left and the other into all those on the right, leaving each rope running parallel and straight. Even when climbing a single crack there are advantages to double ropes. It is often the case that the climber will place a runner at arm's reach above the head, so that for a time the rope runs up to the runner and down to the climber. Using a single rope, an airborne climber in this situation will fall further if the top runner pulls out than one who had clipped a second rope into the penultimate runner below his feet.

There is also the possibility that a climber with failing strength will fall as he pulls up extra rope, before clipping the next head-high runner. He will be held sooner if a second rope runs through the previous runner. When only runners of dubious security are available, double ropes enable the climber to duplicate placements, and so to be held by two ropes at the same time, thus reducing the impact on each runner.

Double ropes also offer extra security for the second, who can protect himself on traversing pitches by using a back-rope. Again, though it is very unlikely during a fall that a rope would snag on a sharp flake and be cut, the occurrence is not unknown: two ropes then have an obvious advantage. Lastly, when retreating from a climb by abseil, it is useful if there is sufficient rope to enable the descent to be made from belay to belay. This leads to the somewhat senseless practice, adopted in areas where use of the single rope is common, of trailing a second rope unused until the descent is begun.

Ultimately, however, the choice between single- and double-rope techniques is up to you.

Right In areas where climbs take devious and wandering lines the use of two differently coloured ropes is common. But, though double-rope techniques give you some advantages, it is easy to make a tangle of them. Here two climbers struggle to manage a double rope on 'A Dream of White Horses', Wen Zawn, Anglesey, Great Britain. **Below** The great advantage of using a single rope is simplicity: there is less rope to tangle, and less weight of rope to drag up behind you. Also, the leader is free to concentrate on climbing, rather than on rope-work.

ABSEILING

Germans 'abseil', French 'rappel' and Americans 'rope down', but the British do not have a word of their own for this method of descent. Once the heart-in-the-mouth fear encountered on the first abseil has been overcome, those new to the game often find the activity more exhilarating than the climb itself, while callus-handed veterans have been known to turn white at the mention of some infamous abseils. Though the technique of abseiling is simple and easily learned, it is unwise to become complacent about its dangers. During the ascent the climber is safeguarded by the rope; when that same rope becomes the means of descent there is no longer any back-up if things go wrong.

All methods of abseiling, whether they employ special devices or the largely redundant traditional techniques, use friction to control the slide down the rope. The classic method generates friction by winding the rope around the body. It is most uncomfortable and little used, but worth knowing if only because it requires no equipment other than a rope and some thick clothes. The rope passes between the legs, and is wound up from behind across the right hip, across the chest, over the left shoulder and down the back to be held in the right hand. The rope running to the anchor is held lightly in the left hand.

A slightly less painful alternative to the classic method is to run the rope from the anchor up through a screw-gate karabiner clipped to the appropriate place on the sit harness. The rope is then passed over the left shoulder and into the right hand or *vice versa*. It is this hand which controls the descent, increasing the amount of friction by bringing the rope forward across the body.

A Dülfer sit harness can be improvised using a large (2.5m [8ft]) tape sling. Pass the sling behind you, running the lower half across the top of the thighs and the other across the small of the back. Bring the two loops to the front across each hip and pull a third loop up between the legs from behind and join them all with a screw-gate karabiner. If a double sling is unavailable, a short sling can be twisted into a figure-of-eight, giving a loop for each thigh. Clip the karabiner into both loops.

The development of friction devices such as the figure-of-eight descendeur (see page 52) has made abseiling safer and undeniably more comfortable. Their universal adoption has not, however, removed the need for care. Make it a habit systematically to check each element in the chain before you commit yourself to the abseil. Make sure that the rope is connected to the anchor, that the descendeur is connected to the rope, and that you are connected to the descendeur. Use screw-gate karabiners and in each case make sure that the gate is closed and locked. Ensure, too, that clothing and hair are not dragged into the descendeur, causing it to jam.

Belay plates and even the Italian Hitch can be used to abseil, though the latter tends to twist the rope badly.

It is also possible to improvise a descendeur using several karabiners. The Karabiner Brake is a useful addition to the repertoire of any climber, but its nuances should be learnt by the fireside and not on the cliff top.

With all these devices it should be remembered that more friction will be required for a controlled descent of a rope hanging clear of the rock or if the climber is carrying a heavy rucksack, and that a single rope generates less friction than two ropes and a thin rope less than a thick one.

SETTING UP THE ABSEIL AND RETRIEVING THE ROPE

Firstly make sure that the anchor to which you intend to attach the rope is secure. Make sure the tree is firmly rooted, that the spike of rock is part of the mountain and that the piton or nut is well set. Abseil points already in place should always be treated with suspicion: pitons corrode, especially those on sea cliffs exposed to salt-laden air, and the strong sunlight of high mountains rapidly weakens nylon rope and tape. No one wants to leave behind expensive equipment but, if there is any doubt, ask yourself how you are going to spend the money you saved when the anchor fails.

An alternative is to back up the anchor temporarily, making sure that the anchor you intend to leave takes all the load and is thoroughly tested by the descent of the first person. The extra anchor can then be removed before the descent of the optimistic second.

Secondly, when choosing suitable anchors for an abseil, bear in mind that the rope will need to be recovered, and that a jammed or hung abseil rope will maroon you on the cliff as effectively as if you had dropped the rope.

Let us imagine that the abseil point you have selected is a small but robust pinnacle of rock. Though the rope would fit neatly in the crack behind the spike, you decide to abandon a tape sling, for then the rope will run easily and you can be more certain of its recovery. Thread the end of one of the ropes through the tape before joining the two ropes together using either a double fisherman's knot, two linked figure-of-eight knots or a reef knot secured by two full hitches. Coil each rope separately and, unless the abseil ends on the ground, it is a wise precaution to tie stopper knots in the ends that will jam in the descendeur and thus prevent the possibility of abseiling right off the rope. Wise also is the use of a prusik knot connected to the harness and fitted to the rope just above the descendeur, so that it will lock unless pulled down the rope by the upper hand. The French prusik is ideal for this task as it can be easily released even when loaded.

If there is a chance that there is anyone below give them warning by shouting, 'Rope below!' Throw the ropes out well clear of the cliff so that the likelihood of them snagging is reduced, and check that they are not tangled and that they reach the ground or the next abseil point. Before the first person descends it is worth reminding each other which of the two ropes will eventually need to be pulled. Pulling the wrong rope will jam the knot up against the anchor.

Unless you have aspirations to be a Hollywood stunt-man, descend smoothly and without hurry. Try not to bounce unnecessarily or to swing from side to side as this will damage the rope, sawing it on any edges over which it might pass. Once down, the first person should pull the appropriate rope to make sure that it runs freely and can be retrieved. The last man down should, as he descends, ensure that the rope above him remains untwisted. Before pulling the rope down, secure yourself to a belay if the situation warrants it and part the ropes to see if they are crossed. Once the rope begins to move do not stop pulling.

Left 'Abseiling', 'rappelling' and 'roping down' are all different names for the same process – a handy, sometimes essential, way to the bottom of a climb. **Below** Abseiling into this climb is much simpler than would be scrambling to the bottom to beat the tide.

77

PRUSIKING

Jumaring — or 'jugging', as it is often called in the United States — is very much a part of everyday climbing on big walls such as those found at Yosemite, California. The climber on the left is following his leader using ascendeurs on a climb called Tis-sa-sack. It is perfectly possible, however, to climb for a lifetime without ever having to resort to such mechanics.

There are some situations when it is either necessary or expedient for the climber to climb up the rope. This technique, known as prusiking, is commonly used on big-wall climbs to speed the ascent of the second man, or on major expeditions when ascending fixed ropes between camps. It is also of use in emergencies: it can be used to extricate oneself from a crevasse (see page 99) or, if a climber falls from an overhang and finds himself dangling in space with insufficient rope to be lowered to the ground, prusiking may well be the only way of regaining contact with the rock.

Climbing up a rope requires the use of two slings, preferably tied from 7mm rope, one short (60cm) and the other long (120cm). These are wrapped around the climbing rope using prusik knots or any of several other friction knots, such as the klemheist,

which will grip when under load but which can be advanced up the rope when the load is released. The short sling is clipped with a screw-gate karabiner to the climbing harness or to a sit sling. The long sling acts as a foot loop, and it is important to tie it to the climbing rope below the short sling. Progress is made by advancing each sling alternately. Standing in the foot loop allows the sling attached to the harness to be moved up the taut rope; the front loop then takes the climber's weight while the foot loop is advanced.

A pair of mechanical ascendeurs, although expensive and cumbersome to carry, make the task of prusiking infinitely easier. They are generally used with a foot loop or étrier fitted to each; because of the possibility that an ascendeur might slip or become detached from the climbing rope, it is a wise precaution to attach both clamps independently to the climbing harness.

1 The climber has arranged two prusik loops: a short one from waist to rope and a longer one for a foot. (The lower karabiner is largely redundant.)

4 Stand up in the lower prusik. This releases the load on the upper prusik and allows you now to slide that loop as high as you can.

2 With your weight resting on the upper prusik, have the foot loop as high as is comfortable.

3 Now, holding onto the rope for balance only, put all your weight onto the lower prusik.

Prusik knots. **Left** The conventional prusik knot, perhaps the most common of all friction knots, has the disadvantage that it tends to jam when loaded. The Klemheist **right** is less susceptible to jamming and is if anything even easier to tie. It also works well with tape slings, which can be useful if you have no prusik loops. A very similar and very versatile knot is the French prusik, tied by simply wrapping a short sling around the rope three or four times and joining the ends with a karabiner.

ARTIFICIAL (AID) CLIMBING

As standards of free climbing have risen, many climbs which were once regarded as possible only by artificial means have had their aid points dispensed with. Sometimes this is a direct result of aids having been used so often in the past: the repeated use of pitons has often widened once thin cracks enough for fingers to be inserted instead of steel. Increasingly, aid climbing has fallen from favour, and those who practise its arcane arts have found their airy stances usurped and their methods banished from all but the most heavily defended territory. Anyone who today pounded pitons into the liberated limestone of Yorkshire's Gordale Scar or into the warm, rough granite of California's Joshua Tree would find themselves very unpopular.

Although aid climbing does indeed allow less athletic mortals to develop a taste for the spectacular from which they would otherwise be barred, it should not be assumed that aid climbing is easy. The most difficult aid climbs are as much ventures towards the limits of the possible as the most difficult free climbs, and aid climbing allows you to do some things you could never even consider if free climbing. It takes a special kind of cool nerve to lead a 50m (165ft) pitch of blank white granite, moving from one creaking copperhead to the next, from rurps to sky hooks rotating on minute flakes and back to rurps again, expecting that at any moment the single tiny point holding you up above the void will suddenly erupt from the rock face so that you hurtle downward in a rush of consuming air...

EQUIPMENT

Except for a few specialized items discussed below, the aid climber's equipment is the same as that used for free climbing (see page 46). However, the quantities required are substantially greater. For example, it is not uncommon for 100 or more karabiners to be needed. (They should therefore be lightweight, although at the same time it is better if they are large enough to provide a comfortable grip for the whole hand, and if they are oval rather than D-shaped.)

Etriers are stirrups, made from knotted or sewn nylon webbing, with three or four steps; originally they were made from cord with wooden or aluminium rungs, but étriers made like this are now found only rarely. Each étrier should be fitted with its own karabiner, from which it hangs – although some favour a fifi hook, which allows remote retrieval from above by means of a thin cord. One pair of étriers per climber is sufficient for most artificial routes, although carrying a third is worth it if the undertaking is a difficult one.

The basic process is that the climber places a point of aid – be it a piton, nut or something more exotic – and then fits it with a karabiner, into which two étriers are clipped. If the climber steps up into the bottom loop of one étrier with the right foot, and then places his or her left foot one loop higher in the second étrier, it is possible to sit on the left heel with the étrier passing on the inside of the left knee, with the right leg thrust forward and kept straight. Using a short sling called a cow's tail means that the hands are freed from the need to hang on; the cow's tail is fixed to the tie-in point on the sit harness, and is fitted with a karabiner or a fifi hook which can be attached to the karabiner on the étrier. After the climber has moved up to sit in the top rung of the étrier, a shorter cow's tail will be necessary, and because of this need for adjustability a chain of karabiners or other variable-length systems are often used.

The climbing rope should be clipped in only when the climber has drawn level with the aid point. Clipping the rope in while you are in the lower steps of the étrier or even before moving on to the aid point means that, should the point fail, you will fall further, and therefore the sudden force on the previous point of aid will be greater.

USING PITONS

Climbing expanding cracks is a nerve-racking business, for pitons tend to force the crack apart, each successive placement loosening those below, including the one from which you are hanging. It is therefore better to rely on nuts or 'Friends'. However, if the use of pitons is unavoidable, then it is a good precaution to clip into the next peg with a sling before you have driven it fully home. Then, even if the one you are hanging from fails, there is a good chance that the top piton will hold.

Fortunately, this is usually unnecessary. Once the next aid point has been placed and the third étrier has been clipped into it, you can test the point's security while still remaining attached to the lower point: you simply bounce a couple of times while transferring your bodyweight.

Pitons are no longer the aid climber's primary tool, their use being limited in the main to thin knifeblade cracks. Modern nut protection, 'Friends' and other similar devices provide alternatives that are faster to use and undeniably less damaging to the rock. Piton hammers have today, therefore, to serve two purposes: placing and removing pegs, and removing stubborn nuts. This latter problem is common in aid climbing, for every placement has borne the climber's weight. Hammers with a slender pick make the task of removal considerably easier.

A perfectly placed piton will sing a rising scale with each blow of the hammer. It is a sound that often brings a feeling of joy and relief. Less elating are the succession of dull, even notes which never rise a semitone and tell of what is euphemistically called an expanding crack, and the vibrating twang emitted when the tip of the peg hits bottom in a shallow or blind crack.

Pitons come in all shapes and sizes. Top row, left to right: a leeper and four sizes of angles. Bottom row, left to right: five sizes, shapes and thicknesses of blades for lost arrows (or kingpins) and two knifeblades. This is but a small sample of the dazzling array available on the market.

Try not to over-drive pitons if their purpose is simply to hold your bodyweight, as this will only make their removal a more difficult and time-consuming process.

Pitons that cannot be driven full into the rock should be tied off with a short loop of tape, using a clove hitch or a larks foot, around the blade at the point where it protrudes, so that the leverage is reduced to a minimum. This is a common requirement, and 'tie-off' loops will often be needed in abundance.

It is faster and more efficient if the second cleans the pitch of equipment while prusiking up the lead rope. This enables a piton to be removed under tension, by clipping an old karabiner and sling into the eye and pulling outwards, while at the same time hammering the piton from side to side in the crack – first in one direction as far as it will go, and then the other.

There is a wide variety of pitons, each type designed for a particular size of crack. A few of these are summarized below (crack size in brackets):

The Realized Ultimate Reality Piton, or rurp (hairline/blind) The smallest piton imaginable. You only need to use one to realize why the name is justified! The rurp's short blade – some are less than 1 cm (2⁄5in) in length – is designed to chisel its way into almost nonexistent cracks.

Off-set – Knifeblade and Bugaboo (hairline to 0.5cm [1⁄5in]) The karabiner eye is set at right angles to the blade, allowing the piton to be used in corner cracks. Lengths range from a little more than 3cm (1 1⁄5in) to 10cm (4in), with Bugaboos being thick and Knifeblades thin.

Lost Arrow (0.5cm to 2cm [1⁄5–4⁄5in]) A beautifully forged robust piton. Both sides of the blade as well as the

face are tapered, allowing the thicker versions to be placed on edge. They vary in length from about 4cm (1 3⁄5in) to 15cm (6in).

Angle (1cm to 3.5cm [2⁄5–1 2⁄5in]) A piton of folded steel with a V-shaped cross-section tapering to a point, giving three points of contact with the rock.

Leeper (0.5cm to 2.5cm [1⁄5–1in]) A Z-shaped cross-section and an off-set eye (as on the Bugaboo) not only give greater security in vertical cracks but enable two or more pitons to be stacked together very effectively.

Bong (3cm to 15cm [1 1⁄5–6in]) A big piton, the biggest being almost as wide as they are long. Bongs get their name because a climber carrying a rack of them sounds like a herd of alpine cattle! They differ from angles only in that the head is riveted together and the larger sizes are usually made of light aluminium alloy drilled with a number of weight-saving holes. They can be placed, although precariously, lengthways across very wide cracks.

A couple of other items of equipment are worth noting.

Sky hooks are small hooks made of hard steel from which the climber can dangle when all else fails. There are many forms – flat and curved, pointed and square – designed to be lodged precariously on small edges, or hooked over the top of a flake or the lip of a pocket. Using sky hooks is sometimes safer than might be imagined, but usually they promote a feeling of great insecurity.

Copperheads, although crude, enable bodyweight-bearing placements to be made in shallow pockets, seams and crackless corners which will take neither nuts nor pitons. The copperhead is a lump of copper or soft aluminium, swaged on the end of a loop of wire, which is hammered into the rock until it is persuaded to cooperate.

CLIMBING WALLS

Indoor artificial climbing walls have transformed British climbing in the 1980s, and have been largely responsible for the explosion of improved technical standards. So popular have they become that climbing on them has almost become a separate subsection of the sport, with particular 'problems' on certain walls gaining 'classic' status nationwide.

The idea of climbing on man-made edifices is hardly a new one. Perhaps the best known collection of 'artificial' climbs is to be found on the college buildings of Cambridge University – and, as such climbing has never been permitted by the college authorities, most of it has had to be carried out at night with great stealth! The 'Railway Wa's' in Edinburgh were even written up in a guidebook – by none other than the late Dougal Haston himself. John Dawes used to practise on an old Fives Court at Uppingham School. The pillars of Telford's Menai Bridge have seen frequent ascents. Ed Ward-Drummond climbed Nelson's Column. Routes have been forced up the outside of cooling towers, and there are countless walls, bridges, embankments, breakwaters and the like throughout the country that have felt the grip of whitening knuckles over the years.

The idea of the climbing wall simply cashed in on this market by providing 'designer climbing' – and, a vital point in the British climate, providing it *indoors*. One of the earliest and best known of these walls was at Leeds University; inauspiciously, it was sited in a corridor. Nowadays, all modern sports or leisure complexes will have a climbing wall on the list of potential facilities, and a fair percentage actually possess one. There have been many different designs; some simply using bricks, some using 'bolt-on holds', some made from natural stone. Perhaps the most successful involve casting natural rock holds and artificial holes and slots into cement blocks which can then be incorporated in standard brickwork.

Most walls 'evolve'; that is, extra holds appear on the brickwork as climbers seek to establish more difficult ways of getting from A to B. This seems to be a factor in the development of increasingly more difficult moves.

USING A CLIMBING WALL

Climbers use walls for three main reasons: to develop appropriate strength and endurance; to develop skill in tackling progressively harder 'problems'; and, last but not least, for *fun*. Most sessions on the wall involve each of these elements, but, in order to minimize the risk of soft-tissue injury, all climbers should have some sort of progressive schedule which they use when training.

Warm-up General exercises (see discussion of training on page 84).
Stretch Stretch all joints after warming up.
Fast, easy traversing Use only the bigger holds and keep moving.
'Problems' Working out moves and sequences of increasing technical difficulty. This is best done competitively with a partner.

A wall such as this will give the fingers and forearms a searing work-out. Even the most innocuous-looking walls often conceal great possibilities. Try them and see what you can find.

'Pump-out' Continuous traversing using small or non-existent footholds. Continue until you drop!
Stretching and relaxation This will minimize muscle soreness after training.

Modern walls are not good places for a beginner, unless you are strong and athletic: the walls are usually vertical and the holds small, polished and awkward to use. Chalk is absolutely essential, as the humidity soon builds up when several people are working hard indoors. Beginners often ask why walls are not made easier – less steep and with bigger holds. There are really two answers: easy walls would rapidly become boring, and less steep walls would be more dangerous in the event of a fall, it being difficult to jump off from them to land on the floor.

Remember, the climbing wall is a very specialized *gymnasium*, and as such is a potentially dangerous place: treat it as such, and not as a playground, and you will find working on the wall both enjoyable and productive.

GRADES

s we have seen, climbers pride themselves on having no written rules: climbers therefore spend much of their time arguing over different interpretations of those unwritten rules! Nowhere is this more apparent than in the inevitably subjective area of grading. Rock is such an irregular medium, and climbers come in such a range of shapes and sizes, that any grade can at best be only an indicator. Grading is more of an art than a science – and some would say a black art!

It all began quite sensibly with the Victorians, who described climbs to their contemporaries using adjectives such as 'easy', 'moderate' and 'difficult' – the original adjectival grade descriptions. Unfortunately, climbers have a habit of 'improving' things. So, with the benefit of their predecessors' knowledge, new techniques and equipment advances, the authors of guidebooks were soon using terms such as 'very difficult', 'severe', 'very severe', 'hard very severe' and finally 'extremely severe'. Furthermore, these descriptions were often subdivided into intermediate shades of difficulty, until you had opaque descriptions such as 'Mild Hard Very Severe'!

This adjectival grading system took all aspects of the climb into account: the difficulty of each move, the number and quality of runners, the problems of route-finding and ease of escape, together with all objective dangers – loose rock, bottle-throwing tourists, spiders, snakes, holly bushes, avalanches, etc.

As standards continued to rise, the category 'extremely severe' was subdivided into E1, E2, E3, and so on, an open-ended system which has currently reached E9. At the same time, there was an increasing demand for the purely technical difficulties of each pitch to be described separately: in other words, that the full description should answer the question: 'What's the hardest "move" I'll have to make?' This rudimentary system has now evolved from one originally used to describe climbs on Clogwyn du'r Arddu, Wales, into a number and letter sequence with each numerical grade subdivided into a, b and c, in ascending order of difficulty. Although, theoretically, it should start 1a, 1b, 1c, 2a..., very few guidebook writers bother to give numerical grades below 4a, which normally corresponds to about 'hard severe'; currently the highest grade thought to exist is 7a or 7b. Using this system, a five-pitch climb might be graded 'E4: 5c, 6a, 6a, 5a, 4b'. 'E4' is an overall, subjective grade taking into account all the factors mentioned above, while the purely *technical* difficulty is quoted for each pitch. This helps uneven climbing pairs to decide who is going to lead which pitch, although any low pitch-grade cited on an otherwise hard climb should be looked at with suspicion! For the 5a and 4b pitches above, although relatively easy, could lack protection, if the overall grade is E4!

The physical effort demanded of the climber by rock such as this is obvious: the need to train for such climbs is equally so.

Unfortunately, the application of grades is not uniform throughout the country – generally, the smaller the crag and the less mountainous the area, the greater the tendency towards an undergrading of technical difficulty.

With this two-tiered grading system now well established in Britain, it should be possible to discern whether or not any particular climb is for you. Cool-headed weaklings with a death-wish can go for routes with relatively low pitch-grades (e.g., VS: 4a), since this implies that the difficulties will be other than technical (no runners, loose rock, difficult route finding, etc.); cowardly body-builders can go for routes with a high technical grade relative to the overall grade (e.g., VS: 5a), safe in the knowledge that their muscles, rather than their minds, will be stressed!

GRADES FOR AID CLIMBING

Pitches of aid climbing are graded numerically in ascending order of difficulty from A1 to A6, with A0 being given to predominantly free climbs that have only one or two points of aid. The grade reflects not only the difficulty of making each placement but also the security of those placements. On a typical pitch of A1, every point of aid would be solid and easy to place, while one of A2 could have one or two insecure placements, or solid placements that are difficult to reach. An A4 placement is one that will only just support the weight of the climber. It follows, therefore, that an A5 placement is incapable of sustaining even that, and would fail under bodyweight. Grades of A5 and A6 are given to pitches which consist almost entirely of A4 placements, where a fall would probably result in the swift 'unzipping' of each point of aid in succession.

TRAINING FOR ROCK CLIMBING

In recent years, top climbers have followed the lead of other athletes concerning training and fitness schedules. However, with no coaches to guide them, many climbers are ignorant of the best and safest methods. Attention to the principles outlined below should enable those who wish to train for rock climbing to do so more effectively and safely.

CARDIO-VASCULAR FITNESS

The importance of heart and lung efficiency in the supply of oxygenated blood to the muscles, and in the removal of the waste products of muscle action, is paramount. The benefits to climbers are enhancement of general muscular endurance and limitation of the effects of muscle cramp. Cardio-vascular training should form a fundamental part of any schedule.

Training techniques Any prolonged exercise of the major muscle groups which exerts the heart and lungs (i.e., makes you puff and pant) is beneficial. Such exercises, which are called 'aerobic', include running, cycling, swimming, squash, easy repetitive weights circuits done at speed, and fast continuous traversing on a climbing wall.

Dangers Apart from the possibility of serious damage to feet, knees and hips through repeated running on a uniform, hard surface such as a road, there is little danger in this area of training for the young and healthy. However, anyone with a heart or respiratory condition should consult a doctor before embarking on such a training programme.

MOBILITY (SUPPLENESS)

Having a good range of movement in all the joints of the body allows whatever strength is available to be applied most effectively. This is obviously an important aspect of fitness for all rock climbers.

Training techniques Increases in mobility are generally brought about by carefully stretching joints beyond the comfortable 'end position'. Two main methods are recommended. One is to hold the 'end position' for about ten seconds before relaxing. The more you do this, the more the 'end position' will be extended. The other method is to stretch to the 'end position' and then try to 'unstretch' against resistance provided by a partner, holding the tension for about six seconds. If you then relax, your partner will be able to extend your 'end position' somewhat.

Dangers Obviously, stretching muscles, ligaments and tendons beyond their normal limits is potentially dangerous, so you must take some precautions: operate only in a warm room; warm up *thoroughly* by running, jumping, hopping, and so on for at least 20 minutes before stretching; work the muscle groups surrounding the joint

before trying to stretch them; and remember that regular sessions of gentle stretching are far better than a weekly or monthly blitz.

STRENGTH

Although this is commonly thought to be the most important fitness element, in practice there are few occasions in climbing when a 'one-off' maximum muscle contraction is called for.

Training techniques Increases in strength (the ability to perform single, maximum contractions) are best achieved by 'progressive overload' using weights. Training should involve working at the limit of strength in one particular muscle group at a time. However, exercises with weights are specific to particular muscle groups, and as climbing involves a wide range of movements, a full spectrum of exercises should be used for a balanced effect.

Dangers When stressed to overload, muscles can tear. That is one worry. Perhaps more commonly, though, the less resilient elements of soft tissue – such as tendons (which join muscles to the skeleton), ligaments (which hold the joints together) and cartilage (the cushion for bones in contact) – can be rendered liable to severe and possibly irreversible damage. Over-powerful muscles can rip tendons, while the enormous loads placed on joints during training can damage ligaments and cartilage. Thorough warming-up and a cautious approach are needed if injury is to be avoided.

MUSCULAR ENDURANCE

This particular aspect of strength training is the most useful in that it allows muscular activity to be maintained for increased periods of time. The aim of training here is independently to develop an efficient cardio-vascular system while working the important muscle groups for longer and longer times. However, muscular fatigue in climbers is usually more a function of mental stress and over-tensioning than of lack of endurance.

Training techniques A good exercise is traversing a good climbing wall or bouldering area: climb quickly and continuously, using moderate-size holds, for as long as you can; then rest and repeat. An alternative or adjunct is to do fitness circuits in a weights room or gymnasium.

Dangers *Climbing can be bad for the body.* Particularly damaging are situations where static loads on cold muscles and tendons are followed by explosive bursts. Arthritis, varicose veins and tendon injury are just a few of the potential dangers. In training, never hang motionless for long periods of time, particularly when you are using weight belts or some other method of overload: this can cause irreparable tissue and joint damage. The fingers are especially vulnerable, particularly when cold and stiff.

SKILL

Without skill, all the fitness training in the world cannot turn you into a rock climber, so it is on skill that the emphasis in any training schedule should lie. Skill is acquired by watching, trying and feeling. Watch skilled performers at work and acquire a mental image of what they are doing. Then try it yourself, experimenting and 'feeling for what seems to work.

Training techniques Bouldering (see page 43) is the best way to develop skills. Artificial climbing walls, natural 'boulders', bridges and buildings can all be used.

Dangers As with any other form of training, first warm up and then tackle more difficult problems progressively. The warm-up becomes increasingly important with age: young climbers can get away with all sorts of mild abuse, whereas after you are beyond the age of 35-40 your body is quite unforgiving of any carelessness in this respect.

Despite all this discussion of the *physical* aspects of fitness, you should remember one paramount truth: the real key to successful and enjoyable rock climbing rests not in the body but in the mind.

Ron Fawcett powering his way up a climb: the physical demands are manifest. Climbs of this order of difficulty will probably never be overcome by natural talent alone. Modern rock climbing requires modern training methods; as the standards continue to rise, so will the intensity of the training.

85

ETHICAL CONSIDERATIONS

Climbing is a game played without rules, played on a field without boundaries, and played within the players themselves. This sums up the curious, even mystical, appeal of what is essentially, if looked at objectively, a rather pointless activity! Of course, there are the obvious 'gymnastic' and 'adventure' elements of climbing, but these are just an attractive lure for the unwary novice. Once hooked, the climber finds himself or herself enmeshed in a web of ethical intrigue and mental struggle.

Although, as we have noted from time to time, the rules of climbing are largely unwritten and are not always essential, they do exist, and most climbers know what they are. The term 'ethics' is used as a substitute for 'rules' probably because climbers are generally an anarchic bunch, and do not see their sport as one in which any concept labelled 'rules' can play a part. However, climbing does need rules, because of the fundamentally artificial nature of the activity in modern times. Getting to the top is no longer the sole goal – it is the act of climbing itself which is both the means and the end. There are, of course, one or two exceptions to this, but with few unclimbed peaks remaining in the world, most of the obvious goals have already been attained.

The rules, which preserve the challenge of the activity, are generally more restrictive the more artificial the nature of the 'game'. For example, what is regular practice in the Himalayas might well be thought of as 'cheating' on a Derbyshire outcrop. Furthermore, as one moves progressively downwards from Himalayan climbing, there is a corresponding tightening of the rules in terms of keeping technological advances at arm's length (although recently the pressure for higher technical standards has led to a slackening of the crag-climbing ethic).

'Style' is an important and widely used concept. It refers to the set of rules used in a particular ascent. 'Good' style describes an ascent according to the most restrictive set of rules in normal operation – for example, 'on-sight, chalk-free, no falls' or 'alpine-style, with no oxygen or fixed camps or ropes'. The description 'poor' style implies that the wrong set of rules has been used.

From the above discussions, progress might be thought to result from two contradictory developments: further tightening of the rules, on the one hand, and on the other the attainment of ever more difficult goals using the same or less-restrictive rules. Most of the great ethical debates which periodically flare up in the climbing press, and which fuel endless discussion amongst groups of climbers wherever they gather, centre on this crucial dichotomy. Those whose aim is to perform the same climbs but under more restrictive rules are usually thought of as 'purists', while those whose goal is to push back the borders of the possible are regarded as 'gymnasts'.

Currently, the following ethics seem to apply to rock climbing in Britain:
- First ascents may involve minimum 'cleaning' of vegetation and genuinely loose rock from abseil pitches. 'Chipping' of holds is not permitted, and the pre-placing of runners is also frowned upon.
- The use of pegs should be kept to an absolute minimum.
- Expansion bolts should never be placed on traditional, volcanic mountain rock, sandstone or gritstone. Their use on limestone and other softer rock such as slate should be seen as a last resort.
- Chalk (light magnesium carbonate) should be used conservatively, and only when needed.
- When repeating routes, the style to aim for is 'on-sight, no falls, no rests'.
- In the event of a fall (or a 'technical' fall, such as grabbing a runner), the climber should immediately lower down to the first place where he or she can 'rest' without aid from the rope, before climbing back up to attempt the moves again.
- Hanging from the rope after a fall before continuing is called 'hang-dogging', and is tantamount to aid climbing. Falling and lowering from progressively higher runners is called 'yo-yoing', and is another form of 'cheating'.

In an attempt to establish a clearer ethic, some climbers are adopting the French 'red-point' technique which allows any amount of 'rule-bending' while the climber 'practises', just so long as he or she eventually makes a 'red-point' ascent with no falls and with no weight placed on any runners. Time alone will determine whether or not this ethic replaces the 'on-sight' one, although it seems that the idea of starting at the bottom and climbing to the top is losing out to the 'clean, inspect, practise and then climb' school. But the only thing which is certain is that the game will evolve, and the very word 'evolution' means change.

All of the above is concerned with the competitive ethic. This is clearly important for competitors, who require the rules if they are to sort themselves out and decide who is the better climber. But there is a second type of 'ethic', the 'environmental ethic', and it is the one which non-climbers are usually more concerned about. Factors to be considered in this category are: the use of chalk, the destruction of vegetation, litter, the wearing of brightly coloured clothes, and the disturbing of bird life. The chipping of holds is a major abuse of both forms of ethic, whereas 'traditional gardening' is a breach of only the environmental ethic. Breaches of the environmental ethic are fundamental, have long-lasting effects, and have repercussions outside the sport. Breaches of the competitive ethic are all in the mind, and in the wider context are actually trivial – but climbers are nevertheless acutely aware of them.

This climber is resting on a runner – a common enough practice. But is it ethical? Does it matter? The climbing game is governed not by rules or referees but by an indefinable code – 'ethics', as climbers somewhat grandiosely call it. These ethics vary considerably according to area, nation, rock type, precedent, history, season and personality.

In all of this the climber has four choices: to observe the rules where possible, to bend the rules to suit, to *pretend* to observe the rules (i.e., to 'cheat'), or to ignore the rules. Fortunately, most climbers are happy to try to observe the rules wherever possible, but with so many people now bending them it is becoming increasingly difficult to identify what the rules actually are. However, this is probably a good thing, provided the environmental ethic is not brutally violated: ideally a climber should feel free to do his or her own thing, and to reject rules imposed by other people.

SNOW AND ICE CLIMBING

Left *Some modern snow and ice climbing gear.* **Right** *Climbing in fine style on 'Body Freeze', Beinn Dearg.* **Far right** *Water ice. Note the runner for protection.*

Ice climbers are users of tools – tools such as ice axes and crampons, which allow them to enter and delight in a crystal world, and without which they would be as handicapped as a skier without skis or a canoeist without a kayak.

Rock is relatively unchanging, but snow and ice are ephemeral – perhaps a water course that has frozen for a few bitter winter weeks, or the verglas encrustation of a rock face. Even the permanent snowfields and glaciers of the high mountains are constantly changing their form, as each successive snowfall slowly metamorphoses into ice. It is this unpredictability that gives snow and ice climbing its special appeal. An ice climb can change from delightful to impossible between one day and the next. In the even shorter term, the control of the climber can melt in an instant, in the time it takes to move the axe from a secure placement to a poor one.

ICE AXE AND ICE HAMMER

Before you opt for any particular model of ice axe, first consider the uses to which it will be put. It will have to perform a number of functions. You will use it as a walking stick when crossing ice that is level or only gently sloping, as a probe in search of crevasses, or totally buried in the snow to provide a belay. The adze can be used to cut steps or belay stances, and the pick not only provides purchase for the ascent of steep ice and hard snow but can in emergencies be used to arrest a slide.

The shaft of a general-purpose axe should be 55-70cm (22-28in) long. Long axes are unwieldy on steep ground, but short axes reduce one's reach and are poor for use in arresting a slide. On all but the easiest climbs you need also an ice hammer. The shaft of the hammer is generally shorter than that of the axe – usually it is 45-55cm (18-22in) in length.

Ice tools are often used for belaying, and so the shafts need to be strong. The traditional hickory and ash have

been largely replaced by light alloys sheathed in plastic or rubber.

There is a bewildering array of bizarrely named weapons from which to choose, but they can be grouped into four categories, according to the type of pick.

First there is the curved pick, which reflects the curved path described by the axe during the most natural and powerful swing, finished off with a flick of the wrist. The relatively long pick allows good penetration when hard ice is overlaid by powder or unconsolidated crud. Picks of this type are excellent for general mountaineering and ice-axe arrest, and for steep climbs, too, as long as the ice is not so thin or brittle as to prevent deep penetration.

Then there is the short straight pick of the Terrordactyl type, angled downwards at 45° to the shaft. This requires a very different arm action. The wrist is kept firm, and the placement is made with a short downward stab. This type of pick is valuable on thinly iced rocks, where penetration is minimal; it can also be inserted into cracks and hooked behind icicles. It is good for the canny tricks devised by the Scots for climbing their winter cliffs. However, on the hard black ice found on winter alpine slopes or reaching over the bulging mushrooms of frozen waterfalls, you are likely to bruise and batter your knuckles because of the shortness of the pick. Moreover, it is not much use for ice-axe arrest.

'Banana'-picked tools allow a more natural swing yet retain all the advantages of Terrordactyls. They are excellent for very steep ice – thick or thin, hard or soft – and their only disadvantages are that penetration through surface layers of snow or rotten ice is poor, while ice-axe arrest is difficult.

The fourth and final pick-type is the tube pick, specifically designed for brittle waterfall ice. Because the displaced ice can escape up the hollow centre of the tube, the ice as a whole is less likely to shatter. Although picks of this type are excellent for climbing frozen waterfalls, they are easily damaged by rock.

Most manufacturers offer matched pairs of tools which differ only in that one has a hammer-head and the other an adze.

The problem with many modern tools is not so much getting them to stick but releasing them for the next placement. A little judicious work with a file will save you from possible embarrassment. The top edge of the pick should be bevelled for several centimetres from the tip, and if necessary round off the teeth on the underside should they be too deep or too sharp.

A wrist loop is essential on all but the easiest snow climbs: not only can it take much of your weight, if you are on steep ice, but on mixed climbs of rock and ice it allows you to let go of the axe so that your hands are free. The length of the loop should be measured precisely so that it gives support to the wrist of the hand grasping the shaft immediately above the ferrule. Most axes have a hole either at the base of the pick or in the head or shaft through which a length of nylon tape can be threaded. The sling should be adjusted to fit your hand clad in your normal gloves or mitts.

Some climbers, for fear of dropping an axe, like the additional security of a leash connecting it to the harness. If you are using two tools, the net effect of this is generally a tangle. However, assuming good placements, such an arrangement does allow you an occasional rest. A good

compromise is to have a cord to the axe alone, which acts as a form of self-belay while you place an ice screw using the hammer. Use the hammer with your stronger hand.

MOVING ON SNOW

Moderately steep snow slopes – up to an angle of about 35° – are usually ascended in a succession of zigzags. You should hold the axe in the uphill hand with the shaft thrust vertically down into the slope. Try to avoid moving the axe and a foot at the same time. The axe is best held with the pick to the rear, ready for self-arrest.

In relatively firm snow, you can slice steps across the fall-line with a forward thrust of your foot. In softer conditions you will have to stamp the snow underfoot until you have created a firm step. Your aim is to produce a platform that slopes in, rather than out, and which is long enough to support the boot from toe to heel.

If you are making a direct ascent, face the slope and kick into the snow with the toe of your boot; hold the heel high so that, once again, the step slopes in rather than out. In descent, face outward using a sort of straight-legged goose-step, keeping the toes up so that the heels cut deep into the snow under the weight of each plunging stride – but do beware of any sudden changes in the hardness of the snow. If the snow is steep or hard face inward, placing the axe low for support, or descend diagonally, keeping the axe in the uphill hand.

ICE-AXE ARREST

On snow, a collapsing step or a momentary lapse of concentration can easily result in a slide, which if not corrected immediately is likely to be fatal. Before ever you venture onto snow-covered hills you should both know the techniques of self-arrest and have practised them rigorously.

Find a safe place to practise: a concave slope with a gentle run-out that has a good covering of firm snow through which no rock or ice protrudes.

Practise without crampons. It is all too easy to stab yourself in the leg or to catch a spike and twist an ankle. Forsake the use of a wrist loop, too, because if you lose control the last thing you want is your axe whipping around your head and body.

Climb the slope and sit down with your heels dug in. Begin with the side you favour, but do not neglect the other. Assuming you are right-handed, hold the head of the axe in your right hand, with your thumb curled around the angle formed between the adze and the shaft. With your left hand grasp the ferrule so that the spike is virtually hidden in your mitted fist. Position your axe such that the shaft runs diagonally across your chest, the adze being above your right shoulder and the pick pointing out to the front. Grip the axe tightly and pull its shaft hard against your breastbone so that it cannot be ripped out of your hands.

Now the fun begins. Slide down on your back and then roll over to face the slope. Always roll toward the head of the axe (if you are right-handed, this means toward the right); if you roll the other way – i.e., onto the hand holding the spike – there is a good chance that the spike will dig into the snow causing you to somersault. Spread your knees apart and lift your feet well clear of the snow – this should become an automatic habit whether or not you are wearing crampons. Do not try to stop your slide down the slope with one mighty blow of the pick. Slow down, and eventually stop, by striking the pick a number of times, each more forceful than the last, into the snow; this is of especial importance if your slide is a fast one and the snow hard, or if you are using a steeply angled pick which is likely to 'grab'.

CUTTING STEPS

Although it is no longer necessary for the climber to hack a continuous stairway of steps whenever confronted by ice or hard snow, a single step can provide a much needed rest, or give you somewhere to stand while placing protection, and at each belay you need to cut stances – perhaps even to give yourself a place to sleep. The adze is the most useful part of the axe for step-cutting. The downward-pointing picks of modern ice tools are less useful in this respect than the straight picks of their predecessors.

Textbooks often give the impression that with three or four adroit blows with the axe you can achieve perfectly formed steps – large and flat and sloping inward. In fact, this is rarely possible. It takes time and effort to chop steps large enough to accommodate the whole boot but, unless you are going to use the step only fleetingly, the effort is worth it.

Before you start, decide exactly where and how big the step needs to be. Try to take advantage of any ice formation that might save you work.

Use a wrist loop when cutting: this not only saves effort but obviates the chance of dropping the axe.

CRAMPONS

Crampons are designed to be fitted to rigid-soled boots: if the soles are not rigid, techniques such as front-pointing are difficult to perform and the crampons are much more likely to break.

Most crampons have twelve points, ten projecting downward from the underside of the boot and two projecting forward from the toe. Crampons with fewer than twelve points are generally unsuitable for technical ice climbing. Some crampons are rigid, supposedly to offer better front-pointing performance, while others are articulated between the heel and the sole. In fact, because a good boot is itself rigid, the difference in front-pointing performance is minimal.

It is vital that the crampon be fitted snugly to the boot – tight enough so that, even with the straps undone, they stay put when the boot is shaken vigorously. The crampon should conform to the curve of the boot's sole, for if there is any gap the metal will flex and in due course fatigue. All modern crampons are adjustable for length, but not all adjust for width at the toe, so make sure that your boots fit before buying a pair.

The front-points should protrude from beneath the toe of the boot a horizontal distance of 1.25-2cm (½-¾in).

Crampons with short points are better for thinly iced climbs because they reduce leverage and hence the strain on your legs, while those with longer points give deeper penetration through unconsolidated snow.

Most manufacturers now produce crampons that are fastened to the boot by means of a toe bale and heel clamp like a ski-mountaineering binding, but the boot must have a pronounced welt. They offer fast fitting and removal, obviating the need to thread frozen straps with frozen fingers; moreover, they reduce the risk of frostbite caused by tight straps inhibiting circulation.

If straps are used, a simple pin buckle is more reliable than one of the quick-release types: the latter tend to loosen during use. Do not cut the straps too short: leave sufficient length for an icy mitt to grasp. Periodically check the straps' tightness, especially during the first hour or so.

The steepness of the slope and the consistency of the snow or ice will dictate the methods of cramponing you use. Flat-footed techniques, which utilize the downward-pointing spikes, are used on slopes up to about 45°. Learn to walk with a gait that is wider than normal, so that the points do not snag the boot or clothing of the opposite leg. Ascend the slope either directly or in a series of zigzags, much as if you were kicking steps; however, the technique differs in that the foot must be placed flat on the surface so that all the vertical points penetrate the ice. To do this you should turn your foot across the fall-line and flex your ankle. Mountaineering boots greatly limit the extent to which you can move your ankle laterally, and so on steeper slopes you have to point the toe a little downhill and turn your hips and knees away from the slope. You do not have to stamp the points hard into the ice: your body-weight is quite enough. Take small steps, so that the transfer of weight from one foot to the other is easier and you can maintain a steady rhythm.

For descent the same applies. Make sure to place your foot flat on the surface: if you rock from heel to toe the vertical points on the heel will meet the surface at an acute angle so that your feet may skid out from under you.

It is not uncommon for soft snow to adhere to a cramponed boot. This 'balling-up' is particularly dangerous in descent. It is possible to clear the snow by lifting the foot and tapping the side of the crampon with the ferrule of your ice axe; if need be, do this at every step.

In either ascent or descent, as the slope steepens it may feel more comfortable to hold the axe across the body using both hands, either in the brace position (spike in snow) or, on even steeper terrain, in the anchor position (pick in snow).

On gradients over 50° one is definitely in the realm of front-point cramponing, but between 40° and 50° it can be less tiring to flat-foot with one foot and front-point with the other. On gradients of this order a second tool becomes welcome. In névé (firn) both axe and hammer can be placed low, with your hands on top of the heads, pushing downward for support. On ice the picks will not penetrate and so a swing above the head becomes necessary: to secure good penetration a flick of the wrist is more effective than the use of brute strength.

Getting to know your crampons and axes. Until you are confident with these tools, play with them on ice of all angles and in all directions – up, down and across.

FRONT-POINTING

Until 1970 all steep ice climbs involved cutting steps because, despite the crampons' front-points, handholds were necessary for keeping balance. With modern axes it is possible to front-point even overhanging ice – bearing in mind that any gradient over 70° is likely to *feel* as if it is overhanging. Front-pointing is basically a very simple technique. There are just a few points to bear in mind:

● a firm tap is more effective than a mighty kick
● for maximum security, try to keep the boot at 90° to the slope
● so that your weight is on your feet rather than on your arms and axe, take small steps up

There is really no great mystique about it, and in good conditions strong arms and calves can be adequate substitutes for skill and experience. Needless to say, good conditions are the exception rather than the rule, while the hardest modern climbs tend to be rock routes with the merest veneer of ice, where both points and picks will be balanced on rock as often as they are embedded in ice.

BELAYING IN WINTER

Often it is possible to use a Sticht plate from the harness just as on a rock climb, but frequently the rope becomes stiff and frozen or thickly furred with snow, and then it is simpler to use a waist belay; in this event, be careful to arrange the rope correctly (see page 66). It may even be worth tying off the rope to a 'tail' at the back of your harness before belaying.

Because anchors in winter are rarely as secure as they (usually) are in summer, it is important to prepare a good stance, so that much of the force of any fall can be absorbed by the body before the anchor takes any strain. On a steep slope, lean back against it, with your feet braced on a good ledge. On a more moderate gradient, the strongest stance is a sitting one, with ledges cut or stamped out for your backside and feet.

With a waist belay, the rope should be passed over the rucksack so that it is around the waist to prevent the upper body being jerked forward. This can be awkward to achieve if the rope is stiff or the sack bulky. If you decide that it is simpler to take the sack off, do make sure it is clipped into the anchor. It is all too easy to drop things in winter, and once they start to slide they are likely to go a long way.

Rock Belays

Even at its hardest, ice is never as strong a material as rock, and wherever possible the ice-climber looks for a rock belay. There may be no rock visible at all, but diligent cleaning and scraping with the axe will often reveal a rock spike or a usable crack. Ethical considerations about the use of rock pegs go by the board in the depths of winter. Partly this is because lengthy excavation may reveal only a hairline crack capable of taking nothing but the thinnest of knifeblades; and partly it is because ice on the walls of the crack can cause a snug-fitting chock to rip out when shock-loaded.

Ice Screws and Drive-ins

There are two basic types of ice piton: those that are screwed in and out of the ice and those (drive-ins) that are driven in using a hammer and then screwed out. The two types have different advantages and disadvantages, and so you should carry both.

Drive-ins are fast to place, something of prime concern on steep ice. The solid steel Warthog piton has a knobbly, angular thread spiralling up its tapered length. This in theory allows the piton to be unscrewed, but in practice, in all but the softest ice, some excavation is required. Also, the Warthog has a tendency to fracture brittle ice as it is pounded in, particularly when temperatures are low and the ice less plastic.

Tubular drive-ins alleviate this problem because a core of displaced ice is extruded up the tube; tapping the screw before removal breaks the base of this core and makes unscrewing easier. Large-diameter tubes are better in all respects than the older narrow ones. The core must be removed before the tube can be reused, something which can be difficult in sunless gullies and on cold north faces; a cigarette lighter is one solution.

Tubular ice screws are slower to place than drive-ins,

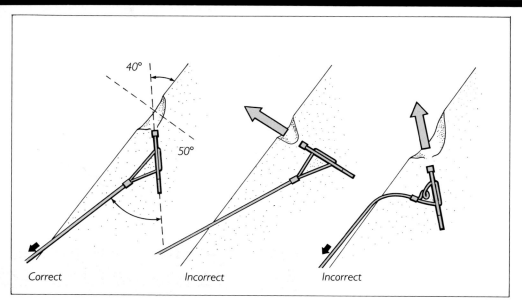

Lower right
The late Dave Cheesmond approaches an enormous cornice on the east ridge of Mt Deborah, Alaska. **Far right** Steep alpine ice in the Cordillera Blanca, Peru. **Left** A deadman placed in flat ground. **Right** Detail of a footbrake.

but are less likely to fracture the ice and generally offer more security than any form of drive-in. Ultimately, however, that security depends more on the quality of the ice than on the characteristics of a particular screw.

When placing an ice screw or drive-in, first clear away any snow or soft or rotten ice. Aim to insert the piton at 90° to the surface, and screw or hammer it in until the head is flush with the surface and pointing down the slope. Frequently the surface layer of ice will fracture while you do this; if so, you must cut away the affected layer to reach more solid ice, and start again.

A few taps of the hammer between turns will help get an ice screw started. Once it is gripping in good ice you will need to use the pick or spike of your axe to provide the leverage to screw it home; if it is possible to screw it in all the way by hand, the hold is untrustworthy.

Whatever the type of piton, if it bottoms on rock, leaving the head proud of the ice, it is important to tie it off by clove-hitching a sling to the shaft in order to reduce leverage. If you are relying solely on ice screws for your belay, use at least two, preferably three, spaced at least 60cm (2ft) apart and equally loaded.

Ice Bollards

It can happen that there is not a rock to be found and the ice is too soft or too aerated to take an ice screw – or it may simply be that you have run out of screws. In such a situation a bollard is a good alternative. Only the time and effort needed to cut one prevents bollards being used more commonly.

When cutting a bollard, aim to make it about 45cm (18in) across, tapering slightly at the foot, with a back wall about 15cm (6in) deep and undercut so there is no chance of the rope or sling riding up. Often you will find there is a bulge in the ice or an easing of the slope that makes a natural place to start cutting. Once you have made your bollard, take a stance well below it so that the pull is downward rather than outward.

The Deadman

The deadman is a rectangular metal plate to the centre of which is attached a length of wire. It is designed as an anchor for use in soft or unconsolidated snow, and should be buried at an angle of 40° to the slope.

Apart from the angle of the plate, the most important thing is to dig the stalk of the T-slot deep enough. Failure to do this means that, when the wire is loaded, it pulls upward on the plate. The strength of this type of anchor depends on the strength of the snow beneath it, so try to set it up from one side and take a stance at least 3m (10ft) below. Always test a deadman before trusting it.

A deadman can be used on flat ground as well as on a slope, which makes it very useful on the plateaux at the top of many ice climbs. In this case it is worth adopting a sitting-type stance so as to keep the angle of pull as close to the surface of the snow as possible.

It is possible to buy 'deadboy' belays, but these are really worth using only in firm snow, where an axe belay (see below) would be just as effective.

Axe Belays

Until fairly recently, an axe belay meant driving the shaft of the axe vertically down into the snow and hoping for the best. In anything except firm névé it had little chance of holding. Much more secure is an axe buried horizontally (pick down) in a T-slot, on the same principle as with a deadman, with the rope or sling clove-hitched to the shaft at the point of balance (slightly nearer to the head than to the spike). Make sure that the clove hitch is tied in such a way that it will not cause the shaft to rotate when loaded, and that the shaft is firmly pressed against the front wall of the slot. As with the deadman, it is very important to ensure that the rope or sling does not impart an upward pull. If you kick extra snow from behind onto the axe and stamp it down you will give added strength to this type of belay, although you must take care not to disturb the snow downslope.

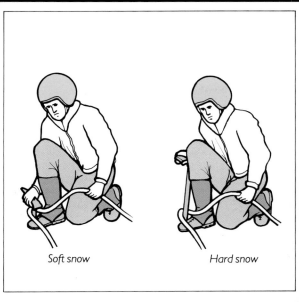

Soft snow   Hard snow

This anchor can be reinforced by placing your hammer vertically downward in front of it at the point where the sling is attached; this constitutes the so-called 'T-axe belay'.

Snow Bollards

These work on exactly the same principle as ice bollards but, obviously, need to be bigger in area and dug to a greater depth. They are very effective in soft snow, but it is crucial that you place your axe and hammer vertically downward at the back to prevent the rope slicing through like a cheesewire. If you are using a bollard to abseil off, a couple of pieces of karrimat from the back of your rucksack are as effective – and a lot cheaper.

WINTER GRADINGS

Traditionally, British winter climbs have been graded from I to V. A Grade I climb would involve no more than steep snow, although you might well find you had a cornice to break through at the top of a gully. A Grade V climb would have several pitches of vertical ice. After a number of years during which climbs of a wider and wider range of difficulty

were all described as Grade V, many modern routes are now described as Grade VI, and there are even a few Grade VIIs.

The problem of grading winter climbs is that they can vary dramatically according to conditions. Any climb can be a full grade easier than expected when there is a lot of well frozen snow banking up ice pitches and chockstones and plastering the ice. Equally, the same climb can be a full grade harder than expected in a year of lean snowfall or early in the season, when the underlying rock is coated only thinly with ice – or alternatively when everything is covered with unconsolidated powder. Grades are no more than a very rough guide to the difficulties that may be encountered.

Jeff Lowe, the accomplished US ice-climber, has suggested a system to be applied worldwide that uses the Roman numerals I to VII to indicate the overall seriousness of a climb; a technical grade of 1 to 6 to rate the difficulty of individual pitches; and the letters 'A' or 'W' before the Roman numeral to indicate whether the ice is of the permanent alpine type or of the seasonal (winter) type.

SNOW SHELTERS

Left *Four snow holes being dug into drifted snow on a lee slope. The excavated blocks make good building material for sealing doors. There's proof in these pictures that the sun can shine even during a Scottish winter!*

Camping on snow is not comfortable. Snow rustles against the tent walls, the fabric flaps in the wind, and the snow you are lying on quickly becomes hard and bumpy. By carrying a shovel, however, you can be equipped to make yourself a shelter that will not blow down, is perfectly quiet, and can be as roomy as you like.

Snow is a variable building material: at one extreme, you can be neck-deep in it with no sign of bottom; at the other extreme, you may find it almost impossible to force a knife into the stuff. So, if you plan to make yourself a snow shelter, you have to be *au fait* with a variety of building techniques. The angle and depth of the snow may exercise constraints, too: the igloo, for example, was developed for the flat Arctic regions, and would be quite unsuitable for a shelter near the summit of K2.

Soft snow is a problem to bivouac in, because of its lack of cohesion. The most effective technique is the 'shovel up', whereby you build a soft-snow mound about the size of an igloo and then hollow it out, using snow taken from the inside to plaster the outside. The movement of snow promotes 'age hardening', and after an hour or so you can dig in. Burying your rucksack in the centre reduces the amount of snow you have to shovel.

Consolidated snow is easier to deal with. Using the adze of your ice axe you can create an emergency shelter for one in 20 minutes or so. These 'caves' are best on slopes of over 30° where there is a good depth of suitable snow; it helps if there is a slope below, making it easier to dispose of debris.

Given the right snow, an adequate slope and a lot of work, there are no real limits to the shape and size of the snow cave you can build. While constructing it, use a large entrance, or even two, since these will make the building process quicker; you can easily block them off later.

The alternative to digging into the snow is to build on top of it. Best known of all snow shelters is the igloo, but unfortunately it is the most difficult to build and the least reliable in varying temperatures. The principle is to quarry blocks of snow and, by spiralling these blocks upwards and inwards, to build a weatherproof dome. The Eskimoes used a smooth bone knife to cut the blocks, but now a serrated metal saw is favoured; ice-axe picks are much less satisfactory.

The varieties of combination cave-and-wall shelters is legion: what you build depends on the nature, depth and slope of the snow. However, here are a few general hints:

● The harder the snow or ice, the tougher is the job that you are taking on.
● While building your shelter, wear as little as possible under your waterproofs.
● Ensure adequate ventilation – people have died in snow-caves from carbon-monoxide poisoning.
● Do your cooking in a well ventilated part of the shelter. Stand the stove on crampons or a shovel, and avoid creating clouds of steam.
● Keep the roof smooth and rounded so that moisture runs down the inside of the walls rather than dripping on top of you.
● Have your entrance as low as possible and your seat and/or bed as high as possible – warm air rises.
● Avoid losing items of equipment. While you are creating your shelter, keep them well out of the debris zone. At night, keep them inside with you.

Right *The depth to which the skis immediately in front of the figure have been buried shows what can happen when wind and snow combine. On the right a new emergency igloo is being built – probably a faster means of creating shelter on flat ground such as this than a snow hole.*

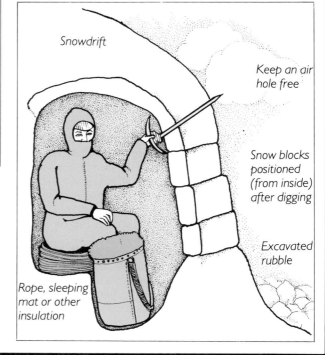

Above *Built under friendlier conditions than the one illustrated at top, an igloo fit for the Ideal Home Exhibition nears completion.*

Right *An emergency snow shelter need be little more than a large hole dug into a snowdrift. Here blocks excavated during the digging have been used to seal the entry. You can enjoy comparative comfort during the wildest of nights in a shelter like this.*

Snowdrift

Keep an air hole free

Snow blocks positioned (from inside) after digging

Excavated rubble

Rope, sleeping mat or other insulation

AVALANCHES

A giant powder avalanche becomes airborne in the Karakoram. Avalanches on this scale can be cataclysmally destructive: any climbers or camps lying in their path are certainly doomed.

The most obvious danger in snow-covered mountains, be they glaciated or not, is that of avalanche. Huge avalanches are obviously lethal, but the sudden descent of even a few cubic metres of snow can injure or kill. The impact is only part of the problem: climbers buried in snow can easily suffocate.

Predicting avalanches is an inexact science and relies on garnering information from a wide variety of sources. It makes sense to consult local mountaineers, who will have watched the snow-pack building up. However, on the hill it is your own observation and judgement that count. 'If in doubt, don't' is a good rule; after all, you have only the one life.

Most avalanches occur during or just after heavy falls of snow. In a maritime climate (e.g., that of the UK), the first 24 hours are the most dangerous, but in colder alpine or polar conditions the danger will persist for days, even weeks, especially on north- and east-facing slopes (south- and west-facing slopes in the Southern Hemisphere). In general, easy-angled slopes – between 30° and 45° – are the most prone to avalanche; the approach can be more dangerous than the climb!

If there has been wind, with or without snowfall, slabs of snow will have formed on lee slopes: the stronger the wind, the harder the slab. Cornices are a sign that it has been windy, and slabs are often found beneath them. The danger of slabs is that, although they form a homogenous layer, that layer is poorly attached to the layer beneath and can easily slide off.

The question of bonding is crucial to the evaluation of avalanche risk; for example, scattered boulders will anchor a snow-mass, whereas long grass gives a much less secure anchor. However, most avalanches occur when one layer of snow slides off another. A hard crust, formed by sun or wind, will create a sliding surface once buried beneath later snowfall; while layers of hoar frost, graupel (pellets of soft snow) or depth hoar (rounded crystals that form within the snow-pack in very cold weather) can all act as lubricants, as they do not consolidate. Where such layers exist, avalanches can be caused by:

● thaws, when water trickles down until it reaches a hard layer, where it acts as a lubricant
● heavy snowfall, which increases the weight of the snow-pack
● the inevitable tension set up by the downward creep of snow

In addition, although many avalanches occur spontaneously, sometimes it is the weight of the climber or skier that provides the trigger.

Experience can give you a 'feel' for avalanche danger, but every avalanche 'expert' has been caught out at some time. If in doubt, dig a pit in the snow to see what layers lie beneath the surface. Look particularly for extreme variations in hardness.

Keep your eyes open for tell-tale signs. Sastrugi (snow eroded into waves) is not in itself dangerous but is an

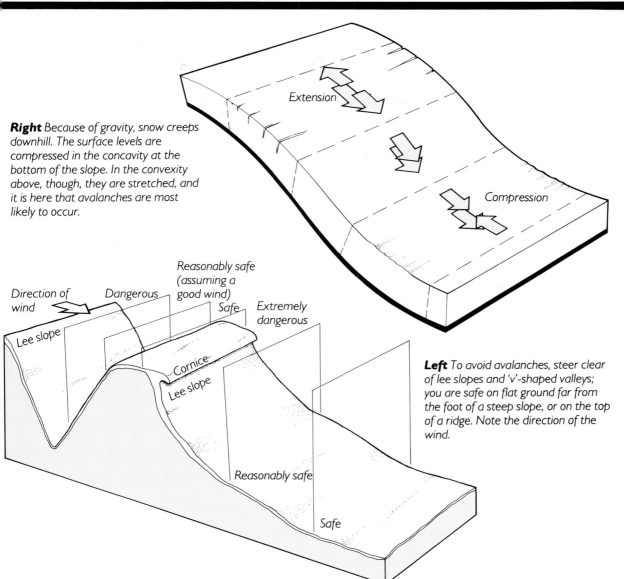

Right *Because of gravity, snow creeps downhill. The surface levels are compressed in the concavity at the bottom of the slope. In the convexity above, though, they are stretched, and it is here that avalanches are most likely to occur.*

Extension

Compression

Direction of wind

Dangerous

Reasonably safe (assuming a good wind)

Safe

Extremely dangerous

Lee slope

Cornice

Lee slope

Reasonably safe

Safe

Left *To avoid avalanches, steer clear of lee slopes and 'v'-shaped valleys; you are safe on flat ground far from the foot of a steep slope, or on the top of a ridge. Note the direction of the wind.*

indicator of recent strong winds. Balls of snow running downslope from your feet or from rocks are a sign of dangerously warm conditions. Watch for snow breaking up in little slabs under your feet and for the very hard, squeaky, slightly rippled surface of hard slab. Choose your routes carefully. Stay on ridges whenever you can, and remember that convex slopes, because they are under tension, are more prone to avalanche than concave ones.

If you do have to cross a suspect slope, do so as high as possible and take some precautions. Do up all clothing, undo the waist-belt on your rucksack and take your hand out of the wrist loop on your axe. Cross the slope one at a time, and do not assume that it is safe just because one person has crossed without accident.

If you are caught in an avalanche, you may be able to run clear. If not, *shout*; it helps your companions work out where you are going. Try to stay on the surface (many people recommend backstroke!); as soon as the slide stops, use a hand to clear a space around your face.

After two hours, the chances of rescuing an avalanche victim alive are slight, so the emphasis must be on self-rescue rather than sending for help. Mark both the point where the victim was swept away and the point where he or she was last seen. Follow this line down to the bottom of the avalanche looking for a hand, a boot or even a rucksack strap visible above the snow. If that fails you will have to try probing with your ice axe, but unless you are a big party or it was a very small avalanche your chances of success are slim. Ski tourers have a better chance because they usually carry shovels and electronic transceivers (or bleepers) which vastly increase the likelihood of their being found.

The whole subject of the structure and behaviour of snow is a complex one, and so the reader is recommended to consult the specialist literature on the topic.

97

ALPINISM

One winter's day on Ben Nevis, a climber who was poking around unsuccessfully under rocks looking for protection, was heard to grumble, 'My second insisted on giving me these nuts for rock belays ... he's a rock climber, you see. Can't be doing with it myself – I'm an ice climber.'

Mountaineering is not about blinkered specialization. It is about using many skills to move safely over all kinds of terrain. When Dougal Haston died in 1977, he was universally recognized as one of the world's leading mountaineers. Unusual nerve, stamina, patience and motivation had taken him to the top of the Eiger Direct, Annapurna South Face and the Southwest Face of Everest; but he also had skill – technical skill learned on the rock and ice of his own Scottish hills. All the great mountaineers have had this ability to translate fundamental skills learned on small crags into a bigger context where they become second nature.

How precisely to define mountaineering is debatable, but let us say that mountaineering takes place on glaciated mountains, where rock, snow and ice skills are required to reach and descend from high summits and passes. We are talking about the 'game' that was invented in the mountains of France, Switzerland, Italy and Austria in the nineteenth century – alpinism. The attractions and possibilities of alpinism are infinite, and if here we stick mainly to practicalities as they refer to the European Alps it should be understood that the same basic principles apply, with obvious modifications, to mountains the world over.

STARTING ALPINE CLIMBING

The easiest and safest way of starting alpine climbing is to do so with an experienced friend; working with an equally inexperienced partner, and hoping to learn by your mistakes, is obviously potentially lethal. Alternatively, find out about one of the many courses for beginners run by guides and by national centres. If you are to get the most out of such a course, you should immediately follow it up by doing some unguided climbs.

Even if you have crag-climbing experience, remember that alpine guidebooks assume an understanding of the additional dangers of rock and ice together, and that the route timings assume a fit party that is moving quickly. In continental Europe, routes are given one of six gradings identified using acronyms based on French: these gradings run from F (*facile*, easy) to ED (*extrêmement difficile*, extremely difficult), with the additional qualifications *sup.* (+) and *inf.* (−) to indicate 'plus' and 'minus'. Crux rock pitches are given numerical gradings from I to VI (although in practice nothing below III is mentioned).

Left *Reaching the summit is always exciting, whatever the climb. In this case it is the Eiger, with the Wetterhorn behind and to the left. Note how the northern, shadier side of the mountain is snow-covered while the southern side has been stripped bare by the sun's heat.*

Right *The Mer de Glace, near Chamonix – the lower reaches of a glacier fed by several glacier basins higher up.*

Below *A steep step on the traverse of the Meije, one of the classics of the Dauphiné Alps. Like many alpine rock climbs, this involves some ice climbing as well.*

The biggest risk when climbing in high mountains is to be so seduced by their beauty that you forget they are potential killers. If you are to enjoy mountains fully you should always be watching yourself in case you make a careless mistake, and always looking over your shoulder to check for possible hazards.

GLACIERS

Travelling over glaciers is an essential part of alpinism.

In summer the lower reaches of glaciers are usually 'dry' – in other words, the ice is bare. Higher up, though, the ice is permanently covered with snow, which masks crevasses. The danger of falling into these is grossly under-estimated: it cannot be stressed too much that, when you are travelling on a snow-covered glacier, you should always be roped.

If there are only two people on the rope, it will be difficult, maybe impossible, for one of them to pull his companion out of a crevasse unaided: the faller has to help extricate himself. You should therefore *always* have prusik loops already attached to the rope, have crampons on your feet and have an ice axe secured to your body. If you have an ice hammer, too, it should be ready in your holster; remember, it is sometimes perfectly possible to climb out of a crevasse using straightforward ice techniques. However hot the sunshine on the surface, it will be bitterly cold down a crevasse, so make sure you always wear a long-sleeved shirt and mittens.

Efficient glacier travel requires good teamwork. Both partners should agree on the best line, avoiding the worst crevasses (even masked crevasses are nearly always visible

An ice-fall. The glacier is a chaos of crevasses and ice-walls.

you know, your partner may be unconscious ... and all the time the rope is pulling uncomfortably at your waist.

Unless you are lucky, and there are other climbers about who can help, you have no option but to construct a belay, which is no easy task. Once you have managed it, use a prusik loop on the rope to transfer the weight cautiously from your waist to the belay. That accomplished, you can untie yourself from the rope and attach it to the belay to serve as a back-up for the prusik. This leaves you free to approach the lip – carefully! – and communicate with your partner. If he or she is already prusiking up the rope, you will be in a position to help them over the lip, where the rope will have bitten deeply into the snow. If on the other hand they have not started to prusik, it will make life easier if you cut away from the lip as much loose snow as possible – well to one side, so as to avoid showering your partner with debris. You can then pad the lip with your rucksack and drop the spare end of rope down into the crevasse so that your partner can prusik up. It is worth tying a knot in the end of the new rope in case the prusiks slip. All of this presupposes that you have both tied-on in the middle of the rope, carrying the spare rope in coils over your shoulder, and tied-off to your harness.

If your partner is unconscious or for some other reason is unable to prusik, you have a real problem on your hands. However, it is not insurmountable. Your chances of a successful rescue will be increased if you were tied-on with about 8m (26ft) of rope between you and each had about 18m (60ft) of rope coiled around your shoulder. Proceed as before, but this time tie the spare end of rope to the anchor. Drop down a bight of rope, taking with you a karabiner which you can clip to your partner's harness. If your partner is unconscious, you will have no choice but to abseil down, clip the karabiner in yourself, and prusik out again. Now clip the live rope through a second krab at the anchor point and run it down to a prusik and krab attached to the live rope as near to the lip as possible. The result of your efforts is a pulley system that will give you a 3:1 mechanical advantage; if you have padded the lip well you should be able to lift your partner out of the crevasse – although it will be hard work. A little pulley, cheap to buy and light to carry, can dramatically reduce the friction involved, making the job that much easier; it is best attached to the bight dropped to the casualty. Another way of reducing friction is to use two karabiners rather than one at the turning points in the rope.

An essential part of any such system is a clutch ('auto-block') which allows the rope to slide through it while you are hauling in but which takes the strain when the prusik on the rope needs to be slid back from anchor to lip. This can be achieved by using a French prusik, where the live rope passes through a krab at the anchor point.

Should you not have enough rope around your shoulder to drop a bight to the casualty, a similar but less effective method is to drop your end of the rope down to them. You do this by passing it through a krab and clutch system at the anchor, down to a prusik and krab on the same rope at the lip, and then back up in the direction of pull. This technique gives you a 2:1 mechanical advantage.

as slight dimples in the snow). Try to avoid moving parallel to the general line of crevasses. When you decide to jump a crevasse, be sure to prepare enough slack in the rope beforehand.

If you have to cross a suspect snow bridge, your best plan is to belay one another across. The form of belay you choose will depend on the snow conditions. If there is ice exposed, or not far from the surface, the answer is an ice screw; an alternative, although a less secure one, is to use the embedded picks of axe and hammer linked in such a way that they take the load equally. You could cut an ice bollard, but this takes a long time and so usually is not worth considering.

On reasonably firm snow the best method is a T-axe or horizontal-axe belay. In deep, soft snow a strong sitting posture will probably be adequate, but if you are really anxious you can always dig out a snow bollard, remembering to strengthen it at the back with axes or a rucksack.

That said, the crevasse you are most likely to fall into is the one whose existence you never suspected. How far into it you go depends entirely on the alertness, preparedness and skill of your partner. The key to safe travel on glaciers is a tight rope. Holding coils in the hand will only increase the distance of a fall and the difficulty of stopping it. The partner's bodyweight, combined with the friction of the rope on the lip of the crevasse, will normally be enough to arrest any fall, but *only* if there is no slack rope.

When it comes to glacier travel there is undoubtedly safety in numbers. On the other hand, the most efficient practice when it comes to the actual climbing is to go roped up in a pair. It is therefore well worth considering in advance what you should do should you find yourself, through bad luck or bad management, lying in the snow in a self-arrest position with your rope running taut from your waist to a partner who is swinging about in a crevasse somewhere below. If life were ideal you would find out first if it were possible to lower your partner to a handy ledge or constriction, or even to the bottom of the crevasse, but in practice it is extremely unlikely that you will be able to hear each other, however hard you shout. You are confronted by a hole in the snow – and silence. For all

Bad weather can materialize from nowhere in the high Alps. The best plan may be retreat.

It goes almost without saying that only practice will reveal to you all the problems you are likely to face and the best ways of coping with them. The best plan is possibly first to try out all the various pulley systems on rock and then on a dry-ice glacier (where you can also practise setting up snow belays) before you finally graduate to a more realistic situation. For this last stage in your education, make sure you are accompanied by a party of friends in case things go wrong, and ensure that you back up all the anchors used.

ALPINE WEATHER

Weather in general has already been discussed on pages 30-31. In high alpine areas storms can be lethal. Some very fine mountaineers have died of exposure after being caught out by big summer storms on Mont Blanc. Modern forecasting has made alpine climbing a safer game, but the forecasters can get it wrong and if you are on a big, remote route, where retreat is difficult, it is wise to carry emergency protection – either a two-man tent sack or individual Gore-Tex bags with zipped hoods. On shorter routes, at least carry light overtrousers (ideally with full-length leg zips) and an anorak.

During hot summer weather, afternoon thunderstorms are common. If possible finish your climb by midday to avoid this danger. If you are caught in an electric storm, get away from exposed ridges as quickly as possible.

Prolonged spells of bad weather can be very frustrating. Rather than hang around waiting for the big routes, be adaptable and move to lower peaks and valley crags, where it is almost always possible to climb.

OTHER HAZARDS

In alpine regions, snow avalanches are primarily a winter danger. In summer one is usually climbing on well-consolidated névé and in the early hours, after a good freeze, it should be safe. Later, when it melts to slush, there is a danger of wet-snow avalanches, particularly in couloirs (the Whymper Couloir on the Aiguille Verte, near Chamonix, is a notorious example). Bad weather brings the risk of powder and slab avalanches. A heavy dump of new snow takes time to consolidate and in mountains the world over it is best, as a general rule, to avoid all big snowslopes during and immediately after a heavy snowfall.

Séracs are the blue-green towers of ice formed in the steepening of a glacier icefall or a hanging glacier. Their behaviour is unpredictable and although they are most likely to collapse in the heat of the day, they do sometimes collapse in the middle of the night. Some ice routes, like the Balfour Face of Mt Tasman in New Zealand, are threatened throughout by séracs, but normally you would expect to be able to find some way around them, or at least ensure that only a short section of your route is threatened. It does require a certain fatalism to cross unavoidable danger zones, and most people reduce the odds by running very fast!

ROCKFALL

Some of the finest rock climbs have to be approached by couloirs which are daily bombarded by loose rocks. On a cold night they are frozen to immobility and one can cross the danger area safely, provided one moves fast and reaches safety before the sun hits the offending rocks above. The other big danger is from other climbers. The best escape is to avoid popular routes and, needless to say, *always wear a helmet*.

ALPINE TACTICS

The essence of summer alpine climbing is speed – not a frantic, panicky rush, but a steady, efficient, smooth movement. Most alpine routes can be climbed in a day. By moving quickly you can guarantee completing the climb on schedule and avoid carrying anything but the barest emergency bivouac protection. That means a light rucksack and, if we start from the premise that climbing should be enjoyable, there is a lot to be said for a light sack. There are other good reasons for speed, which should be apparent from the foregoing section on alpine dangers. Rockfall, collapsing séracs, avalanching couloirs and thunderstorms are all most common late in the day. By leaving early, usually before dawn, and moving fast you can minimize your risk. But, apart from the dangers, moving efficiently across difficult terrain is simply very satisfying.

Speed depends partly on fitness, but it depends far more on good route finding and on being familiar with equipment: putting crampons on quickly, avoiding snagged ropes and belaying quickly. On a pitched climb, don't put runners in every two feet – there isn't time. Clip into main belays with a clove hitch, which is quick to tie and adjust for length. Whenever possible, move together, either putting in a few runners as you go or, on a rocky edge, shortening the rope and always keeping it looped over blocks between you to help arrest a fall. Moving together on snow ridges requires a lot more nerve, and many British and American parties resort to soloing.

A point of note concerns abseil slings. Take your time over these. Never trust *in situ* abseil slings, which are often dangerously weakened by sunlight. Add your own.

Left *The Bertol hut, high in the Swiss Alps. The spectacular situation renders it safe from avalanche.*

Below *A snug site for a bivouac on the east ridge of the famous Mt Huntington, in Alaska.*

Front-pointing up an alpine ice face. Technically straightforward, front-pointing is tiring on calves and nerves, especially when you are a few thousand metres up!

BIVOUACS

In many areas of New Zealand or North America there are no huts and you will need to sleep out at the foot of your route; even in the European Alps huts are expensive and can be very crowded, so that often it is more comfortable to sleep out. Sometimes it may be necessary to bivouac actually on a route. On big winter climbs or Himalayan climbs several bivouacs are the norm.

Bivouacs can be ghastly, especially when it is cold or when you are on a steep snowslope being drowned in spindrift and pushed repeatedly off your inadequate ledge. In a storm the best shelter is a dry snowhole. However, if the weather is clear and you have some room to lie down, bivouacs can be sheer contentment.

The old adage, 'Any fool can be uncomfortable', is particularly true of multi-day routes. The bigger the route, the more important it is to look after yourself. It is always best to stop early at a good ledge, rather than carry on climbing till dark: an early start the next morning is much easier from a comfortable, organized bivouac. The best site will be on rock (which is warmer than snow), but will have snow or ice within reach to melt for hot drinks, and will be sheltered from rockfall. Take time over clearing a good space and always keep everything, including yourself, tied on. The best food requires no cooking – cheese, salami, bread, butter, biscuits, chocolate and dried fruit. Keep the cooking for liquids – tea, coffee, fruit juice and instant soup (instant noodles add bulk). One of the best stoves for bivouacs is a hanging gas stove with built-in windshield, but some people prefer liquid-fuel ones.

EQUIPMENT

Choice of equipment is a very personal thing and after years of experiment most of us are still vacillating endlessly about exactly what to take. For the mountaineer there is a constant juggling of the two considerations of weight and safety. A few suggestions are given below for two different sets of equipment, taking two very different routes to illustrate the point.

Traverse of L'Evêque L'Evêque is a small peak (3,716m [12,192ft]) in the Pennine Alps, above Arolla, where the terrain is approached across a glacier to the southwest ridge, a short rock climb with several pitches of grade III and one of IV. The descent is by the glacial north flank. The climb is graded AD inf. (−) and the expected time for the round trip is about 5 hours.

The anorak (see list below) would probably be worn for the pre-dawn start across the glacier. Leather boots are quite adequate for this sort of route and much more comfortable than plastic. On the glacier you would wear crampons and have your ice axe in hand. You would be roped up, with prusik loops attached to the rope, and one long and one short sling (with karabiners) round your neck (not stuck under rucksack straps) ready for use in an emergency. At the start of the rock ridge, you would take off crampons, pack them away with the ice axe, get out the rock gear and by now probably remove some clothing and put on sun cream and sunglasses. After climbing the 300m (985ft) rock ridge to the summit, you would re-equip for the glacier descent.

Personal Gear
leather mountaineering boots
crampons
ice axe
harness and prusik loops
helmet
warm breeches or salopettes
shirt
fibre pile jacket or jersey
light overtrousers
woollen gloves or mittens
anorak
sunglasses
suncream
handtorch
small rucksack

Communal Gear
one 45m (150ft) rope (10 or 11mm)
2 long slings
3 short slings
5 assorted nuts
8 karabiners
full water bottle
a little food
minimal first aid kit

Upper right
Crampons. Left to right: articulated between front and rear (also adjustable at toe and centre); with toe bale and ski-type heel clip; fully adjustable, rigid; adjustable for length and at centre. **Right**
Sunglasses, nosepiece and side flaps are ideal eye protection. Goggles are useful in strong winds.

Far left *A banana-picked axe; ideal for technical ice climbing, with a large inclined adze useful in soft snow. The screw at the top enables the pick to be changed for a conventional pick.* **Left** *A matching hammer.*

Below *The Eiger. The famous north face is the dark triangle on the left; descent by the* voie normale *is down the west flank, to the right of the north face. The Eiger is one of the test-pieces of the Alps, with hard climbing on both rock and ice, and is made even more serious by the ever-present danger of stonefall.*

The Eiger North Face – 1938 route

This is a historic serious climb up a huge wall, 1,600m (5,250ft) high and graded ED. Thought by many to be the finest route in the Alps, it has nearly 2,000m (6,500ft) of fantastic rock, mixed and ice climbing, but conditions can be very variable.

The equipment below was taken by one party for a September ascent, when the face was well iced-up and temperatures were cold, so that the notorious Eiger stonefall was almost nonexistent. However, whenever a storm rolls in, spindrift avalanches can be a great problem, and escape to the top or retreat to the bottom very serious undertakings. You would not normally expect to bivouac more than twice on the face, but big storms can pin you down for longer.

The equipment list, below left, would be similar for other big mixed climbs the world over; for instance, the south face of Mt Hicks in New Zealand, one of the big north faces in the Canadian Rockies, or many moderate-sized faces in the Himalayas.

The party started the route in mid-afternoon when running water on the lower wall was a problem. All warm clothes were packed away in rucksacks and just nylon overtrousers and anoraks were worn. At the first bivouac the climbers put on all their warm clothes and in fact kept on longjohns and salopettes for the rest of the climb. Duvet, spare socks, overtrousers and bivvy bag provided extra insulation and shelter at night. Dachstein felted wool gloves were worn for all but one or two awkward rock sections, like the difficult 'Brittle Crack'. Their fibre pile clothing and snowproof mittens remained in the sack, in reserve for bad weather. Crampons were worn throughout. The hardware was ample to supplement *in situ* pegs and protect every pitch safely.

RESCUE

In the European Alps the rescue helicopters are run by commercial organizations. If you do have to be rescued, the bill will be enormous. There was a famous case of a well-known English climber who broke his leg in the Dolomites. He was uninsured and his friends had a tough race to rescue him from the Italian rescue service, who were eagerly touting for business. Most people prefer to take out insurance cover. The Alpine distress signal is: 6 whistle blasts (or torch flashes) at ten-second intervals, followed by one minute's silence, followed by another six blasts at ten-second intervals, and so on. If a helicopter approaches, signal using the international code, made of any large materials to hand. The main signals are:

Personal Gear	Communal Gear
helmet	2 50m (165ft) 9mm (⅓in) ropes
ice axe	2 long slings
ice hammer	6 short slings
crampons	10 assorted nuts
plastic boots	3 'Friends'
gaiters	5 pegs
brake/descendeur	6 titanium ice screws
harness and belay	22 karabiners
longjohns	spare abseil tape
thermal vest	gas stove with 3 cylinders and pan
halena salopettes	mug
fibre pile jacket	penknife
very light overtrousers	spoon
anorak	3 days' food rations
woollen gloves	small first aid kit
snowproof mittens	photocopy of route description
balaclava	and topo cut out portion of
Gore-Tex anorak	map and compass for descent
dry socks	
duvet jacket	
bivouac bag	
karrimat	
sunglasses	
sun cream	
55 litre rucksack	

△	Safe to land here
I	Require a doctor
↑	Proceeding in direction of arrow
X	Unable to proceed
NN	Nothing found
II	Require medical supplies
IIIII	Require assistance
LL	All well

WINTER ALPINISM

Some people dismiss winter alpine climbing as perverse masochism. In fact there are any number of good reasons to take to the mountains in winter. You may want to enjoy a day's ski touring on powder snow through Washington's Cascade Mountains, or you may want a gruelling multi-day challenge on Mt Blanc's Peuterey Ridge Integrale to train for a major Himalayan expedition. In both cases the terrain will be transformed by powder snow and if the weather is fine the air will have a crisp clarity lacking in summer. The glaciers will be frozen to immobility, the summer clatter of stonefall will have ceased and the traffic and crowds will be far away.

There are endless possibilities for winter climbing, but some of the main categories are:

- ski ascents: using skis to ascend and descend snow peaks
- ice and mixed faces: these are often little changed by winter conditions, although the ice can be iron-hard and black
- rock walls: intense cold, coupled with powder in cracks, can make the technicalities of climbing a real challenge
- classic ridges: these are often transformed by huge snow mushrooms
- dangerous couloirs and runnels: some superb lines that are stonefall deathtraps in summer can be climbed perfectly safely in winter

If you enjoy speed and movement, ski mountaineering is probably the most satisfying sport in winter and spring. But skis are also the ideal way of approaching a remote climbing route, provided that you plan to descend the same way. If you are descending the far side of the mountain you may need to use snowshoes, which can be carried up the route.

For all its attractions, winter climbing is a very serious game. Even in fine weather, long nights and extremely low temperatures necessitate carrying lots of warm bivouac gear. A bad winter storm can last for many days and test

Left Note the huge quantity of powder snow that has had to be cleared in order to create a stance on this winter climb.
Lower left An enormous cornice bars the way on the east ridge of Mt Deborah, Alaska.
Below Ice falling from a sérac high on Mt Huntington sets off a huge avalanche of powder snow. Such avalanches can become airborne and travel spectacular distances.

survival abilities to the limit. The biggest single danger in winter is avalanches. This is particularly true in the American and Canadian Rockies, where devastating powder avalanches are very common. Often it is necessary to deviate from normal summer approaches and descents to avoid avalanche-prone slopes. Keep away from the mountains during times of heavy snowfall and always listen to the warnings of local experts: they may sound like kill-joys, but they are nearly always right. *Avalanches and Snow Safety* by Colin Fraser (Murray, 1978) is an excellent study of the subject and makes sobering reading.

EXPEDITIONS

Left *Porters wait to start the day on the Baltoro glacier.* **Below** *At high altitudes even summer climbing has the same 'feel' as the Alps in winter.*

There are countless reasons for travelling to the greater ranges of Alaska, Greenland, the Andes, the Greater Himalayas (or even Antarctica for the very lucky and determined) but for most dedicated alpine climbers there is a common desire to attempt unclimbed peaks or new routes in far-away places, where problems of remoteness, scale or altitude stack the odds more heavily against the climber, and even minor alpine-scale peaks can be serious. There are for instance, peaks in Peru's Cordillera Vicanota as small and easy as the simplest Alpine climbs; but they start at 5,000m (16,400ft) above sea level, they are two days' walk from the nearest road and there is no rescue helicopter standing nearby. The greater ranges are for practising and expanding, not learning, mountaineering skills.

On the world's highest mountains, the dangers of avalanche, cold and exhaustion increase with height; but the one potential danger to all expeditions going above about 4,500m (14,750ft) is altitude sickness. Pulmonary oedema (water retention in the lungs) and cerebral oedema (the same on the brain) have killed many experienced mountaineers. The risk at 8,000m (26,250ft) is extreme; at 6,000m (19,700ft) proper acclimatization makes oedema very unlikely.

Acclimatization requires climbing in slow stages, giving the body time to adapt to decreased air pressure and oxygen content. As a guideline, most people can acclimatize up to about 5,500m (18,000ft) in two weeks if they move up in slow stages. Mild headaches and nausea are common on reaching a new height and are a warning to wait a day before moving higher. Chronic headaches, loss of vision, lapses of consciousness and bubbling in the lungs are all indications of oedema, for which the only reliable cure is to *go down immediately*.

PLANNING A MAJOR EXPEDITION

This is a checklist for an expedition to a 6,000m or 7,000m (19,700-23,000ft) peak in Pakistan, India or Nepal.

Research The easiest way to choose an objective is to consult someone who has been to your chosen area; but there is a mass of information available in journals and magazines and the more research you do the more fascinating it becomes. The most useful sources are the *Himalayan Journal, Alpine Journal, American Alpine Journal* and *Mountain*.

Permission Contact the relevant authority in your country of destination (addresses from your own national climbing organization) well in advance. (Pakistan, for instance, requires peak fees to be paid at least 6 months in advance, which means applying 9 months in advance.)

Visas Check requirements with relevant embassy.

Transport Book flights. Arrange for any air freight. Find out about local road transport and porter rates.

Insurance A Himalayan accident can result in enormous rescue, medical and extra transport costs. Pakistan actually demands a cash deposit against possible helicopter rescue.

Medical Start inoculations one month before departure. Find out anti-malarial requirements. Prepare first aid kit. Ideally a member of the expedition should be a doctor, or at least trained in first aid – a climber seriously injured on a remote peak may have to wait two or three weeks for outside medical help.

EQUIPMENT

Tents Ideally geodesic domes which can be pitched easily on snow.

Climbing gear You may need to cover for long abseil descents. Spare axes and crampons are advisable, to cover against breakage.

Mending kit Adequate for repairing tents and clothing.

Clothing To cope with enormous extremes of temperature: light pyjamas and sun hat for the approach; down gear, etc., on the mountain.

Liaison officer You will probably have to equip your liaison officer. Allow for this in your budget.

Cooking Primus stoves can be bought in all Himalayan countries and paraffin is always available. Gas stoves and cylinders are usually unavailable. It is illegal to carry cylinders in aeroplane-hold luggage – make special freight arrangements. Pressure cookers are essential for base camp cooking above 4,000m (13,100ft).

Books Boredom can be a big problem during spells of bad weather.

Photographic If you are sponsored, it is essential to fulfil your obligations and get first-class photographic coverage.

Above A camp at 7,000m (23,000ft) on Annapurna II, in Nepal. Behind is the sacred peak of Machapuchare ('The Fish's Tail'). The weather is clearly unsettled, boding ill for the climb. **Left** The view from a snow cave on the east face of Mt Huntington, Alaska.

Maps Often the most useful are climbers' sketch maps from the journals. Take plenty of photocopies.

Packaging A large selection of different-sized, tough polythene bags is extremely useful.

Food All basics can be bought locally, but you may want to take some high-altitude food, which is hard to obtain in the Himalayan countries – e.g., instant soups, potato powder, good chocolate, freeze dried meals, tea bags. Locally bought fresh vegetables like onions, carrots, potatoes and garlic will last for several weeks if protected from frost – well worth the extra weight if you can afford the portage. When working out food quantities, use a guideline of 1kg (2.2lb) per man day.

PART TWO

VENUES

The following pages are pointers to those great arenas of the world wherein the climbing games are played. They are intended as whetters of appetites, tasters, come-ons, seductions. After that we hope they will fire the imagination, nudge an idea, foster a plan and then help you take the first step — although there is much more that you will need (and want) to know before embarking on the journey. In a way, your journey begins even before that first step, with the planning and the research and all the delights of daydreaming that accompany those preparatory things.

If, though, these pages supply only fun or feed merely dreams, they will have done half of their job. And if they spring your first step, then their task will have been well done. Good daydreams make good plans, and good plans make good luck.

Evening sun on the Aiguilles above Chamonix, France. Beautiful mountains — but, Scottish Highlands to Himalayas, Kenya to Karakoram, Andes to Alaska, the world is full of beautiful mountains.

THE BRITISH ISLES

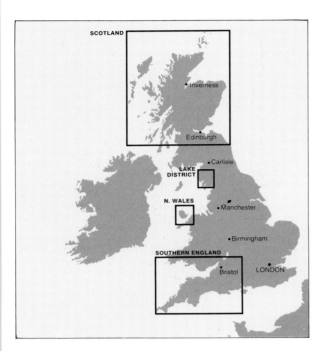

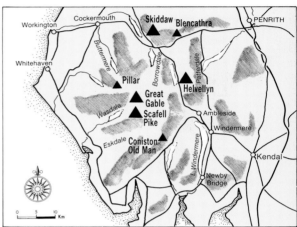

Geography and geology have been generous to the British Isles; for though these islands are small in area and rise to no great height, they have been blessed with a fabulous variety of mountaineering treasures from sunny south-facing sea cliffs to sunless ice-hung winter walls – and much more in between.

THE LAKE DISTRICT

The Lake District is nicknamed the 'birthplace of rock climbing' because of the ascent in 1886 of Napes Needle by W. P. Haskett Smith. Tricouni nailed boots and a hemp rope tied around his waist were his only items of climbing gear. After his ascent, new crags were soon discovered and climbed on, and in due course they were almost completely explored. However, even today new crags are being found, some of them 'excavated' from hillsides of steep grass and heather.

Roadside crags abound in the Lake District. A few typical ones are Castle Rock of Triermain, Shepherd's Crag, Falcon Crags and Raven Crag. 'Middle-distance' crags – i.e., those less than an hour's walk from the road – include Gimmer Crag, Pavey Arc, Dow Crag, Heron Crag, Dove Crag, Goat Crag and Black Crag. Crags on the higher mountains – e.g., Scafell, Great Gable, Pillar and Bowfell – take a little more than an hour to reach from the road.

Here we look at some of the main centres from which you can explore the excellent rock climbing of the Lake District. All areas are well supplied with youth hostels.

Langdale

The main crags you can reach from here are Raven Crag, White Ghyll, Pavey Arc, Gimmer Crag, Neckband Crag and the Bowfell Crags. There are hotels, but less expensive are the many guesthouses and farms in the valley, and there are also camp sites. Various climbing clubs have huts which nonmembers can use if they book in advance, assuming they are members of a club belonging to the British Mountaineering Council.

Borrowdale

Borrowdale, which runs south from Keswick, gives access to plenty of crags, the main ones being Falcon Crags, Shepherd's Crag, Black Crag, Great End Crag, Eagle Crag and Goat Crag. Bed-and-breakfast accommodation can be found in a number of farms and guesthouses, especially near the head of the valley (i.e., the south) in the picturesque hamlets of Rosthwaite, Stonethwaite, Seatoller and Seathwaite. There are good camp sites at Grange and Stonethwaite, and the valley has a number of climbing-club huts.

Buttermere

The three main crags you can reach from Buttermere are High Crag, Eagle Crag and Grey Crag; there are a number of smaller, grassier crags. Buttermere is a peaceful, charming valley with good camp sites and a few farmhouses that offer bed-and-breakfast accommodation; there are a few small hotels as well as a couple of climbing-club huts.

Wasdale

All the Scafell and Gable crags, as well as the approach to Pillar and a few minor crags, can be done from Wasdale, which has good camping facilities, a fine hotel with a barn annexe, some farmhouses where bed-and-breakfast

Right *Steep and strenuous Lakeland rock.*
Below *A view across the gritstone edges of the Peak District of Derbyshire, home of countless fine rock climbs.*

accommodation is available, and a number of well sited climbing-club huts. The valley is renowned for its screes and for having the highest mountain (Scafell Pike, 978m [3,210ft]) in England.

Patterdale and Other Bases

There are many smaller and more esoteric crags accessible from Patterdale, but the main ones are Dove Crag, Scrubby Crag and Eagle Crag. This is a more secluded area than Langdale, Wasdale and Borrowdale, but it has fine camping and farmhouse accommodation as well as a number of good hotels.

Other bases are to be found in Eskdale, Ennerdale and, for the superb Dow Crag, Coniston. Eskdale provides the start for the shortest walk to Esk Buttress, a magnificent crag. On the peripheries of the Lake District there are crags which are worth thinking about if the weather is poor or if you are simply not feeling on form; examples are Chapel Head Scar, Farleton Knott and Trowbarrow Quarry.

Winter Climbing in the Lake District

Although winter climbing in the Lake District is not so grand as in Scotland, some snow and ice climbs are minor classics – e.g., Inaccessible Gully on Dove Crag. The vagaries of the winter weather allow waterfalls to be climbed even when there is no snow around. When conditions are right there are many good climbs to suit all standards and tastes.

THE PEAK DISTRICT

This roughly rectangular area runs from Sheffield in the east and Buxton in the west south to Matlock and Ashbourne. Climbing here is almost exclusively on outcrops: limestone in secluded valleys and gritstone on exposed edges. The outcrops are within easy reach of major cities such as Sheffield and Manchester, whose rock-climbing enthusiasts find them ideal for a day's or even an evening's workout.

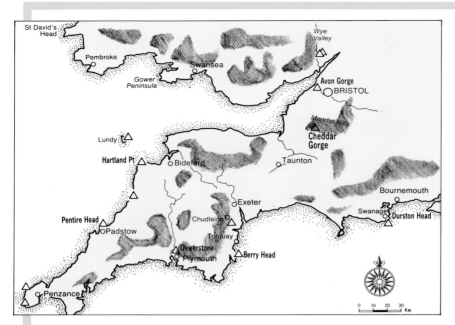

THE YORKSHIRE DALES

This large and varied area is noted for the spectacular limestones of Malham Cove, Gordale Scar and Kilnsey. Brimham is renowned for its weird gritstone pinnacles such as the Turtle Rock and Indian Turban. Almscliff is an aptly named cliff if you substitute an 'r' for the first 'l'!

THE SOUTH OF ENGLAND

Southern England may boast no great peaks, but there are plenty of outcrops and sea cliffs to climb. Even Londoners have easy access to some of these: around Tunbridge Wells there is a plethora of small sandstone outcrops, as well as the famous 'rock gymnasium' of Harrison's Rocks, where many alpinists have started their careers.

Sea-cliff climbing in Britain really began at the end of the last century, although the first recorded climb was as early as 1858. Thanks to improvements in both protection and skills, the sport is very popular today, being carried out on a wide variety of rock, from the soft chalks of the South East to the solid granite found in Cornwall. Access is generally difficult, and so it is worth reading the relevant sections in the various guidebooks with some care. Many sea cliffs have seasonal restrictions in order to protect nesting birds.

The South East

Although there are a few good outcrops in the South East, such as Harrison's Rock, there is comparatively little for the sea-cliff climber. However, near Swanage there is an excellent stretch of limestone cliffs running for about 8km (5 miles) westwards from Durlston Head to St Alban's (or St Aldhelm's) Head. Camp sites abound, as do bed-and-breakfast establishments and youth hostels. The major cliffs are Subliminal, Boulder Ruckle, Cattle Troughs, Cormorant Ledges and Guillemot Ledges; there are plenty of others worth climbing. Climbs on all of these tend to be steep.

The South West

There are numerous crags in the South West, most of which are perhaps better classed as major cliffs. Of especial note are those of Avon Gorge (near Bristol), the 120m (400ft) cliffs of the Cheddar Gorge (in the Mendip Hills, south of Bristol), the large granite cliff of Dewerstone (near Plymouth), Chudleigh (near Exeter), Wintour's Leap (near Chepstow) and Wyndcliffe (in the Wye Valley, South Wales). All of these crags are limestone, with the exception of Dewerstone, which is granite.

Between Babbacombe, just by Torquay, and Berry Head, near Brixham, there are good sea cliffs, the main ones being Babbacombe Long Quarry Point, Daddyhole and the impressive Berry Head itself. All climbs are on limestone. There are surprisingly few camp sites nearby, but there are youth hostels and plenty of bed-and-breakfast establishments.

Cornwall is a marvellous area for sea-cliff climbing. Most of it is in West Penwith, an area to the west of a line drawn between Penzance and St Ives. The main crags, all granite, are Chair Ladder, Carn Les Boel, Pedn-Men-Du (Sennen), Bosigran and the Great Zawn area. The area is blessed by warm weather, and has good accommodation – camping, youth hostels, bed-and-breakfast establishments and the Climbers' Club hut, the Count House, at Bosigran.

Lundy is a small island, about 5km by 1.5km (3 miles by 1 mile), in the Bristol Channel, and is a lovely 'away from it all' area: apart from a few private dwellings, there are only a pub, a shop, a church and a hotel – and there are no cars. Lundy sports many excellent climbs on granite sea cliffs of all grades. The island is approached by boat or helicopter, but permission is required in advance: write to the Agent, Lundy Island, via Ilfracombe.

In the climbing area of North Devon and North Cornwall – the area between Padstow (Cornwall) and Ilfracombe – the sea cliffs include Pentire Head, Tintagel Head, Sharpnose, Hartland Point and Baggy Point. The rock is either slate or sandstone, varying from cliff to cliff, but, either way, it gives weird and wonderful rock contortions and excellent climbing, with slabs, walls and loose cracks. There are many good camp sites, youth hostels and bed-and-breakfast establishments.

SCOTLAND

Wild and rugged, Scotland provides some of the finest climbs in Britain on both rock and ice. Most crags involve long walks. The weather tends to be rather harsher than elsewhere in Britain, but periods of sunny hot days frequently dry out the vast mountain crags of Ben Nevis (1,343m [4,406ft]), Shelter Stone Crag, Creag an Dubh Loch, Sron na Ciche, Buachaille Etive Mor (1,020m [3,345ft]) and others. Winter climbing in Scotland is unparalleled and world-famous: Ben Nevis, Creag Meaghaidh (1,128m [3,700ft]), Creag an Dubh Loch and Lochnagar (1,154m [3,786ft]) are just a few of the many excellent sites.

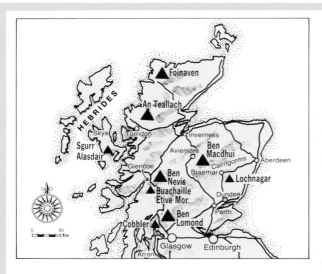

Western Scotland

Arran, an island in the Firth of Clyde, is remarkably quiet. It possesses some fine granite crags, such as Cioch na h'Oighe, Meadow Face on Beinn Tarsuinn (825m [2,706ft]), the south face of Cir Mhor (798m [2,618ft]) and some fine ridge traverses. Also of note is Goat Fell (874m [2,866ft]), the highest mountain on Arran. Accommodation of all kinds is plentiful. There are frequent sailings from Ardrossan.

Arrochar, at the end of Loch Long, is like Arran a favourite venue with Glaswegians. It is famous for Ben Arthur (881m [2,891ft]), nicknamed 'The Cobbler'. The cliffs, although short, have some really good climbs on silica schist. There is plenty of accommodation of all kinds.

Glencoe is perhaps the most popular Scottish venue, and is famous for the Three Sisters – Beinn Fhada (934m [3,064ft]), Gearr Aonach (966m [3,168ft]) and Aonach Dubh (950m [3,118ft]). Buachaille Etive Mor stands guardian to the entry to the valley and sports many classic easy and hard climbs, while Gearr Aonach (966m [3,168ft]) and Aonach Dubh (950m [3,118ft]) are splendid spurs of rock jutting forward into the glen. There are plenty of winter climbs, especially in the higher corries of Stob Coire nan Lochain (1,115m [3,657ft]), Bidean nam Bian (1,148m [3,766ft]), Stob Coire nam Beith and The Lost Valley. A winter traverse of the Aonach Eagach ridge is an experience not to be missed.

The best slab climbing in Britain is to be found at nearby Glen Etive on the Trilleachan Slabs (Etive Slabs), an idyllic spot some 120m (400ft) above the head of Loch Etive.

Ben Nevis, rising above Fort William, is the highest mountain in Britain. Summer or winter, there are climbs for all. There are a couple of shelters, one at the top and one in Coire Leis, to protect people caught out should the weather turn foul. Beneath the mountain's magnificent ramparts – cliffs 600m (2,000ft) high – is a climbing-club hut belonging to the Scottish Mountaineering Club (SMC). Known as the CIC Hut, it has been the saviour of many poor souls, although to make a planned stay in it you need to book first with the SMC's Secretary. Aside from staying in the hut, you can camp either high or in the valley, or use local bed-and-breakfast establishments or the youth hostel in Glen Nevis.

In the south of the island of Skye, in the Inner Hebrides to the mainland's west, there is a compact and beautiful mountainous area, the Black Cuillin. Winter climbing is unpredictable. Gabbro crags exist, notably Sron na Ciche, which is only an hour's walk from the main camp site in Glen Brittle. The complete ridge traverse is the best in Britain, summer or winter, and to spend a couple of days on it is to create a memory that will last a lifetime. In Glen Brittle there is, as well as camping, bed and breakfast, a youth hostel and the British Mountaineering Council's Memorial Hut. There are other good camp sites, and the Junior Mountaineering Club of Scotland has a hut near Loch Coruisk.

Wild and virtually unspoilt, Torridon is an area of remote crags, such as Coire Mhic Fhearchair. The rocks are mainly sandstone, but on this crag the sandstone is topped with quartzite. Camping, bed and breakfast, youth hostelling and bunkhouse accommodation are all easy; the SMC has a hut in Torridon, but this needs to be booked.

Eastern Scotland

The Cairngorm Massif can provide tough tests of your navigational and survival skills should bad weather come on, which it can do very abruptly. In general the crags are remote, the major ones being Creag an Dubh Loch, the Shelter Stone and Lochnagar (1,154m [3,786ft]). There

Left The Cioch, on the Isle of Skye, one of the Inner Hebrides off the western coast of Scotland. This is Scotland in its gentler summer guise.

Scotland in winter is another thing altogether! **Far left** Climbers scrambling on the Aonach Eagach Ridge in Glencoe, Scotland. **Top** A sparkling vista of névé in Stob Coire Nan Lochain, also in Glencoe. **Above** The Cuillin Ridge. People come from far afield to enjoy the climbing on the Isle of Skye.

are many other fine crags. The main centre is Aviemore. A good camp site at Glenmore, youth hostel, bunkhouse, bed-and-breakfast establishments and occasional bothies comprise the locally available accommodation.

Winter climbs in the Cairngorms tend to be more serious than elsewhere in Scotland owing to the remoteness of the crags and the likelihood of a sudden Arctic storm.

To the northeast of Scotland lie the Orkney Islands, one of which, Hoy, boasts the famous sandstone stack called The Old Man of Hoy (140m [460ft]). The unspoilt island is most welcoming with its accommodation – camping, hostel or bivouac.

Other Scottish sea cliffs of note are to be found at Longhaven (near Peterhead), Greg Ness (near Aberdeen) and Fort Castle (on St Abb's Head, northwest of Eyemouth).

WALES
To the climber, the interest in Wales centres largely on the north. However, as we shall see, South Wales too has climbs of some interest.

North Wales
North Wales is well favoured with superb crags that are less than 20 minutes' walk from the nearest road. Some of them have brilliant easy climbs. Milestone Buttress Direct is a particularly fine example, one of the best of its grade in Britain; it is found on the flank of Tryfan (917m [3,010ft]), overlooking the A5 road at Ogwen. Good mountain crags abound, one of the best being Clogwyn du'r Arddu on the north face of Snowdon's west ridge. (Snowdon, at 1,085m

[3,560ft], is the highest mountain in Wales.) This crag is steeped in tradition; in fact, it was on 'Cloggy' that the first recorded rock climb took place, in 1798. Most climbs on it are in the harder grades, and they are undeniably of great character.

The crags in North Wales are possibly more favourably sited than those of the Lake District in that it is possible to climb on the edges of Snowdonia at Tremadog or the sea cliffs on Anglesey when the mountains are shrouded in mist and rain. On the other hand, access to the crags is sometimes more of a problem than in the Lake District. New climbs are constantly being discovered both as techniques improve and as ideas of rock-types to be climbed vary; for example, slate is popular at the moment, and exceedingly hard climbs have been accomplished on this generally smooth rock.

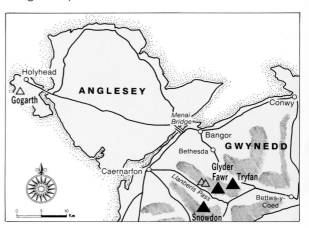

Below *The Old Man of Stoer, seen in summer.* **Right** *Wild winter in the Cairngorms.*

Anglesey

Gogarth, perhaps the most celebrated of all the British sea cliffs, is on the island of Holyhead, thrusting out into the Irish Sea. Development started in 1966-7, and many superlative climbs have been made. The rock is quartzite. Climbing in this region is very popular because the weather is generally better than in nearby Snowdonia. Access to the climbs can be tricky until you know your way around. There is camping outside Holyhead; otherwise you can use youth hostels or bed-and-breakfast establishments.

Llanberis Pass

This centre is famous for its 'three cliffs', Dinas Cromlech, Carreg Wastad and Clogwyn y Grochan. Other major cliffs on the south side of the pass are Dinas Mot and Cyrn Las; there are smaller cliffs and a couple of large broken

Wales in a few of its many guises.
Far left *Clogwyn D'ur Arddu ('Cloggy'), one of Britain's foremost rock playgrounds.*
Left *Sea and space on 'A Dream of White Horses', Wen Zawn, Gogarth.*
Below *Winter conditions make a scramble more serious on Grib Goch, Snowdon.*

mountain crags on the flank of Crib Goch ridge. Lliwedd is easily reached from the top of the pass.

Llanberis can also be used for the approach to 'Cloggy'. You follow a road to limited parking facilities at Hadodty Newydd, and then the Snowdon Mountain Railway line to Halfway House, before striking across to the cliff.

The climbing area in North Wales is very compact, so Llanberis can be used as a centre for other crags. The town is also handily situated for climbing's newest game – the vast paradise of the slate quarries of Deiniolen and Dinorwic, which are currently yielding hundreds of superb new routes; a paradise indeed, though something of an esoteric one.

Ogwen and Other Areas

The main crags accessible from Ogwen are Tryfan (with the Milestone Buttress on its flank), Idwal Slabs and Walls, and Glyder Fawr (999m [3,279ft]). Also, it is usual to use Ogwen as a base for the Carneddau Crags, the main areas being Llech Ddu, Black Ladders (especially in winter) and Craig yr Ysfa.

Farms provide camp sites as well as bed-and-breakfast accommodation; there are hotels of varying standards in Capel Curig and Bethesda; and climbing-club huts can be booked in advance with the club concerned.

The other main areas – Cwm Silyn, Cwellyn and Tremadog – are easily reached by a short drive from

bases in Llanberis or perhaps from a quiet camp site in the Gwynant Valley, near Beddgelert.

Minor areas include the Moelwyns, which rise above Blaenau Ffestiniog; the slate quarries of Llanberis, which provide some difficult modern climbs; Lledr Valley, near Dolwyddelan, which has a few isolated cliffs; Dolgellau, where there are some crags; and, on the fringe of Snowdonia, Llandudno, near to which there are sea cliffs and popular low-level crags.

Although North Wales is not favoured by long cold winters, some snow and ice climbs do exist. If you pick your time, these can provide some excellent expeditions at all standards – some rival the length, difficulty and quality of the harder Scottish climbs.

The Gower Peninsula

Situated in South Wales, west of Swansea, this area is ideal for married couples with children. The climbs are generally easy and they rise from golden sandy beaches: while the kids play in the sand, the parents can play on the cliffs. The rock is limestone and very solid.

Pembroke (Dyfed)

This is a very fashionable area for modern sea-cliff climbing, running from Tenby to Fishguard. The rock is limestone in the south and gabbro (the roughest of all rocks) around St David's Head. The main limestone crags are Mother Carey's Kitchen, Stackpole, Mowing Wood, St Govan's Head, Crickmail Point and Mewsford; some of these crags lie in the Castlemartin firing range and so access is restricted. The main gabbro crags are Trwyn Llwyd, Carn Porth Llong, Mur Cenhinen and Craig Coetan. There are plenty of camp sites, youth hostels and bed-and-breakfast establishments in both areas.

IRELAND

Climbing did not really get under way in Ireland until after World War II; even today there is much less activity than in, say, England. This is one of Ireland's great appeals to the hill walker and rock climber – the lack of other people.

The highest mountains are Macgillicuddy's Reeks, in County Kerry, extending west of the Lakes of Killarney; their highest peak is Carrantuohill (1,041m [3,414ft]). However, the red sandstone of these hills is not particularly suited for climbing. Better are the granite cliffs of Glendalough, in the Wicklow Mountains, County Wicklow. The Poisoned Glen in County Donegal has some fine climbs. Northern Ireland boasts the Mourne Mountains (County Down) and an important rock-climbing venue, Fairhead, which is one of the biggest cliffs in the British Isles – and, as any Ulsterman will tell you, one of the best.

There are good sea cliffs in western Ireland, notably in Mayo, Donegal and Kerry.

THE ALPS

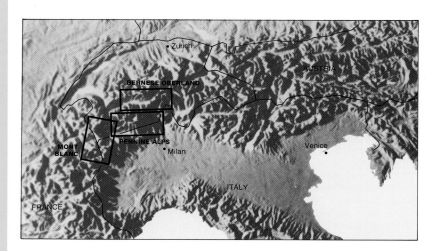

Approaching a sizeable rimaye (bergschrund) on the Bossons glacier above Chamonix, France. Rimayes on this scale can be problematical in both ascent and descent.

The Western Alps are the highest and most heavily glaciated region in Europe. Talking generally, it consists of the Mont Blanc Massif on the French/Italian border (see page 124), the Pennine Alps on the south side of the Rhône Valley, spanning the Swiss/Italian border (see page 126), and, in Switzerland, the Bernese Oberland, which is to the north of the Rhône Valley (see page 128).

As you travel south through regions like the Vanoise and the Dauphiné, or east through the Bregaglia and Austria, the weather improves and, with less snowfall, the mountains become rockier; by the time you reach the Julian Alps in Yugoslavia, the Maritime Alps in France or the Dolomites in Italy (see page 138), there is virtually nothing by way of permanent snow. Although there is fine climbing in all of these places (see below), the Western Alps are the main goal of alpinists the world over.

As long ago as 1871 Leslie Stephen described the Alps as the 'Playground of Europe'. Today they have been heavily developed to enable us to play more easily – albeit to the detriment of the mountains themselves. Many of the railways and *téléphériques* built to cater for the ski industry are used also by walkers and climbers in the summer. High on the flanks of the mountains, an elaborate system of huts, serviced by helicopters, has grown up to allow climbers to move in the mountains with the minimum of equipment. Huts are not as spartan as they might sound. True, accommodation is in large communal platform-bunks, and sheets are not provided with the blankets, but some can house up to 200 people and it is possible to buy meals, wine and beer for not much more than in the valleys. Alternatively, you can give the guardian your own food to cook, carry a stove and cook your own (although this is not allowed in Swiss huts), or simply buy hot water and live on instant soups and bread and cheese. Many huts are hideously crowded in July and August, and in good weather it is infinitely preferable to bivouac. To arrive with plenty of time to find a site that is comfortable and safe, to cook in the warmth of the evening sun, to watch from the warmth of your sleeping bag as the day fades and the stars come out – all of this makes up an important aspect of the alpine experience that can never be enjoyed from the clamour of a hut.

Newcomers used to climbing on outcrops can find the effort involved in alpine climbing disconcerting. It is a strenuous pastime. You may typically walk for three hours up to a hut and then have to set off the next morning before daybreak to ensure good snow conditions or simply in order to have plenty of time for the climb. The climbing day will involve a minimum of six hours' sustained movement and often as many as twelve – longer, if things go wrong.

To a large extent, whether or not you enjoy the Alps depends upon your physical attributes and personal preferences. Some revel in 'the magic of long days', in the utter content that comes at the end of an exhausting climb. Other people, more suited to the bursts of explosive energy needed for high-standard rock climbing, find that the steady rhythm of an alpine climb holds few attractions. The British alpinist Dorothy Pilley, who climbed well into her seventies, put it in a nutshell when she described 'that mixture of ecstasy and weariness and discomfort that from the beginning to the end is the basic quality of the Alpine experience'.

Fitness is essential if you are to enjoy a holiday in the Alps. Something you cannot prepare for, though, is the effect of the altitude – in other words, the lack of oxygen. It is common to suffer from headache and a loss of appetite the first night in a hut, and, unless you want to feel thoroughly miserable, you will not choose a 4,000m

(13,000ft) peak for your first route. However, most people quickly acclimatize: after a few days the altitude usually ceases to be a problem. The rate of acclimatization does vary from person to person, though, in a way unrelated to the individual's fitness. A few people find it impossible to adjust at all, and for them Diamox (acetozolamide) may provide an answer.

Because alpine routes are long and the weather rarely settled, safety depends largely on speed. Storms can blow up from nowhere in a matter of a couple of hours and can be so violent that you have no chance of moving either up or down. More commonly, rock climbs become plastered with snow, making them desperate if not impossible. Moreover, electric storms, originating over the plains, are common occurrences in the afternoons even in good weather. All in all, in order to avoid being caught by bad weather or by nightfall, it is necessary to cultivate a sense of urgency not usually encountered in outcrop climbing – not for nothing do the French refer to the start of a climb as *l'attaque*! Chiefly the matter of urgency is a state of mind, a determination to get up and go, but there are technical ramifications, too: you should move together with a shortened rope and a handful of coils wherever feasible, rather than climbing pitch by pitch.

MONT BLANC

Right and far right Two Alpine scenes from the Argentière Glacier Basin, high above Chamonix, France.

Mont Blanc (4,807m [15,772ft]) is the highest mountain in the European Alps. Its rock, a rough orange granite, is a delight to climb on – unlike that in many other areas of the Alps. There is a huge number of climbs of all sorts – rock, ice and mixed (all meticulously recorded in the French *Vallot* guides) – though in such a heavily glaciated region you usually need, for even a rock climb, an ice axe and crampons for the approach and descent. Some climbs are approached from Courmayeur, on the Italian side of the range, where villages, camp sites and huts all have a 'quieter' feel. However, by far the most important base for the majority of the range is Chamonix, in France. From here mechanical transport makes access to almost everywhere easy. Railways run from Chamonix up to Montenvers, overlooking the Mer de Glace, and from St Gervais up onto the north spur of Mont Blanc itself. The Aiguille du Midi *téléphérique* gives access to the Vallée Blanche, the heart of the massif, and other cable cars up and down the valley ensure that climbers never have to walk far to reach a hut unless they particularly want to.

For all of these reasons Mont Blanc has ever been a forcing ground in alpinism, climbers from all over the world congregating in an atmosphere of great competition. Rock climbs like the Bonatti Pillar on the Dru, the Walker Spur on the Grandes Jorasses, and the high and remote Central Pillar of Fréney are renowned test pieces, while the Argentière basin – containing the north faces of the Triolet, Courtes, Droites and Verte – has a collection of ice routes rivalled only by the Lauterbrunnen Wall in Switzerland. Climbers who want long, serious but technically less difficult routes are recommended to try the south side of Mont Blanc, which offers not only the magnificent 1,500m (5,000ft) Brenva face climbs but also a series of incomparable ridges: the spiky Diable Ridge of Mont Blanc du Tacul, the Frontier Ridge of Mont Maudit,

the Brenva Spur, and – a long way from anywhere – the ridges of Peuterey, Innominata and Brouillard. And then there are the famous and aptly named Aiguilles (needles), which have plenty of rock climbs in the middle and upper grades.

CLIMBS FOR BEGINNERS

Beginners will find rather fewer suitable climbs, but 'fewer' does not mean 'few'. Classics include the Forbes Arête on the Chardonnet, the Midi-Plan traverse, and the traverse of Les Courtes. The ascent of Mont Blanc by the standard route over the Dôme de Gouter cannot be recommended, if only because it is so popular: the Gouter hut bulges at the seams every fine night in the summer. Indeed, crowding is the main problem on Mont Blanc: any route mentioned in Gaston Rebuffat's *One Hundred Best Climbs*, however hard, is likely to have a queue on it, which means that the ambience of the climb is destroyed, the risks of injury due to stonefall are increased, and there are chaotic tangles as faster parties, rightly concerned about time, overtake slower ones. This aspect of modern alpinism is undoubtedly one reason why both solo climbing and winter climbing have become so popular, especially around Mont Blanc.

THE PENNINE ALPS

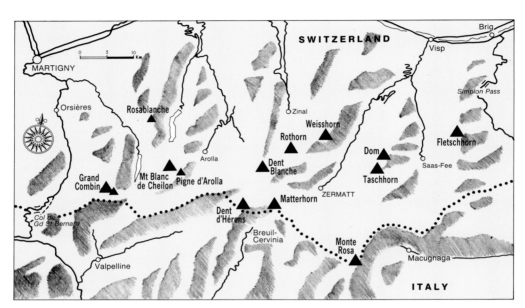

Nearing the summit – and the sun! The effect of sunshine at alpine altitudes can be fiercely discomforting. Take plenty of liquid, apply suncream liberally, and always wear sunglasses or goggles to protect your eyes.

The most famous peak in the Pennine Alps – and a distinctive feature of the view from any other part of the Alps – is the Matterhorn (4,477m [14,688ft]). However many photographs you may have seen, the reality never fails to impress: it will be an unusual climber who does not feel a mixture of dread and desire when contemplating it. Sadly, though, the reality belies the promise. The Matterhorn is notorious for the looseness of its rock, and both the Hörnli and the Italian ridges have been marred by fixed ropes and wires placed by local guides to make them accessible to everyone, assuming he or she can afford it.

The Fürggen is regarded as the hardest of the four ridges, but the Zmutt is the classic. Technically speaking it is not difficult, but in bad weather it is made very serious by a zone of slabs that are difficult to protect. The north face is one of the great faces of the Alps, and has become a popular winter route because it is best climbed in cold conditions, when the rock is frozen into place.

However, the Matterhorn is far from being the only peak worthy of attention in the Pennine Alps, which stretch for some 110km (70 miles) from the Grand Combin in the west to the Fletschhorn in the east – with convenient valley bases in Arolla, Zinal and Saas Fee, not to mention Zermatt on the Swiss side and Macugnaga, Alagna and Cervinia on the Italian side. The highest peaks and the greatest concentration of climbing are to be found around Zermatt but, because much of the rock is poor, the

area has traditionally been unpopular with 'hard men'. Nevertheless, there are many snow climbs suitable for beginners, and no shortage of fine mixed ridges.

The highest peak is Monte Rosa (4,633m [15,203ft]), a sprawling mass of a mountain with three summits, Nordend, Dufourspitze and Signalkuppe. Its east face, towering 2,400m (8,000ft) above Macugnaga, is not particularly steep but is nevertheless the biggest wall in the Alps. Signalkuppe has the dubious distinction of possessing the highest-built building in Europe – the Margherita hut.

Nearby is the Lyskamm, described in the English guide as 'a superb snow mountain, one of the most beautiful in the Alps and Himalayan in character'. The traverse of its twin summits gives an easy but serious route 4.5km (5,000yd) long. In the nineteenth century this ridge became known as the 'man-eater', but the double cornices which gave it the name seem less common these days.

To the north are other fine peaks, such as Dent Blanche, Rothorn, Weisshorn, Dom, Taschhorn – all of them names to conjure with. In particular, the Dom-Taschhorn traverse is rated by the guidebook as 'one of the finest expeditions in the Pennine Alps'.

THE HIGH LEVEL ROUTE

The High Level Route is a glacier journey from Chamonix to Zermatt, and is nowadays most commonly done in the spring on skis. Essentially it is a traverse of the range. After a two-day section from Chamonix you can travel by car or

bus to Bourg St Pierre, below the Grand St Bernard Pass. From here you ski for four strenuous days over a shoulder of the Grand Combin and through the heart of the range to a grand finale, skiing under the north faces of the Dent d'Harens and the Matterhorn down into Zermatt. A popular alternative, avoiding the steep slope above the Valsorey hut on the Combin, but traversing the Rosablanche and the Pigne d'Arolla, is to start from Verbier, rejoining the traditional route at the Vignettes hut. The High Level Route is equally enjoyable in summer, when the flowers provide an added interest; even in this season, however, the glaciers need to be treated with respect.

THE BERNESE OBERLAND

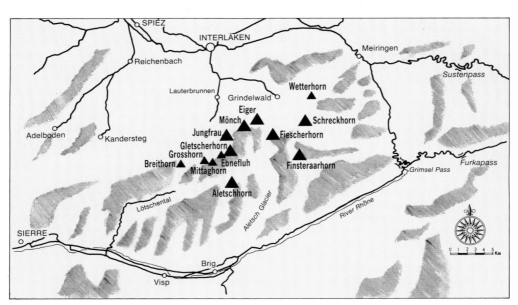

First-time visitors to Switzerland usually view the Bernese Oberland initially as the wonderful panorama seen from Interlaken of the north sides of the Jungfrau (4,158m [13,642ft]), Mönch (4,099m [13,448ft]) and Eiger (3,970m [13,025ft]) (the 'maiden', 'monk' and 'ogre'), but behind that impressive façade lie other and equally imposing peaks such as the Schreckhorn (4,078m [13,379ft]), Finsteraarhorn (4,274m [14,022ft]), Fiescherhorn (4,025m [13,205ft]) and Aletschhorn (4,195m [13,763ft]). The core of the range is a broad snow basin, the Konkordiaplatz, after which Concordia, at the Baltoro Glacier in the Karakoram, was named. Geographically, it is a remote place with a long approach from any direction, be it the Lotschental in the west, the Grimsel Pass in the east or the Aletsch Glacier (the longest glacier in Europe) in the south. However, since 1912, when a railway was tunnelled under the Eiger and the Mönch to the Jungfraujoch, access has been easy – albeit expensive. Nowadays the Konkordia and Finsteraarhorn huts are as crowded as any in the Alps.

The area is very popular during the spring with ski-mountaineers. There are many peaks on which skis can be used most of the way to the summit, and on some, such as the Ebnefluh (3,962m [12,998ft]), you can ski the whole way to the top. In terms of climbing, these routes are obviously very suitable for beginners, although in summer crevasses are more open and glacier travel more difficult than in spring.

Climbers and armchair mountaineers the world over, to whom the name 'Bernese Oberland' means little or nothing, nevertheless instantly recognize the Eiger and recall the grim history of its north face. Its notoriety has made Grindelwald almost as popular a tourist resort as Chamonix or Zermatt. For climbers, though, Grindelwald is a useful base only for the Eiger and the Wetterhorn (3,700m [12,142ft]). Of greater charm and offering a wider variety of climbing is Kandersteg – from where a railway leads under the mountains to the Rhône Valley and the Pennine Alps, cars being taken through the tunnel on railway trucks – while the Lötschental is a lovely valley, even if it offers relatively little climbing.

Lauterbrunnen is the starting point for some of the finest ice climbs in the Alps. Dropping from the summits of the Breithorn (3,782m [12,408ft]), Grosshorn (3,762m [12,343ft]), Mittaghorn (3,895m [12,779ft]), Ebnefluh and Gletscherhorn (3,983m [13,068ft]) is a north wall that is continuously steep for 9km (5½ miles). This was the stamping ground of the great Willo Welzenbach, who in the 1930s created routes which were only rarely repeated until the 1970s, when the advent of curved picks for axes and hammers made ice climbing both faster and safer. Now that the ice faces have been tamed, the spectacular waterfalls lower down the Lauterbrunnen Valley have become a venue for modern ice-climbing challenges.

SCANDINAVIA

Scandinavia is a sadly neglected climber's paradise, and all we can do here is give an indication of the area's scope. There is such a vast amount of good rock and alpine climbing that people have tended to explore only the more familiar regions. However, more recently such areas as Ulvik, Egersund (with its thousands of granite domes) and Setesdal have been developed.

Tromsø is perhaps the town with the finest local crags. The Hollenderen Massif on the Kvaloy Peninsula provides world-class climbing on crags such as Baugen. The most popular crags around Oslo are Kolsas (routes of all standards), Vardossen, which has 120m (400ft) slabs, and Fjell (short hard routes of up to 40m [130ft] and grade 10- [British 7a]). Further west, the 200m (660ft) cliffs of Andersnatten present classics such as Den Hvilte Stripa (the White Stripe; grade 6+), which is also popular in winter (use bolt belays).

Stavanger has some fine cliffs at Dale (up to 60m [200ft]) and, near Tau, Svao (up to 16 pitches). From Trondheim you can cross the fjord to Selnes (a local guidebook is available) or work on local test pieces such as Skygebua (grade 8+) on Korsvika sea cliff.

The Jotundheimen ('Home of the Giants') boasts Norway's two highest peaks, Galdhøppigen (2,468m [8,097ft]) and Glittertind (2,452m [8,045ft]). The area is characterized by easy alpine-type climbs, but Vesle Galdhøppigen has a difficult and serious south face (grade 6-). Further east, valley bases at Eidsbugarden and Gjende offer fine scrambles on shapely peaks such as Knutsholtind and Urdanostind – take crampons. The Hurrungane region to the west has a concentration of hard mountain challenges: Store Skagastølind (2,404m [7,888ft]) holds climbs ranging in difficulty from the route used by Cecil Slingsby (the 'Father of Norwegian Mountaineering') in 1876 – he was not only the first to attain the peak, he made the ascent solo – to various south-face climbs such as the modern Nytid (grade 7). Nordre Midtmaradalstind has several hard climbs on its east face (grade 6) and Store Midtmaradalstind gives classic problems, including its East Pillar (grade 5+) and Jubilee Wall (grade 6+). Centraltind and Store Styggedalstind have difficult mixed north faces. Other classics include Storn west face (grade 6), Søre Dyrhaugstind southeast face (grade 5) and Midtre Dyrhaugstind's northeast pillar. Austabalatind and Store Ringstind are rarely visited, but are well worth investigating.

ROMSDAL
Romsdal, famed for the stupendous Troll Wall, has routes of all standards and degrees of commitment, from roadside crags such as Hornaksla and Mjølva, through classic scrambles such as the Ordinary Route on Store Trolltind (1,795m [5,888ft]) and the traverse of Søre Venjatind (1,842m [6,045ft]) to multi-day big walls. Recommended routes include Kvanndalstind southeast ridge (grade 2+, 360m [1,180ft]), Romsdalshorn north wall (grade 3, 300m [985ft]), Stighorn west wall (grade 5-, 600m [1,970ft]) and various climbs on the west wall of Goksøyra (grades from 6- to 6+). Of the famous 'Three Pillars of Romsdal' Trollryggen East Pillar (grade 6-, 2,400m [7,875ft]) is the classic. On the Troll Wall the Rimmon Route (grade 6) is the Big Wall Trade Route, but the Swedish Route (grade 7-) is among Europe's finest big-wall routes. Both are now free-routed, but nevertheless many parties resort to a little aid. Other big-wall challenges are Mongejura's south pillar (grade 6), Kongen east face direct (grade 6+ [British A3]) and the magnificent Sondre Trolltind north wall (grade 6+ [British A4]).

In winter Romsdal provides plenty of opportunities for climbing frozen waterfalls. The most popular climb is Skogagrova (grade III) in upper Romsdal, opposite the unclimbed 800m (2,625ft) Dontfossen. Other winter venues include Hemsedal – with big routes such as Gratenfossen (grade IV/V), above Ulsak – and Laerdal, with its many falls and the nearby Vettifossen (grade VI),

Left *The great Trolltind Wall of Romsdal, Norway, offers some of the longest rock climbs in Europe (over 1,000m [3,300ft]) and some of the hardest. Access is easy and the area is unglaciated. However, Romsdal suffers fickle weather.*
Below *Climbing high on the Troll Wall.*

climbed in 1977 by Barber and Taylor.

North of Romsdal is Innerdal. This area is popular among Norwegians and boasts classics such as Skarfjell south wall direct (grade 6) and the southeast pillar of the massive Hastadnebba (grade 5, 1,500m [4,920ft]).

TYSFJORD AND OTHER REGIONS

The Tysfjord region has an abundance of huge granite faces. In Skjomdal there are fine routes on Haugbakktind and on Durmålstind. The Jegervasstind group has a tradition of alpine- and Scottish-style winter climbing, largely thanks to the fact that marines train in this area. North again, the alpine peaks and rock walls of Øksfjord have received attention. Finally, the Lofoten Islands have enormous potential, and many impressive climbs have been recorded there.

FRANCE

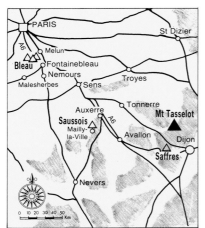

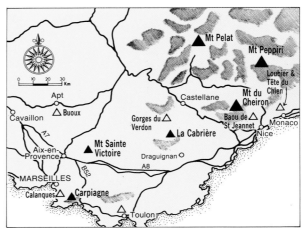

Two vintage French venues, each brilliantly different. **Below** *Buoux and the best limestone imaginable.* **Right** *Gorges du Verdon in Provence is currently a Mecca for European rock-climbers.*

132

The majority of French rock climbing – especially in the south – is on limestone, on cliffs of anything up to 350m (1,150ft) in height. However, there is also a sandstone region spreading from the Paris basin to the German border in Alsace, and this offers climbing mainly on small outcrops and boulders up to 50m (165ft) high.

Rock climbing in France is of world importance: its development since the free-climbing revolution in the late 1970s has been incredible. An individual style, drawn from an international menu of ethics and ideas, has evolved so that France is nowadays responsible for some of the hardest free climbs in the world. The 'French style' concerns itself totally with movement. Worries about placing complicated and intricate protection devices have been virtually eliminated, since almost all routes are pre-equipped with protection. For an ascent, only kara-biners and quick draws are required – in France an ascent is a climb that begins at the bottom and ends at the top without falls or lowering off – and on the hardest climbs even the quick draws can be preplaced to minimize effort, leaving nothing to interrupt your concentration or disrupt the physical flow of climbing. As a result, climbs tend to be well rehearsed, with the moves all planned in advance. While such advance planning is obviously very necessary on the hardest routes, it is sad that it is now part of almost all French rock-climbing. However, on-site ascents of grades up to 8a (British 6c) are becoming more common.

The grades system in France refers to the hardest moves on pitches. There is some regional variation in grading assessment, but the following is a general guide. The French grade is given first, followed by the British equivalent in brackets: V+ (5a), 6a (5b), 6b (5c), 6c (6a), 7a (6b), 7b (6b), 7c (6b-6c), 8a (6c), 8b (6c-7a).

Fontainebleau, a wooded sandstone area that offers three-season climbing, is nicknamed 'Bleau' and its regular climbers are known as 'Bleausards'. The area is centred on the town of Fontainebleau, some 40km (25 miles) south of Paris and just east of the A6 autoroute. Climbs are up to 15m (50ft) in length and are colour-coded for difficulty.

The climbing in Saussois, possible during three seasons, is on polished limestone; routes are up to 70m (230ft). The cliffs are near Mailly-la-Ville, 32km (20 miles) from Aux-erre and 3km (2 miles) southeast of Mailly-le-Château.

Saffres is 5km (3 miles) northeast of Vitteaux and 40km (25 miles) west of Dijon on the N5. Here there are limestone cliffs up to 30m (100ft) high which offer climbing from late spring to late autumn.

Salève is a cliff about 1km (½ mile) southeast of Collonges-sous-Salève, which is just south of Le Coin, 11km (7 miles) down the road from Geneva to La Croisette. The rock is limestone, the season is summer, and the routes are up to 100m (330ft) in length.

About 10km (6¼ miles) south of Apt and east of Bonnieux in the Massif du Luberon is the limestone gorge of Buoux; it is France's premier outcrop, with routes of length up to 100m (330ft). It has become very popular in recent years, with two adverse results: the rock has become highly polished, and local residents have become fed up with climbers! You can receive on-the-spot fines for

illegal camping, and your car can be impounded if you park it in the wrong place. There are several other well developed crags in the vicinity, such as Cavaillon (20km [12½ miles] southeast of Avignon) and Menerbes (20km west of Buoux). All offer year-round climbing.

Like Buoux, Gorges du Verdon is a prime limestone area. The gorges comprise a series of cliffs, mainly on the north side of the Verdon River between Moustier and Castellane. Spring and autumn are the best seasons and, since most climbs are approached by abseil, a very long rope is useful; nuts and 'Friends' are recommended for the longer traditional routes (some as long as 400m [1,300ft]).

Montagne Sainte Victoire, a limestone mountain 15km (9 miles) east of Aix-en-Provence, offers all-year climbing on routes of length up to 300m (985ft). Protection is often widely spaced, and nuts are useful.

The coastal cliffs between Marseilles and Cassis have long been popular. This is a vast area, with three sections of special interest: Morquou, Sugiton and En Veu. All offer year-round limestone climbing with routes of up to 150m (500ft). Nuts and 'Friends' are essential, because the salt water corrodes any fixed protection. Approach is from either Marseilles or Cassis.

THE GERMANIES AND CZECHOSLOVAKIA

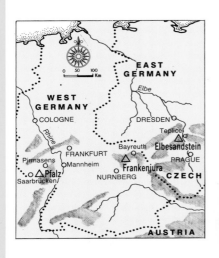

WEST GERMANY

There are two main climbing areas in West Germany: the Pfalz in the northwest, which is sandstone, and the Frankenjura in the southeast, a scattered series of limestone outcrops to the north of Nuremberg. The climbing is safe, with large well placed bolts for protection, but you should carry a small rack of nuts and 'Friends'. Generally, the easier the route the less well protected it will be.

The Pfalz is a superb sandstone region near Pirmasens – 90km (56 miles) southwest of Mannheim on the west bank of the Rhine – which provides fine climbing in picturesque settings. It is a continuation of the French and Luxembourg sandstones, but possesses vastly more extensive outcrops. More climbing is found east of Pirmasens, between the towns of Hinterweidenthal and Annweiler. The main town, in the centre of the region, is Dahn, where there is a camp site – although the most popular base is the Barenbrunner Hof, a large and attractive complex of farm buildings, bunkhouse, eating house and camping area reserved especially for climbers and walkers and located about 8km (5 miles) east of Dahn. Climbing in the region is possible from late spring to early autumn. The types and styles of routes are varied – a welcome respite from the steep limestone of most other areas.

The Frankenjura, or Frankische Schweiz, 45km (28 miles) north of Nuremberg, is an extensive area of limestone cliffs and pinnacles with a large number of routes. The climbing is invariably hard, but it is well protected. Most cliffs have only a few routes, so it may be necessary to visit more than one cliff in order to get in a good day's climbing. Most towns and villages in the region have camp sites; it may well be worth moving from one to another, as the area is quite large. The existing guidebook is written in German and has few illustrations and maps, so the best sources of information are back issues of the magazines *Alpin* and *Rotpunkt*.

EAST GERMANY AND CZECHOSLOVAKIA

An extremely picturesque region of sandstone walls and spires straddles the border between East Germany and Czechoslovakia. This is the Elbesandstein, whose cliffs have a long tradition of climbing. The main climbing is in the valley of the Elbe between Dresden and Teplice.

Climbing on the towers is strictly controlled: apart from rope, boots and harnesses, the only items of equipment allowed are jammed knotted slings. There are placed bolts for protection but, as these are a minimum 5m (16½ft) apart, falls of up to 15m (50ft) are not uncommon. Routes are up to 75m (250ft).

You need a visa to reach the area from the West, but the effort is well worth it. The best idea is to go to Dresden in East Germany and there obtain a visa for Czechoslovakia; however, it is a good idea to check this out before you go. An East German visa can be obtained from Berolina Travel, London; a Czech visa can be had from the Czech embassy in your country. You have to book your accommodation well in advance if you are to qualify for a visa, but the said accommodation can be camping.

Left and **above** Elbesandstein, in Falkenstein, East Germany. Here there is a long tradition of very hard free climbs on rough sandstone. The ethics in the area are strict: 'free' means exactly that, and nothing less is tolerated.

SPAIN

Spread around Spain are well over 300 cliffs. The climbing is varied and extensive, including limestone, granite, conglomerate and sandstone. Spain has recently become popular with climbers from other European countries during the winter, when cheap flights are available.

Because there are so many crags and locations it is not possible here to do justice to the whole of Spain: the following selection of venues is merely an introduction. If you wish to explore the matter of climbing in Spain further you should read a series of articles on the subject by Nico Mailander which appeared in the British magazine *Mountain* (nos. 112-15) and a topographical guide in German and English by the same author.

PEDRIZA

This superb granite area lies between Madrid and Segovia on the southern foothills of the Sierra de Guadarrama; from Madrid you drive about 60km (37 miles) along the A6 or the E25. Climbing is on cliffs as well as on countless blocks and boulders; there are well over 1,000 routes, some of them up to 250m (820ft) long. Camping is available near the cliffs.

VALLE DE LEIRA

Leira is a big limestone cliff on the edge of the Cordillera Subetico Plateau, some 30km (19 miles) southwest of Murcia, near Alhama de Murcia. The site overlooks the E26, the main Murcia-Granada road, and faces southeast, getting the sun. The climbing is on steep good-quality limestone on routes up to 170m (558ft), and is possible at all times except the height of summer. It is a good idea to take along a full set of nuts and 'Friends' as some of the fixed protection is old and in a poor state.

There is camping near the cliff. Also, numerous local

hotels offer excellent cheap board and lodging.

CALPE

This large town – 60km (37 miles) northeast of Alicante on the E26 – is a good centre for rock climbing, especially in winter, when several tour operators offer cheap package holidays in the area. The climbing is varied and extensive – with, importantly, much for the middle-grade climber – and is to be found in a variety of locations ranging from the Renon sea cliffs to the gorge at Mascarat. There are several camp sites in Calpe and it is possible to camp 'wild' in the hills.

MONTANEJOS

Near the village of Montanejos, 100km (60 miles) north-west of Valencia and 50km (30 miles) north of Segorbe, lies the valley of Mijares, which contains a superb series of limestone gorges. In spring and autumn climbing takes place in two gorges just north of the village where the routes are all in the higher grades (5b and above). Most of the protection is fixed, requiring only quick draws.

There is a camp site at Montanejos. However, you can camp for free at a ruined settlement on the bank of a reservoir 3km (2 miles) north of the village.

MONTSERRAT

This is a superb series of conglomerate walls 60km (37 miles) northwest of Barcelona; there are over 1,000 bolt-protected routes of all grades, and they provide a superb alternative, in spring and autumn, to southern France (see page 133). Camping is possible near most of the cliffs; also, there are some official camp sites in the neighbourhood.

MALLOS DE RIGLOS

This is another area famous for its conglomerate towers and walls; it is about 4km (2½ miles) southeast of Santa Maria de la Pema. The more popular climbs are now protected by large bolts; beware, though, of some of the less used routes, where the protection is older and consequently not so reliable. Large falls can occur. Descents are often by abseil, so double ropes are advised. There is camping in the village of Riglos and a hut to the south of Santa Maria (on the lakeside).

ITALY

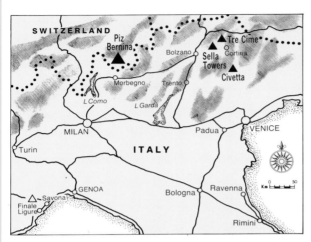

The Dolomites – popularly known as the 'Dollies' – were for many years famous for their long, steep aid climbs. Today they are enjoying a renaissance as a free-climbing playground.

Italy has many climbing regions, of which several deserve specific mention: these are the Dolomites, Arco, Sandrio and Finale, all of which are in the north of the country.

THE DOLOMITES

This is a semi-alpine region of limestone peaks and spires. The range occupies a wide area of northeastern Italy, south of the Austrian border and east of the towns of Trento and Bolzano. There are many centres, some of the more celebrated being Canasei (for the Sella Towers), Allegre (for the Civetta) and Cortina (for the Tre Cime).

Although the Dolomites' alpine nature should never be underestimated, they can be considered separately as a rock-climbing venue (summer only). The climbs can be up to 1,000m (3,280ft) or more, and are often subject to bad weather and summer storms: even in summer it is not unusual to find ice in summit chimneys.

Most climbs can be done in a day by a fast party; otherwise, allow for a bivouac. You can expect equipment to be in place on the more popular climbs, but it may well be of doubtful quality, so you would be advised to be experienced, well equipped and well prepared! At the least you should take karabiners and quick draws, but you will find on many climbs that you need also nuts, 'Friends' and sometimes pegs and bolts.

Camp sites exist in most towns, and there is a good network of alpine huts. For some climbs, however, it is necessary to walk in and bivouac or camp near the face.

ARCO

The Arco climbing area is just to the southwest of the Dolomites, on the northern tip of Lago di Garda. It offers a low-level alternative to the Dolomites, and has better weather: three-season climbing is possible. The centre is Arco itself, 3km (2 miles) north of the tip of the lake. Most climbing routes are up to 150m (490ft), but a few are as long as 800m (2,625ft); as a general rule, the longer routes are less well protected than the shorter ones.

Beneath the major cliff, Cima Colodri, 1km (1,000 yards) north of Arco, there is a superb camp site.

SANDRIO

South of the Badile, in the Bregaglia Alps, is the climbing region of Sandrio, where fine climbing on granite walls can be found. The main centre is Val di Mello, a valley just to the north of Morbegno. The region is 100km (62 miles) north of Milan and 20km (12½ miles) east of the northern tip of Lake Como. Access is fairly easy, and there is camping available near the town of San Martino.

Unfortunately, the climbs can suffer from mountain weather, and so the region is regarded as a summer venue only. Routes are mostly up to 100m (330ft), although there are some up to 500m (1,640ft).

FINALE

This is a limestone area on the Mediterranean coast 80km (50 miles) east of the French border: the main coastal autostrade from Nice to Genoa runs right through the area; exit at Finale Ligure. Four-season climbing is possible, although winds can be a problem in winter. Routes are of lengths up to 300m (985ft), and all are equipped with protection.

There are two camp sites in Finale Ligure, but they are rather expensive. Out of the holiday season you can camp beneath the main cliff of the region, Monte Cucco.

Italian granite at Val di Mello, one of the best of Europe's 'new discoveries'. Here is a roadside crag with hundreds if not thousands of metres of granite bathed, it seems, in sunshine all through the summer months.

139

UNITED STATES OF AMERICA

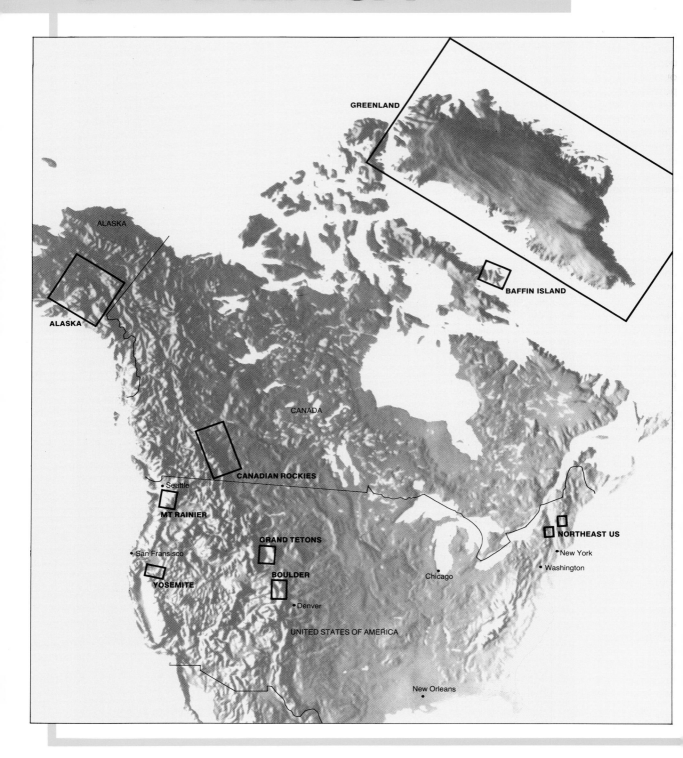

For two centuries the vast spaces of North America have teased the souls of its inhabitants. Even today, getting from one corner of the United States to another can take a week by car – double that if you include Alaska. For the past seven decades or so US climbers have been criss-crossing the country, tirelessly searching out climbing areas.

Within the 9,372,614 square kilometres (3,618,772 square miles) you can find innumerable climbing areas, each with its own unique character. To cover all of them would require a separate book, and so here areas have been chosen that are both historically important and outstanding for climbing. There are plenty of other popular areas – sandstone bluffs in the Southeast, desert spires in the Southwest, remote mountains in the Rockies … Readers interested in such sites are recommended to Chris Jones' *Climbing in North America*, published by the American Alpine Club in 1976. Sites in Canada are discussed in the present book on pages 154-157.

A quick glance at North America's topography reveals a series of parallel mountain ranges running north-south. On the east coast are the Appalachian mountains, an ancient range now eroded down to be rounded and forested hills, with heights rising to about 1,800m (6,000ft) on occasion. The Rockies include over 50 peaks of height around 4,300m (14,000ft), but ironically only a few are steep and compact enough for technical climbing. The mountains of the West Coast include two long chains of igneous peaks and a network of volcanoes – the Coast Range, the Sierra Nevada and the Cascades – both types of mountain attaining 4,300m (14,000ft) on occasion. Each of these major ranges contains a wealth of cliffs. Rock types include various sandstones, quartzites and granites, with the granites generally dominating. Also to be found are glaciated peaks offering a truly alpine character.

Over the years since the origins of US roped sport-climbing in the 1910s, when it was learned from the Europeans, and the first serious cross-pollination of ideas and experience in the 1950s, several important climbing centres have emerged: the Northeast, Colorado, California and the Northwest. Climbing in each of these regions developed more or less independently.

Until recently, when rock climbing became accepted purely for its own sake, most US climbers were oriented entirely towards mountaineering; even those who had developed their technical skills exclusively on small crags felt that they were merely training for future mountain adventures. Lately, though, crags of all sizes have come into their own. Younger climbers are increasingly focusing their attentions on rocks that barely rise above the trees, and some modern climbers go so far as to shun the mountains altogether. A great number of crags that until recently were totally ignored are now popular venues, and rocks have been unearthed and even devegetated to make room for hard new routes. The other side of the coin is that fewer climbers seem to find their way to the quiet reaches of the wilderness mountains.

One thing is certain: in a country the size of the United States there is never a lack of places to climb.

North America has many alpine routes. Here is one of the best of them – the Exum Ridge of the Grand Teton (4,196m [13,766ft]), Wyoming. The Teton range is so-called because of the ribald nickname given to its three principal peaks by early trappers – les trois tetons, or 'the three breasts'.

THE TETONS

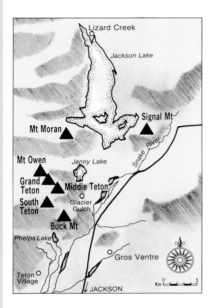

A scene in the Tetons: Perry Williams on 'Irene's Arête'.

The new generation of US climbers that emerged in the 1950s began to travel much more widely than had their predecessors. And, no matter where else they visited, the Teton Mountains on the Wyoming-Idaho border formed their most important gathering point and social centre. Around the officially designated Climbers' Campground stories were told of adventures far and wide: the latest Yosemite big-wall exploits, a particularly horrendous roof recently climbed in the Shawangunks, a big storm on Mt Assiniboine... all would come alive again in the flickering light of a campfire in the cool Wyoming air.

In this compact cluster of mountains – the entire range is contained within an area a mere 22km (14 miles) wide by 65km (40 miles) long – rise dozens of ragged peaks. Tallest is the 4,196m (13,766ft) Grand Teton, which towers over 2,100m (7,000ft) above the arid Western sagebrush and cowboy country of Jackson Hole. Other peaks of note include Cloudveil Dome (3,666m [12,027ft]), Middle Teton (3,903m [12,804ft]), Mt Owen (3,940m [12,928ft]), Mt Moran (3,842m [12,605ft]) and South Teton (3,814m [12,514ft]). Most climbing is on solid granite and gneiss, with some routes following ice couloirs and snow faces. Routes up the larger faces generally take a day of climbing from a high camp (i.e., a round trip of two or three days from the valley), but the round trip for many shorter climbs takes only a day from where you park your car. Routes of all grades abound, and there are both easy and difficult climbs tackling spectacular ridges and steep, exposed faces – climbers who want it can find plenty of vertical rock and exposure. Should the joys of rock climbing temporarily pall, climbers can visit the wilderness of neighbouring Yellowstone National Park.

Although the Tetons no longer enjoy the same level of popularity as they once did – modern rock climbers are less interested in approach walks and mountain weather – they will always remain one of the most spectacular and enjoyable mountain ranges in North America.

From late June to the middle of August you can expect warm sunny weather, sometimes punctuated by afternoon thunderstorms and hailstorms: be prepared and carry rain clothing. In a good year, the season can last from late May to late September.

Climbers usually stay at the American Alpine Club's Climbers Ranch, just south of Jenny Lake, which operates on a first come, first served basis. Before any climb you must register with the Park Rangers. There are guide services available: Exum Mountain Guide Service, in Wilson, and Jackson Hole Mountain Guides, in Teton Village.

Above *The Teton range as seen from Jackson Hole.* **Right** *Jim Evans on the Exum Ridge of the Grand Teton. The Grand Teton is probably North America's most popular rock summit and the Exum the most frequented of its 20 or more routes. The long (1,200m [4000ft]) but easy east ridge and the often icy north ridge are also classics.*

143

BOULDER, COLORADO

To the east of Boulder, Colorado, the pancake-flat cornfields and prairies of the Midwest stretch out for over fifteen hundred kilometres (a thousand miles); to its immediate west are the Rocky Mountain foothills. The population of Boulder, the hub of Western climbing activities, contains an extraordinary number of climbers from elsewhere – not just elsewhere in the United States but also from Europe. They have come here because no other city in North America – perhaps even the world – is within striking range of so much good and diverse rock.

Within ten minutes' drive of downtown Boulder are the Flatirons, Flagstaff Mountain and the world-renowned Eldorado Canyon – all very solid sandstone – while even closer to town are the numerous granite crags of Boulder Canyon. An hour away, in Rocky Mountain National Park, there are granite faces on peaks of height 3,700-4,300m (12-14,000ft), while within two hours one finds the rough granite crags of Vedauwoo and South Platte as well as the soft sandstone spires of the Garden of the Gods. Going further afield, within five to eight hours' driving from Boulder there are five further major climbing areas, including the granite chasm of the Black Canyon of the Gunnison, 600m (2,000ft) deep; the phenomenal red sandstone spires and walls of the Canyonlands; and the Devil's Tower, the ultimate crack-climber's paradise.

Eldorado Canyon's metamorphosed sandstone offers by far the most famous and popular climbing in the region. The sandstone has a near-silky texture that adds to the pleasure of the intricate face climbing on the coloured rock. There is a strong feeling of space under one's feet as one swiftly ascends routes of two to eight pitches on nearly vertical rock. Though Eldorado is often crowded, the atmosphere is very comfortable, the sound of rushing water in the stream below is soothing, and Colorado's famous sunshine floods the cliffs with warm light.

Eldorado Canyon can be climbed all year, although April to June and September to November generally offer the mildest weather. There is no convenient camping, but you can telephone the Forest Service for a list of camp sites further away. The KOA at 5856 Valmont, in Boulder, is expensive and sterile, but does have showers. An alternative is Boulder International Youth Hostel.

ROCKY MOUNTAIN NATIONAL PARK
Equally exciting are the most accessible rugged mountains in the United States: the high peaks of Rocky Mountain National Park. Here there are superb climbs on excellent rock. Routes ascend 300m (1,000ft) faces, knife-edge ridges and 250m (800ft) spires. Because of the altitude –

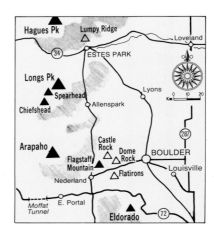

summits can be 3,700-4,300m (12-14,000ft) above sea level – climbers planning to attempt challenging routes must be in good physical condition and properly acclimatized. Afternoon thunderstorms are common, so it is a good idea to set out from the trailhead before dawn and to move quickly.

Despite its altitude and weather, the Park has no glaciers and only a few permanent snowfields. During the summer its high altitudes offer only rock climbing, with a few exceptions such as Kiener's route on the east face of Long's Peak, which ascends a 450m (1,500ft) 45° snowfield before you reach rock. Lower in the Park are the crags of Lumpy Ridge, whose sundrenched granite overlooks the mountains and whose easy accessibility and mild weather make it very popular with modern rock climbers.

The Park is best for climbers from June through to September, with July and August being the favourite months. For the high peaks, warm clothing and rain protection could quite literally be life-savers.

The nearby Estes Park area has numerous camp sites, and there is also a youth hostel.

ICE CLIMBING
There is some good ice climbing in the Boulder region, Rocky Mountain National Park starts freezing up in late November and offers a few moderate gullies, but most of the Park's ice climbs tend to be steep and difficult, whether on the rare waterfalls or on the more common icy runnels on mountain faces. Boulder Canyon offers a few moderate waterfall climbs up to 30m (100ft); these are best in midwinter. More extensive ice climbing on larger frozen waterfalls can be found two hours away in Glenwood Canyon.

Top *A proffered hand 4,250m (14,000ft) up on Long's Peak in the Rocky Mountain National Park is a welcome sight indeed.* **Above** *'Mickey Mouse Direct' (5.12A) in Eldorado Canyon, Colorado.* **Right** *Climbers on the Yellow Spur in Eldorado Canyon. Eldorado is a rock climbers' paradise with rough red rock and almost permanent sunshine.*

145

MOUNT RAINIER

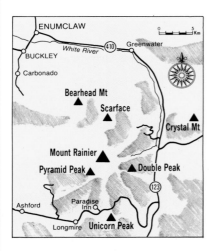

Liberty Bell (about 2,290m [7,515ft]) in the Cascade Range, Washington State, an area blessed by superb granite peaks and cursed by bad weather.

Wild and powerful, the Cascade Mountains of the Northwest are the most glaciated and rugged peaks in the United States (outside Alaska). The greatest concentration of these peaks lies just south of the Canadian border in Washington State's North Cascades National Park. Here hundreds of mostly granitic summits have been carved by nearly 800 different glaciers. Although the mountains rarely top 2,750m (9,000ft) above sea level, the actual height from valley floor to mountain summit is usually much greater than among the 'higher' peaks of the Rockies in Colorado. All this glaciation, as well as the lush forests in the valleys below – trees can reach heights of 75m (250ft) – is made possible because the region receives a tremendous amount of annual precipitation. Indeed, bad weather is the curse of Cascades mountaineering through much of the year. However, there are often long spells of fine conditions in midsummer.

When the clouds clear, one peak stands out among all the rest. The Indians named it Tahoma, 'The Mountain That Was God', but settlers renamed it Mt Rainier. It is an inactive volcano standing 4,392m (14,410ft) tall and soaring some 2,500m (8,200ft) above its minor subpeaks. In good weather it is spectacularly visible even from Seattle, 80km (50 miles) away.

In all respects Rainier commands attention. Many consider it to be the single most impressive North American mountain outside Alaska. Its sheer immensity is awe-inspiring, its volcanic-cone shape is exquisitely beautiful, and the amount of ice that flows down its flanks is unbelievable. Each year Rainier receives more than 14m (45ft) of snow, which contribute to its 26 named glaciers.

In any one year some 4,000 climbers may ascend to Rainier's summit. This is testimony not just to the mountain's attractiveness but also to its accessibility. With 30 or

more routes leading to the summit plateau, climbers have choices that range from simple glacier walks to steep rock and ice climbs. However, even the easiest routes demand caution, for the dangers of crevasses, hanging glaciers, avalanches and storms are very real indeed: this mountain truly makes its own weather. Though good physical condition is more important than technical skill for climbers tackling Rainier's easier routes, mountain experience and knowledge of crevasse rescue can be critical should anything go wrong.

The first complete ascent to the summit, by P.B. Van Trump and Hazard Stevens, was in 1870, and before the turn of the century a guide service had been formed – one of the first in the United States. Mt Rainer National Park, founded in 1899, was one of the earliest of the nation's parks. When registering with the Park Rangers before a climb (this is obligatory) you can learn the latest news about the conditions on the mountain.

By far the most popular route is the Ingraham Glacier/Disappointment Cleaver, including a high camp at the John Muir Hut at 3,000m (10,000ft). For this route, starts at midnight or in the wee small hours are common, so that a return can be effected before the snow is softened enough by the sun that snow bridges over crevasses are weakened. For most other routes a high camp and an early start are likewise recommended.

The favourite season is June/July, after which the ice becomes increasingly hard and rockfalls more common. May and September can offer good climbing, although these are transitional months and the weather is likely to be even less predictable than usual. Winter temperatures in this area are not severe, but the sheer quantity of snowfall can make climbing difficult and hazardous.

Ice axes and crampons are necessary for all routes. Prusik slings or ascenders are needed in case of crevasse

rescue. Emergency shelter, a sleeping bag and extra warm clothes should be taken, as well as sunglasses, extra food and the normal mountain necessities. There are numerous camp sites: ask at the gate to the National Park.

Below the snow and ice, the lower flanks of the mountain are draped with fields of wildflowers and laced with hiking trails. Even if the weather turns sour, this part of 'The Mountain That Was God' is a joy to walk on.

Nearby there are a few other mountains to explore: among these are Mt Adams (3,751m) [12,306ft]) and Mt Stuart (2,866m [9,403ft]). Also nearby is Mt St Helens (2,950m [9,677ft]), but this is, for understandable reasons, little climbed these days.

Above Mt Rainier (4,392m [14,410ft]) is an inactive volcano. **Left** Jim Brigham on Mt Stuart (2,866m [9,403ft]), also in the North Cascades National Park.

147

THE NORTHEAST

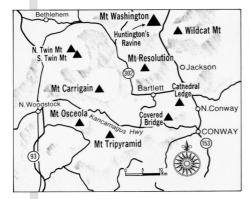

John Harlin on 'Layback', at the Shawangunks. The 'Gunks', a limestone crag, are characterized by steep – indeed, often impressively overhanging – climbs, some of which turn out to be surprisingly straightforward. Mind you, others are surprisingly difficult!

Perhaps it is because they are only a two-hour drive away from the teeming streets of New York City that the Shawangunks (or 'Gunks', as they are generally called) are the most heavily climbed crags in North America. That is the cynical view: in fact they offer some of the finest rock climbing in the United States. Indeed, the crowds are not the main problem in this area – it is the wet weather, whether it be rain or summer humidity. However, this wetness has its good points so far as winter climbers are concerned: oozing water freezes solid. The blue waterfall ice of northern New Hampshire, Vermont and New York is thoroughly tattooed by crampons each year: as with the rock, this is some of the most used ice in North America but also among the continent's finest.

The landscape of the eastern United States is very different in character from that of the West, the area more commonly associated with climbing. Instead of open prairies, massive cliffs and rugged mountains, the East has gentle slopes and hides its climbing gems in a blanket of forest. Autumn is the finest time to visit the mountains of the East, when the forests change from the rich greens of summer to the reds and golds of an artist's palette. The summer humidity and the area's notorious bugs have

disappeared, the air is fresh and invigorating, and the colours are nothing short of spectacular.

Crags are found throughout the Northeast. Most are of granite and several are of world class in terms both of quality and of climbing history: think of the Adirondacks, the North Conway area and Mt Desert Island. But the quartzite cliffs of the Shawangunks are clearly the centre-piece of rock climbing in the East. The band of quartzite-conglomerate, 75m (250ft) high, extends, with interruptions, along 11km (7 miles) of escarpment in the Hudson River Valley. The average angle of the cliffs is just shy of vertical, while numerous roofs jut out horizontally so that at first sight you might think they would completely block your passage – in fact, the rock is so liberally endowed with edges for face climbing that almost every roof can be overcome. The face climbing is good not just on the most difficult routes but also on the easiest. The Gunks are among those extremely rare crags where beginners can taste the clean, solid and exposed climbing normally reserved for experts.

In the Gunks you will encounter many fixed pitons: treat these with suspicion, because many of them are old and the prevalent humidity tends to rust them badly.

The Gunks are most popular from April to June and

from September to November. The high temperatures and humidity can be stifling in July and August. Especially in spring, rain can plague a visit, and insect repellent can literally save your life in late spring and early summer.

There is a small daily charge for hiking and climbing at the Shawangunks, which lies on the private property of the Mohonk Preserve. Keep a few dollars in your pocket to cover this fee, which also includes camping. Most climbers camp in their cars along dirt sideroads near the Gunks, set up tents in a reserved area, or toss out sleeping bags along the base of the cliffs.

ICE CLIMBING

In winter the ice climbing further north is similarly approachable for all enthusiasts. Beginners can pick from low-angle gullies and ice-smeared faces, while experts can tackle vertical candlesticks of ice that plummet from 150m (500ft) cliffs. Approach walks are very mild: most frozen waterfalls can be reached within a few minutes of your leaving your car, with even the longest approaches, to gullies in Mt Washington's Huntington ravine, taking no more than about three hours. This ravine is popular because of its rugged setting: at 1,917m (6,288ft), Mt Washington is the highest point in the Northeast.

Above *The Skytop area of the Shawangunks.*
Left *Eastern ice near North Conway, New Hampshire.*

Cold temperatures keep the ice in shape through most of the winter, although occasional thaws and midwinter rains can swiftly ruin it. The North Conway area of New Hampshire is by far the most popular – its ice is plentiful, the hotel lodging is comfortable and there are nearby equipment stores. If ever winter ice could rival the popularity of summer rock, this is the place for it.

The ice is best between December and March, although the tail ends of the season are variable in quality. Note that, even in the dead of winter, rain is a possibility up here. Hotels are the most popular accommodation option; on popular weekends you need to book in advance.

YOSEMITE VALLEY

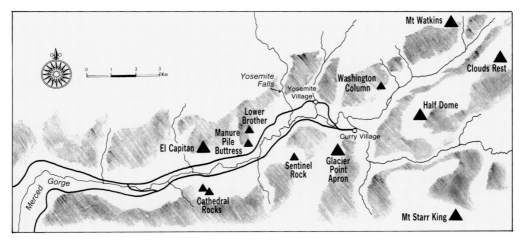

Below left
*Yosemite Valley.
The Half Dome
is clearly visible
(centre
background).*

F ramed by rock monoliths that brightly reflect the intense Californian sunshine, Yosemite Valley is without equal in the rock-climbing world. Its perpendicular walls reach a dizzying 900m (3,000ft) in height as they shoot skyward from the open forests and meadows of the flat valley floor. Even the most jaded world travellers, as they crane their necks to take in the full expanse of rock, find themselves awestruck by what US climbers simply term 'The Valley'.

Yosemite is blessed with incredibly clean and smooth granite, easy access and superb weather. Although the changing trends in ultrahard climbing, towards short face climbs, have taken some of the glamour out of Yosemite's long cracks, 'The Valley' has for decades been the Mecca for anyone serious about the sport. This 11km (7 miles) by 1.5km (1 mile) rock climbers' valley is the object of pilgrims from all over the world. The climbing can be good all year round, although the most popular months are April, May, September and October.

Yosemite reigns supreme in Californian climbing. The sheer scale of its cliffs and its keystone position in climbing history assure its position. Not all climbers, however, come for the 900m (3,000ft) walls of El Capitan, the 600m (2,000ft) face of Half Dome or the miscellaneous other cliffs over 300m (1,000ft): there are also hundreds of short climbs on smaller features and routes that scale only short distances on the big cliffs. Most climbers, no matter how experienced, spend a while on shorter climbs while getting to know the peculiar intricacies of Yosemite's polished granite – and some climbers never bother with the multiple-day excursions and aid climbing involved in tackling the bigger walls, preferring instead to stick exclusively to the short stuff.

Yosemite climbing is dominated by cracks on polished rock with a low friction coefficient. If you are not accus-

Left El Capitan, in Yosemite, has one of the most famous and certainly one of the most impressive rock faces of them all.

Below Eric Perlman pits his abilities against a route at Joshua Tree.

tomed to jamming you need several days – preferably weeks – to learn the skills; tape on the hands helps while you are learning those skills. Because of the uniform size of the cracks it is often essential to take with you a good stock of pieces of the same-sized protection. For the bigger walls, appropriate multiple-day wall-climbing equipment is necessary.

In an area as spectacular as this one must expect crowds – certainly on the valley floor. The historical climbers' ghetto, Camp 4 (officially named 'Sunnyside Campground' – available on a first come, first served basis), has been granted some special rules to help climbers. However, other camp sites – even those outside the National Park – may be more attractive to some visitors. During the summer, these latter have to be booked in advance; for information on them, read the guidebooks (see page 186).

There is a guide service available from the Yosemite Mountaineering School, in Curry Village: it covers both Yosemite and Tuolumne.

With a little care and flexibility in terms of route choices and camping locations, Yosemite will offer you an awesome climbing experience.

TUOLUMNE MEADOWS

Yosemite Valley was carved by glaciers out of the western slope of the Sierra Nevada range. Just above the valley's rim you find subalpine coniferous forests, green meadows and sparkling lakes. Sprouting from this gentle countryside are the amazing granite domes of Tuolumne Meadows. If you have never been to 'The Valley' and want some idea of its wonderful crags, imagine lumpy upside-down bowls – perhaps the rejects from a pottery class – that are 60-275m (200-900ft) tall and polished white by glaciers. Summers in Tuolumne are cool, a relief from the hot summer weather of nearby Yosemite, and the bolt-protected face and friction climbing here are a delightful diversion from the strenuous cracks of 'The Valley'.

JOSHUA TREE NATIONAL MONUMENT

When winter's occasional storms render Yosemite too chilly for taste, climbers migrate south to Joshua Tree National Monument, named after the weirdly shaped yucca plants that dominate the flat, sundrenched Mojave Desert. Scattered over the landscape are coarse granite boulders that reach 60m (200ft) in height; they are laced with crack climbs and studded with face routes.

This area is best between October and April. Guide service is available from Vertical Adventures, Redonda Beach.

ALASKA

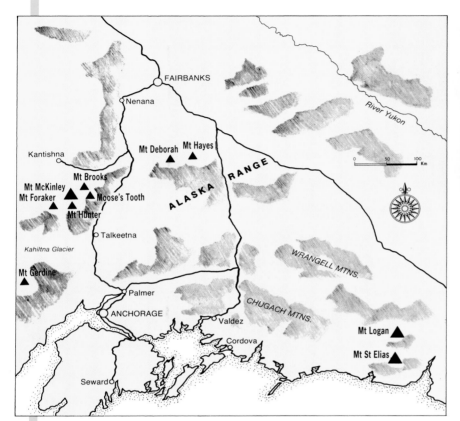

Above *Rob Collister prepares to abseil off a snow mushroom from the summit of Mt Deborah (3,822m [12,540ft]) after the first ascent of its east ridge.* **Right** *A well-established camp on Mt McKinley (6,194m [20,322ft]). To the rear rises Mt Foraker (5,304m [17,402ft]).*

A large proportion of Alaska is mountainous. The Brooks Range in the far north and the Wrangells and Chugachs in the south are relatively low, offering interesting terrain for ski-touring or travelling with dogs. In the east the enormous St Elias Range in the Yukon and the Fairweather Range in British Columbia both encroach into Alaska.

However, the range best known to climbers is the Alaska Range, where Mt McKinley (6,194m [20,322ft]) dominates the landscape, standing head and shoulders above its highest neighbours – Mt Foraker (5,304m [17,402ft]) and Mt Hunter (4,442m [14,573ft]). Altitude is a serious problem – 6,000m on McKinley feels more like 7,000m in the Himalayas; this may be a result of the reduced depth of the atmosphere in the polar regions. McKinley is, in addition, noted for the ferocity of its weather and the Kahiltna Glacier is notorious for crevasses. Although hundreds of climbers annually attempt the mountain by its technically easy west buttress, many fail.

Most of the early climbs in the Alaska Range, even on the lower peaks, were made using siege tactics and a great deal of fixed rope – both on faces and on the long, heavily

corniced ridges that are a feature of the region. More recently, though, the trend has been towards bold and difficult alpine-style ascents on peaks such as Huntington (3,731m [12,240ft]), Dickey, Moose's Tooth (3,150m [10,335ft]) and Rooster's Comb – not to mention, at the east end of the range, peaks like Hayes (4,216m [13,832ft]), Hess (3,668m [12,030ft]) and Deborah (3,822m [12,540ft]).

MT MCKINLEY

By world standards Mt McKinley, although the highest peak in North America, is not especially high ... above sea level, that is. However, no other mountain on this planet towers a full 5,000m (17,000ft) over its base (Everest, for example, rises only 4,000m [13,000ft] above the Tibetan Plateau). Often called by its Indian name, Denali, 'The Great One', McKinley is a magnificent mountain.

McKinley's massive bulk so dominates the range that its surrounding peaks appear as mere foothills when viewed across the flat tundra of the Mount McKinley National Park. Because of its height its weather is dangerous, so that normally peaceful walk-up routes can suddenly be con-

verted into lethal battle zones. Most climbs involve several weeks on the mountain, with long waits in storm-bound camps along the way to the summit. Even in clear weather the temperature can hover around −40°C (−40°F).

Despite the hardships of scale, weather and altitude, climbers swarm in from all over the world to tangle with Alaska's peaks, and in particular with McKinley. The west buttress is the route of choice for 700 or more climbers each year, because it takes a fairly direct and easy line between the Kahiltna Glacier ski-plane landing site and the summit. (Round-trip flights can be arranged with pilots in the village of Talkeetna.) The fact that so many people climb by this route is upsetting for those who come expecting a pristine, frozen wilderness: trailside faeces and garbage-filled crevasses are relatively commonplace. Climbers who thrive on good climbing away from the crowds need only, however, wander away from the most popular routes to find their own space.

The best weather is from late April to early July. As noted, storms are likely, but they usually last only a few days each. However, climbing in the Alaska Range in midsummer can be like midwinter alpinism anywhere else.

You should travel equipped with double boots, a good tent, sleeping bags rated to at least −30°C (−20°F), shovels, sleds and other equipment for surviving a long time in extreme cold. Before starting on any climb you must check in with the Park Rangers at Talkeetna Ranger Station.

Why do the hordes descend on Mt McKinley? A main reason is of course the mountain's pre-eminent position, but in addition there is the fact that on the way to it visitors will discover the wonders of the Arctic landscape, especially if they allow themselves a little time to explore the tundra away from the mountains. Land that seems barren from a distance is, up close, teeming with caribou, fox, grizzly bear, miniature flowers and innumerable species of birds. Early-season climbers will arrive before the tundra wakes up from its winter torpor, but they may be privileged to see the Aurora Borealis as it dances overhead at night. If you bring skis, the Ruth Glacier provides some of the most magnificent summer ski touring and mountaineering in the world.

THE CANADIAN ROCKIES

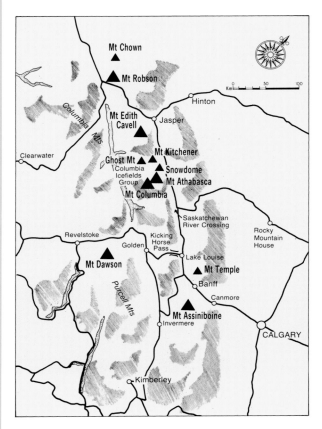

Contained in the Canadian Rockies are some of the finest mountain-climbing challenges in the world. There is something here for everyone, from big alpine north faces to warm summer rock climbs. In addition, there is the winter sport, developed in this region during the 1970s, of climbing frozen waterfalls.

In summer, temperatures can vary from extremely warm during the day to well below freezing at night. You should dress accordingly, and make sure that you are familiar with the sudden changes in weather that are a feature of the Rockies. Because of the possibility of rockfalls, a crash helmet is necessary on all routes. For most of the mountains in the Canadian Rockies, good alpine climbing equipment is essential. If you wish to climb frozen waterfalls, you need modern short ice-climbing tools, rigid boots and crampons; adequately equipped, you can climb vertical and even overhanging ice.

The easiest approach, especially for those coming from outside Canada, is *via* Calgary, which has an airport and a

youth hostel. It is easy to rent a car in Calgary – indeed, because of the distances involved when climbing in the Rockies, a car is almost a necessity. Alternatively, you can catch a bus, train or plane to a centre such as Banff or Jasper. It is best to buy most of your food in Calgary. Mountaineering stores in Calgary and Banff stock all types of rock and ice gear as well as guidebooks, and are a useful source of local gossip and information about conditions.

It would be impossible to describe every good climb in the Rockies, so the peaks described in the next few pages must be regarded as only a brief selection. In addition to the peaks mentioned here, Mt Andromeda (3,444m [11,300ft]) and Mt Edith Cavell (3,363m [11,033ft]) are particularly worthy of note.

MOUNT ASSINIBOINE

Assiniboine (3,618m [11,870ft]) is one of the most famous and most photographed peaks in the Canadian Rockies; it is often called the 'Matterhorn of the Rockies'. It was first climbed in 1901, the ascent being by the southwest face and the descent being by the north ridge. Today the north ridge is regarded as the standard route for both ascent and descent. The north and east faces were for a long time considered to be too difficult to attempt, but in 1967 Chris Jones, Joe Faint and Yvon Chouinard climbed the north face with surprising ease, and in 1977 Raymond Jotterand did the first winter ascent solo on it in only three hours! Nevertheless, the north face is a classic alpine climb, and attracts a number of parties each year. The east face, much more difficult, was finally conquered in 1982 by Tony Dick and David Cheesmond.

You can charter a helicopter from Canmore to fly you to the meadows below Assiniboine. Alternatively, you can walk, cycle or (in winter) ski from Canyon Creek, which is a short drive from Canmore. Most parties base themselves in the Hind Hut, above the headwall. The preferred approach to the hut is up a scramble route which goes up to the right of the prominent couloir that splits the headwall. In good cold conditions the couloir itself gives a fast approach, but it is exposed to falling rock and ice. From the Hind Hut the climbs are approached across the glacier; it takes about an hour to reach the north face and ridge, and about two to three hours for the east face.

As you look up at the mountain from the Hind Hut, the north face is the major face on the right. It is a classic, easy north face which takes most parties about six hours to climb. The route starts up a snow gully on the right-hand side of a pillar on the left of the face, trending up and right from the top of the gully, to finish either left or right of a

Left Mt Assiniboine – nicknamed the 'Matterhorn of the Rockies' – viewed from the meadows. The north ridge runs down towards the camera; the north face is to the right and the east face to the left. **Below** A climber tackling a typical frozen waterfall during winter in the Canadian Rockies.

steep buttress below the summit. Descent is either by reversing your tracks or, better, by the north ridge.

The north ridge bounds the north face on the left. To ascend it you start up the right-hand side to gain the crest and then follow through some steep steps to the summit; the climb takes about five hours. Descent of the north ridge is the best way off the mountain.

To the left of the north ridge is the east face. The climb follows the depression in the middle of the face, deviating only once, at the steep rock band in the centre. This is the most difficult route on Assiniboine, with pitches of grade 5.9 (A2).

MOUNT TEMPLE

Wherever you stand in the town of Lake Louise, the skyline is dominated by the huge mass of Mt Temple (3,544m [11,626ft]) – often referred to, because of its size, as the 'Eiger of North America'. The iced-up north face seems to have few natural weaknesses, and even the

flanking ridges end in rock steps and hanging ice cliffs. The ascent *via* the south and southwest faces, by contrast, is little more than a walk, although care is needed as there have been a number of accidents on these slopes owing to avalanches.

The north face of Temple has always appealed to climbers. Even in high summer, the face gets little sun. There are now five routes and variations on it. If you plan to climb the north face you should drive from downtown Lake Louise to the Paradise Valley parking lot. For the standard route (i.e., the ascent on the south and southwest faces) or a direct ascent of the east ridge you should drive on to the end of the road at Moraine Lake.

The north face is approached by walking from the parking lot along the Lake Annette trail for about two hours until you reach the lake itself. From here it takes a further half hour, straight ahead, to get onto the north face, the most popular route being to follow the central couloir (the Dolphin) up onto the rock headwall. This ascent has

155

sections of hard rock climbing as well as some snow and ice in the lower part. Most parties do the climb in a long day from a camp below the face.

To climb the east ridge direct you begin on the hiking trail leading through the forest between Moraine Lake and the Chateau. After walking for about half an hour, you strike up the slope in the direction of the east ridge, which now forms the skyline to your right. You keep on up until you are at the base of a series of gullies leading onto the ridge crest. You then follow the crest over the Black Towers onto the summit icecap, where you will need to put on crampons for the trudge to the top. The time for the climb is usually about ten hours.

For the standard route, you walk to Sentinel Pass, on the west side of the mountain. From the pass you follow a vague trail up scree slopes towards the ridge that descends from the summit. By crossing some snow slopes and passing through a gap you gain access to the summit slopes and so to the summit itself. The climb is a good one-day round trip from Moraine Lake; the descent is the usual way off the mountain for climbers who have ascended *via* more arduous routes.

MOUNT ATHABASCA

Since the turn of the century one of the premier areas in Canadian mountaineering has. been the Columbia Icefields. From the Icefields/Athabasca Glacier parking lot you find yourself looking almost directly up at the north face of Athabasca (3,491m [11,452ft]): although it was by the north ridge that the mountain was first climbed (1898), the north face is today by far the most popular climb. This route requires competence on snow and ice as well as good mountain judgement. The standard route (used in all descents from the mountain) is by the north glacier. This requires care, because of dangers from crevasses and avalanches.

The north ridge is gained by crossing the glacier below the notch and then climbing up a slope. From here you follow the ridge, some rock and later some snow to the top.

For the north-face and north-glacier routes you walk up the snowmobile tours road for a couple of kilometres (about a mile), leaving the road after you cross the stream which comes from the north side of Athabasca. You then follow the moraine up until you gain the glacier. From the centre of the glacier, for the north-glacier route, you simply pick the easiest line up to the col at its head, and then follow scree and snow slopes to the summit. Descent is by the same route.

In order to climb the north face, you get onto the glacier, as described above, and then veer towards the left, passing either to the right or to the left, depending upon conditions, of the central spur low on the glacier. The face itself has a relatively easy lower section, after which there is a gully through the rock band at the top involving some mixed climbing. All in all, it is a good day's outing.

Mt Andromeda, close by Athabasca, provides good climbing as well.

MOUNT ROBSON

Mt Robson (3,954m [12,972ft]) is the highest peak in the Canadian Rockies. The first ascent, from the south, was achieved in 1913 by Conrad Kain; the mountain's Kain face is named in his honour. The standard route has become the south face, a surprising choice as the climb is threatened by horrendous séracs (ice-cliffs) in more than one place. The route probably attracts people because of the convenience of the hut at its start.

The second classic climb on Robson, the north face, was first done in 1973: Pat Callis and Dan Davis climbed it in a time that is rarely bettered today. The number of ascents of this route have confirmed it as one of the most popular north faces in the Canadian Rockies.

The last major face to be conquered was the Emperor face, to the right of the north face. This yielded in 1978, but has yet to be reclimbed – although a somewhat easier route, rather to the left, has since been climbed.

For the north face you go first to the beginning of Berg Lake, cross the river to the south shore and then go up scree slopes towards the spur that descends between the two tongues of the Berg Glacier. You scramble up the spur to gain the glacier, and then continue to the col between Robson and the neighbouring mountain, The Helmet

(3,414m [11,200ft]). Most parties camp on the west of the col so as to get an early start on the next day. The route follows the centre of the 60° slope, moving right at the top to avoid cornices, and, depending on the season, it may be almost all snow or almost all ice. From camp to camp, assuming a descent down the Kain face, it takes about a day.

The Kain face is at the head of the Robson Glacier, up which it is approached. After reaching Berg Lake you gain the glacier and then ascend it to its head in the Robson Cirque. You begin contouring around to the right until you are on the plateau above the Dome. Most parties camp here so that they can get an early start the following morning. From here you move up towards the bulging ice barrier that comes down from the southeast ridge, which you gain by climbing left of the bulges but right of the rock bands. You then turn right on the ridge and follow it directly to the summit. When descending *via* this route, watch carefully for the point where it is necessary to drop off the ridge. If you choose the correct place, climbing down is easy and should require no abseiling.

The Kain face is best in late summer, although there have been winter ascents. Earlier in the summer there is danger from avalanches. From Berg Lake the climb takes about six or seven hours.

Two views of the Canadian Rockies. **Above left** *The north face of Mt Temple, as seen from Paradise Valley. Mt Temple – nicknamed the 'Eiger of North America' – was first climbed in 1894.* **Above** *The north and Emperor faces of Mt Robson. It was not until 1973 that the north face was climbed; five years later, in 1978, the Emperor face finally yielded.*

GREENLAND AND BAFFIN ISLAND

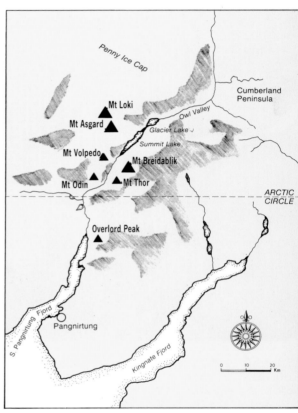

GREENLAND

Greenland is basically an enormous dome of ice 3,000m (10,000ft) high ringed by a rocky mountainous coast. The weather is just warm enough for animals, plants and a human population of under 55,000 to survive. Of its 2,175,600 square kilometres (840,000 square miles), only 341,700 square kilometres (131,930 square miles) are ice-free. As every schoolchild knows, Greenland is the world's largest island.

Although good climbing has been found in the Cape Farewell region in the extreme south and in Peary Land in the north, as well as at several points on the west coast, most attention has been focused on the east coast. The two highest peaks in Greenland – Gunnbjorn's Fjeld (3,700m [12,139ft]), in the Watkins Mountains, and Mt Forel (3,360m [11,024ft]), north of Angmagssalik – are very remote and have been ascended only rarely, despite a number of attempts. Further north, the Staunings Alps received a lot of attention in the 1960s, enough to warrant

a guidebook of their own (see page 186), although recently the Danish authorities have restricted public access to this region.

Expeditions to Greenland are not cheap, because of the cost of travel and the high price of the necessary insurance against the expenses involved should you need to be rescued. There are scheduled air services from Copenhagen to Thule and Søndre Strømfjord on the west coast, and from Iceland to Angmagssalik on the east. Onward flights by light aircraft or helicopter are extremely expensive, and access by boat is strictly limited to the summer months – even then sometimes being impossible because of pack-ice. Transport by dog sledge is available from some of the major settlements.

However, if you can get there, climbing in Greenland is an attractive proposition, with 24 hours of daylight through part of the year, long spells of good weather, immense glaciers sweeping down from the icecap to fjords studded with icebergs, and a true wilderness atmosphere.

BAFFIN ISLAND

Baffin Island, the fifth largest island in the world (507,451 square kilometres [195,927 square miles]), lies to the north of Hudson Bay; its terrain is largely tundra. Like that of Greenland, Baffin's coast is indented by numberless fjords. The whole of the island's north coast is backed by heavily glaciated mountains. The most exciting climbing is to be found in the Cumberland Peninsula, where mountains like Asgard (2,011m [6,598ft]), Thor and Overlord offer granite walls as impressive as those in Yosemite but in far more serious circumstances.

Baffin's weather is at best unsettled, and in summer mosquitoes can be a problem. However, when the sun shines the scenery can be incomparable. Access is by air from Montreal *via* Frobisher Bay to the settlement of Pangnirtung, and from here by skidoo or small boat (depending on season) up the South Pangnirtung Fjord.

The area is a National Park, and permission to climb there must be sought.

Greenland is ringed by mountains that rise immediately from the sea. The biggest island in the world has a vast wilderness of remote mountains. Although access is difficult, a determined expedition will be well rewarded.

AUSTRALIA

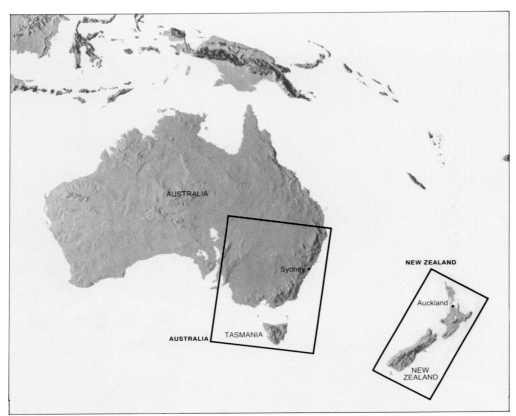

There is little mountaineering of note in Australia, but during the past few years much has been written about Australian rock climbing: fraught with adventure and populated by strange animals, the country has fascinated the world's media. Areas like Mt Arapiles, the Grampians and Frog Buttress are becoming increasingly common destinations on the international circuit – and with good reason. Near-perfect weather all the year round, short approaches and an abundance of great routes have all contributed to this growing popularity. This is truly a rock climbers' paradise.

The system of bolting used in Australian rock climbing may be most charitably described as peculiar. Few bolts are equipped with fixed hangers, a fact that usually brings a shocked look to visitors' faces. On many routes first bolts may often seem dangerously out of reach; prior consultation with a local expert, proficient in the long-stick technique, may very well save your life!

Throughout Australia the Ewbank system of grading is used. This is a numerical system, larger numbers indicating more difficult routes. The system starts at 1 and currently goes up as far as 32.

MOUNT ARAPILES

The area around Mt Arapiles, with nearly 2,000 climbs of all grades, including the bulk of the country's hardest routes, is without doubt Australia's major climbing centre. Spring and autumn are the most popular seasons, since they offer the best weather, but climbing is possible all year round – a proliferation of gullies giving respite from the searing summer sun and open faces providing welcome warmth in winter.

The rock is a solid quartz sandstone and is noted for its absence of cracks but generous supply of small edges. It affords almost unlimited potential for new routes, although good new ones are, as you might expect, rare at the easier end of the spectrum.

Camping is the only form of accommodation at the crag, and facilities are primitive – no toilet block or running water, and the only shade coming from a plantation of dying pines. That said, the advantages are that there are no fees and no petty restrictions! Morning comes abruptly to the camp: first light stirs the myna birds and kookaburras, which erupt into raucous chatter. Even the fervent curses of waking campers fail to drown this racket.

THE GRAMPIANS

A group of crags of enormous variety, the Grampians are close enough to be visible from Mt Arapiles. In fact, this group is an hour closer in the car to Melbourne than is Arapiles, but for some reason has never enjoyed the same popularity and has yet to be properly developed. Certainly their neglect is not due to any lack of fantastic climbing. During the summer – when temperatures at Arapiles can rise to well over 40°C (104°F) – the cooler weather of the Grampians is an added bonus.

The rock is sandstone, although it varies widely in solidity. At its best it is superb, featuring a host of difficult natural lines. At its worst, though, it is atrocious.

Of the crags in the Grampians, Bundaleer is perhaps the most popular and established: what it lacks in stature is

more than compensated for by its atmosphere. South-facing, it presents a sombre and shady aspect which, combined with its bristling overhangs, can intimidate even the most stout-hearted party.

At the left-hand end of Bundaleer there is a large camping cave whose water supply is a seasonally intermittent spring. A stay here adds immeasurably to the 'Bundaleer experience'.

MOUNT BUFFALO GORGE

Mt Buffalo Gorge lies in the Victorian Alps some 300km (190 miles) northeast of Melbourne. Although it is not particularly high, its 1,500m (4,900ft) elevation makes for perfect climbing temperatures in the summer; in late spring and early autumn, however, the weather can be so severe that climbing becomes a frozen nightmare.

The coarse granite offers a variety of different climbing styles, from tenuous slabs and faces to soaring crack-lines and big walls. As a general rule, view all cracks with suspicion: this is no glacier-polished Yosemite (see page 150). The best advice, if you want to keep a few tatters of skin on your fingers, is to regard a jam with the same degree of respect as you would the jaws of a shark. Liberal taping is mandatory. The safest way to ensure a pleasant visit is to stick to arêtes and face climbs.

In the summer the camping is idyllic: the site is on the shores of Lake Catani in the middle of aromatic eucalypt woods. Whatever the time of year you stay here, there is a fee for camping: the sole benefit you receive for this is that you contribute to the salaries of the people employed to collect it. Despite these minor problems, an Australian climber's year seems incomplete if the granite delights of Mt Buffalo have not been savoured at least once.

BOOROOMBA ROCKS
It would be difficult to find a more boring city – from a climber's point of view – than Canberra, Australia's national capital, were it not for the city's one redeeming feature: its proximity to Booroomba Rocks. The granite of Booroomba may lack the grandeur of that in Mt Buffalo Gorge, but nevertheless it offers a wealth of elegant face routes on fine-grained stone. Temperatures are pleasant during most of the year, although snow may fall in winter. Camping is in attractive bushland, near where you have to leave your car; the lack of facilities and running water means that you have to bring everything in with you. From the camp site you can reach the top of the crag with a gentle 20-minute uphill walk.

THE BLUE MOUNTAINS
Melbourne may be Australia's best destination for the purely climbing-minded, but Sydney, the country's biggest city, runs it a close second.

For those with a penchant for adventure, a trip to the local sea cliffs is a must. Walls of flexing rotting sandstone are sculpted not just by the elements but by the decaying urban environment; you can find yourself in one moment floating in a bubble of isolation above the sea and, in the next, mantling into the back yard of an apartment block. All bolts should be treated with extreme distrust, whatever their outward pretensions, and camping is impossible. Still, here you have the chance of creating new routes on blanks of malleable stone – inspired either by the thought of the first person to ascend the cliff or by a nightmare!

The Blue Mountains, also on Sydney's doorstep, may be more to your taste. A night spent in the Imperial Hotel at Mt Victoria can give a welcome respite from camping (although it is not cheap), while good cafés and restaurants can be sampled without shattering your budget.

The Blue Mountains abound in routes of a relatively conservative nature. The area is much like the Grampians (see page 161); there are dozens of different crags. The best established climbing is to be found in the inner mountains, between the townships of Katoomba and Mt Victoria; on crags such as Mt Piddington and Narrowneck the earliest Australian routes were pioneered, and many are still test pieces.

The crags are remarkably alike throughout the mountains: sandstone escarpments boasting, usually, only one pitch. Most of the harder routes tackle bolt-protected faces and arêtes, while the easier climbs follow cracks.

The weather tends to be far from perfect. Winters are usually wet and cold, while summers are invariably hot. An afternoon or two spent by the Blackheath pool does a lot to alleviate the summer conditions, but winters are, quite frankly, best spent elsewhere.

FROG BUTTRESS
Elsewhere could well be southeast Queensland. Far enough north to be almost tropical, Queensland has a winter that, for comfort, rivals a European summer. The standard dress for climbing at any time of year consists of shorts and a T-shirt, although in summer, when the humidity approaches 100%, the T-shirt is likely to double up as a towel.

The classic crag of the area is Frog Buttress. Composed of rhyolite columns up to 50m (165ft) in height, Frog is best known for its continuous crack climbs. More recently, attention has focused on its closed seams and arêtes, with, generally, surprising success. Most routes tend to follow natural lines, and so fixed gear is kept to a minimum. Climbers can no longer camp above the crag – the Park Service has prohibited it for reasons beyond the ken of humankind – and so now you have to camp outside the park boundary.

Left Martin Scheel on 'Dinosaurs Don't Dyno' on Mt Stapylton in the Grampians.

Above Dave Fearnley leading 'Voices in the Sky' (grade 26) on Frog Buttress. **Right** The east face of Frenchman's Cap; this is truly serious climbing.

FRENCHMAN'S CAP

A problem of a different kind, which has to date received scant attention from overseas visitors, is Tasmania's Frenchman's Cap. The face itself is only 400m (1,310ft) high, but a combination of access and logistical problems, some of the worst weather in Australia (over 750cm [295in] of rain per year) and an unpredictable rock type (quartzite) all combine to make for truly serious climbing. To date the east face boasts only three routes, although all of them are difficult. Frenchman's Cap, which is free from snow and ice in the summer, is perhaps the only alpine rock in Australia – which, in a land of heat and dust, makes it a special challenge.

MOONARIE

This important area is situated deep in the heart of the Flinders Range some 400km (250 miles) north of Adelaide. The setting – pine-clad rolling hills – is dramatic and inspirational, and the area enjoys fine, stable weather, with annual rainfall rarely exceeding 40-50cm (15-20in).

The main climbing is to be found on the impressive walls that crown the rim of Wilpena Pound. These walls reach 120m (394ft) high, and present the climber with some powerful and imposing natural lines. Spectacular corners, cracks and chimneys, roofs and intimidating overhangs are the trademarks of this remarkable area. The climbing is generally very steep, but the rock – a fine sandstone – is almost universally sound.

There are climbs of every grade, from the classic 'Nervine', a 115m (377ft) corner climb, grade 11, to routes such as 'Languish in Anguish', a fine grade 25 on the Great Wall. You can camp in the area, but there are no facilities and precious little water. If you plan to camp, you must tell the Park Authorities.

NEW ZEALAND

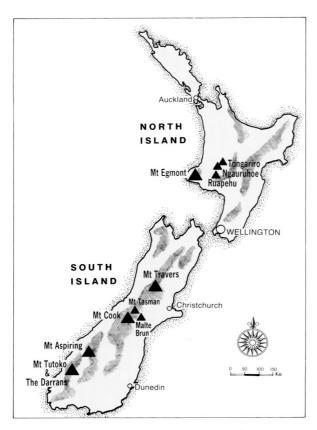

By world standards the mountains of New Zealand are not high, but nevertheless they command respect from even the most experienced mountaineers. There are four main climbing regions: the North Island volcanoes, Mt Cook and Westland national parks, the Mt Aspiring region, and the Darrans.

It is worth noting that a north face in the Southern Hemisphere is equivalent to a south face in the Northern Hemisphere.

Gradings in New Zealand follow the Ewbank system (see page 160) for rock climbing. For alpine climbing a system has been devised running from −1 to 6+; this system is intended to be open-ended.

NORTH ISLAND VOLCANOES

Standing alone in the western corner of Taranaki, the dormant volcano of Mt Egmont (2,518m [8,261ft]) offers a wealth of rock and ice climbing. In the summer months the mountain is virtually free from snow, and excellent rock climbing can be found on a number of bluffs low down on it – Warwick's Castle and Humphries Castle are pre-eminent. Winter turns the mountain into an ice climber's

paradise, particularly within the crater itself, where numerous climbs of all grades are possible. The east ridge, a moderate rock scramble in summer, becomes an exciting climb in winter, the prominent Shark's Tooth providing a fitting climax.

Some distance to the east is the Tongariro National Park, a climbing area consisting of three peaks, Ruapehu (2,797m [9,176ft]), Ngauruhoe (2,291m [7,516ft]) and Tongariro itself (1,968m [6,547ft]). These rise dramatically between the barren wastelands of the Desert Road, to the east, and the luxurious bush to the west. All three are active to some extent, and Ngauruhoe almost continuously emits clouds of sulphurous smoke, making a prolonged stay on the summit somewhat unpleasant. Of the three, Ruapehu has the most to offer the mountaineer seeking thrills on snow and ice. The area called Te Heu Heu gives the best climbing.

The lower slopes of Tongariro offer some rock climbing, but the main haunt of New Zealand rock climbers is an hour's drive to the north – Whanganui Bay, situated on the shores of Lake Taupo. Its climbs tend to be quite short and steep, but are generally solid; there is a variety of grades to suit all climbers. The climate is remarkably warm, and so it is usually possible to climb whatever the time of year.

MOUNT COOK AND WESTLAND NATIONAL PARKS

This is by far the most important mountaineering area in New Zealand, not least because it has as its centrepiece the highest peak in Australasia, Mt Cook (3,764m [12,349ft]) – known to the Maoris as Aorangi ('Cloud-piercer'). This peak is situated on a backbone of mountains, the Main Divide, that stretches some 700km (435 miles) along the length of South Island. The Main Divide's proximity to the sea in the west gives it severe weather patterns not unlike those in Patagonia (see page 166). The summit of Mt Cook is only about 15km (10 miles) from the sea. The prevailing wind comes from the northwest across the Tasman Sea; when it blows you are advised to forsake the mountains in favour of the pub! It is not uncommon for the weather to be very mild for a week or more, leaving in its wake mountains covered in rock-hard green ice.

The rock in these mountains is generally unstable, although good climbing can be found on Malte Brun (3,176m [10,421ft]), Aiguille Rouge (2,911m [9,551ft]), Mt Walter (2,903m [9,524ft]) and the north face of Mt Hicks (3,183m [10,443ft]). The region is noted for its long mixed or ice climbs. The Caroline face of Mt Cook is some 2,000m (6,560ft) long and of a very serious nature. The grand traverse of Mt Cook is a highly recommended outing, beginning in the Hooker Valley and traversing the low, middle and high peaks of Mt Cook to finish at the Plateau Hut, on the mountain's east side. The simplest way

Looking east from a point near the summit of Mt Cook (3,764m [12,349ft]). Behind and below the climber is the icefield of the Grand Plateau, from the right-hand side of which spills the Hochstetter Ice Fall. Still further below is the mighty Tasman glacier.

up Cook is by the Linda Glacier route: though technically straightforward, this climb has a high risk of ice-cliff avalanche.

Near Mt Cook is the second highest peak in Australasia, Mt Tasman (3,498m [11,475ft]). It offers some fine ice climbs, of which the route over the Balfour face is the most difficult. Mt Hicks offers excellent ice climbs on its south face. Mt Douglas (3,081m [10,107ft]) also has a south-face route worthy of attention. The area abounds, too, with fine easy peaks for the less ambitious, particularly the Franz Joseph and Murchison glaciers; as elsewhere in the region, though, glacial travel tends to be rather complex.

Access to these mountains is usually very time-consuming, and it is well worth considering the idea of hiring a ski-plane, especially if the weather forecast is marginal or if you have time only for a short visit. There are plenty of small unguardianed huts, which are adequate except at busy times of the year. You have to register at Park HQ before embarking on a trip. The summer climbing season runs from December to April and the winter season from June to September.

THE MOUNT ASPIRING REGION
This area, about 200km (125 miles) to the southwest of Mt Cook, offers some interesting mountaineering. From the northwest, Mt Aspiring has a Matterhorn-like appearance. Though only 3,027m (9,931ft) high, it is in a remote and serious setting. Other peaks worthy of attention include Rob Roy (2,606m [8,550ft]) and Mt French (2,341m [7,680ft]).

The region has a number of very small, unguardianed huts; parties planning to use them are advised to book in advance through the New Zealand Alpine Club. Throughout the region, huts are quite a long way from the peaks.

THE DARRANS
The Darrans are tucked away in the southwest corner of South Island. They are the main mountain mass in an area called Fiordland, where steep-sided peaks rise sharply almost 2,000m (6,560ft) above sea level. As a climbing area its potential is enormous. Perfect granite walls are in abundance for the summer visitor, and there are 1,000m (3,280ft) ice climbs for the winter connoisseur. The highest peak in the area is Mt Tutoko (2,750m [9,022ft]), and the ascent from Turner's Bivvy of its southwest ridge gives an excellent mixed climb with, for starters, an exciting dawn foray through the Madeline icefall.

Unfortunately, the region's weather is poor: the average annual rainfall is about 772cm (285in), and it is not uncommon for it to rain in tropical proportions for days or even weeks on end. In these conditions the unwary can find themselves unable to move for long periods, hemmed in by swollen rivers it would be too dangerous to cross.

From a base at Homer Hut it is possible to climb on some marvellous peaks. Mts Moir (1,960m [6,430ft]), Talbot (2,120m [6,955ft]), Marian (2,110m [6,923ft]), Sabre (2,170m [7,119ft]) and Barrier (2,050m [6,726ft]) all have first-class rock climbs in inspirational settings. For ascents of the more remote peaks it is necessary to camp or bivouac. Be sure you take some form of well proven weatherproof shelter.

165

SOUTH AMERICA

The Andes form the natural boundary between Chile and Argentina, and are characterized by many isolated volcanoes, such as Tronador (3,470m [11,385ft]) and Llaima (3,124m [10,249ft]). The range's greatest peak is Aconcagua (6,960m [22,835ft]), the highest mountain in the Western Hemisphere, a complicated mountain first ascended in 1897 by the Swiss guide Mathias Zurbriggen, who climbed the easy side. (The mountain is rarely visited: apart from other difficulties of access, it is in an Argentinian military zone.) This region typifies the Andes, as the actual range is very narrow and you can usually get within a day of the base of any mountain by road or dirt track.

The mountains in the cordilleras of Bolivia and Peru are among the most beautiful in the world. The weather and the topography combine to offer snow and ice climbing on steep slopes and narrow ridges. As with most of the Andes, the peaks should be attempted only by experienced mountaineers; there are no rescue services. Particularly important areas include the Cordillera Real (including Illimani, 6,462m [21,201ft]), Vilcanota (including Ausangate, 6,384m [20,700ft]), Vilcabamba/Urabamba (including Salcantay, 6,271m [20,574ft]), Huayhuash (including Yerupaja, 6,634m [21,765ft]), and the most popular, extensive and highest venue, the Blanca.

In Ecuador the character of the mountains changes. Here you find such famous volcanoes as Chimborazo (6,267m [20,561ft]) and Cotopaxi (5,897m [19,347ft]), which provide mountaineering problems concerned more with altitude than with any technical difficulty. In fact, the majority of mountains of interest in Colombia and Central America are the high volcanoes. Though many of the Andes are difficult, the volcanoes of Ecuador and the cordilleras, particularly the Blanca, offer many easier snow climbs for the experienced alpinist who wants to climb outside Europe.

PATAGONIA – THE FITZROY REGION

At the southern end of the Andes, in Argentina, you find one of the world's most impressive alpine landscapes. This area of southern Patagonia is a stormy land with an environment of great contrasts. There are bizarre formations of granite spires, while the character of Fitzroy changes constantly with the weather.

The area is a national park. Access is *via* dirt roads across the pampas from Rio Gallegos, then along the shores of Lake Viedma. Base camps can be as much as a day away from the roadhead. The weather at base is often good, but a few kilometres into the mountains the conditions can deteriorate rapidly, thanks to the ferocious winds from the icecap. These abruptly changing conditions make climbing dangerous and often futile. You should have a barometer (or altimeter) with you: a rise in atmospheric pressure

South America provides the finest challenges in the world outside the Himalayas and Karakoram – with the big advantage that the peaks are much more readily accessible. The vast majority of mountains of interest are in the Andes, a chain stretching some 7,250km (4,500 miles) from Tierra del Fuego in the south to Ecuador and Colombia in the north. As you might expect, weather and climbing conditions vary greatly – as indeed do the characteristics of the mountains.

The steep rock spires of Patagonia offer some of the finest 'super-alpine' climbing in the world; though the weather is appalling, the challenge of the huge granite rock walls attracts many top mountaineers. There are two distinct areas; the Cordillera del Paine in Chile and, 150km (95 miles) north, the Fitzroy region of Argentina. The highest point in the Paine is Cerro Paine (3,050m [10,007ft]), near to which are the famous 'three towers' of Paine.

Left The Towers of Paine in Chilean Patagonia. Here there is some of the finest 'super-alpine' climbing in the world. However, Paine is no climbers' paradise: the weather is as bad as the granite is good. The most spectacular peak, the Paine Grande, was first climbed in 1958.

indicates one of those rare spells of good weather, when you should start to climb immediately; if a drop occurs while you are climbing, bad weather is on its way, and your only sensible course is to descend. Good weather in this area rarely lasts more than three days, yet when the weather is good the area provides some of the best climbing in the world. The best times are midsummer, particularly December and January.

The highest peak of the region is Cerro Fitzroy (3,375m [11,073ft]). There are now more than a dozen different routes on the mountain, and possibilities exist for more. The most popular ascent routes are the Californian 1968 route and the Argentinian 1965 Super Couloir route. All around Fitzroy are superb sharp rock peaks: Aiguilles Poincenot (3,085m [10,120ft]), St Exupery (2,580m [8,465ft]), Mermoz (2,574m [8,445ft]) and Guillamet (2,593m [8,507ft]). All have been climbed, but there are still possibilities for finding new routes.

Just to the west, overlooking the icecap, is Cerro Torre (3,128m [10,262ft]) – arguably the most spectacular peak in the world, with its vertical rock walls, plastered with ice, rising over 2,000m (6,600ft) above the glacier. The peak has a tangled climbing history. In 1959 Cesare Maestri claimed its ascent *via* the northeast face in an epic climb in which his partner, Toni Egger, was killed during the descent. His claim is widely doubted. In 1970 Maestri was back to create a controversial bolt ladder up the southeast ridge using a compressor driven drill. It took many weeks and was a tremendous feat of endurance in appalling

conditions, but was regarded by most mountaineers as a 'murder of the impossible'. Now it is the most popular ascent route! Not until 1974 did an Italian party reach the top from the icecap side, and this is usually treated as the first conquest of the peak.

The surrounding mountains include Torre Egger, Cerro Standhart, Aiguille Bifida and Pier Giorgio. These provide similar mountaineering challenges.

Now that equipment is much lighter and safer, and bad-weather clothing has improved, harder and longer climbs are being attempted and existing routes are being repeated in remarkably fast times. The area has vast potential for the expert climber. Bureaucracy is minimal, although you may meet political problems. Travel *via* Buenos Aires to the south of Argentina is clearly expensive but, once you have bought food in Rio Gallegos, there are few further costs.

PERU – THE CORDILLERA BLANCA

The Blanca is one of the most magnificent mountain ranges in the world. It is roughly 180km (110 miles) from north to south and on average only 20km east to west. In 1975 the area became the Huascaran National Park. It is a paradise for the alpinist, walker and naturalist alike: there are 30 peaks over 6,000m (20,000ft), hundreds of glacial lakes, rivers and waterfalls, and an abundance of flora and fauna.

The area lies in the department of Ancash, on the eastern side of the Santa Valley. In its centre is the large town of Huaraz, used as base by the vast majority of visiting mountaineers. The usual way of reaching Huaraz is to fly to Lima and then ride the last 400km (250 miles) to Huaraz on one of the comfortable daily buses; the journey takes about 12 hours.

There are several reasons why the Blanca is so accessible. The range is very narrow, and all parts are relatively close to roads and small villages. As the Blanca is in the tropics it has a warm climate, so that glaciers rarely extend below 4,850m (15,900ft). Approaches are through beautiful grassy valleys rather than across moraine-strewn glaciers. Finally, many valleys (*quebradas*) traverse the range in an east-west direction from the Santa Valley. These *quebradas* provide ideal routes between 3,800m (12,500ft) and 4,400m (14,500ft) for walkers and climbers. They lead past all the major peaks and give access to the eastern (Amazon) side of the range.

The weather in the region is typically good, especially in the dry season ('winter'); climbing therefore extends from the beginning of May to the end of August, with June and July being the ideal months. Afternoon storms are common, but rarely last more than a few hours and usually are not severe enough to stop climbing; thankfully they are not electric storms. Nevertheless, they can cause problems in the high mountains, and temperatures can drop dramatically at night, so take warm clothing and a good sleeping bag and mats.

The vast majority of the Blanca's peaks are snow-covered, and the challenges are the steep snow and ice faces and narrow, dangerously corniced ridges. Notable features on the faces are the extremely steep flutings brought about by avalanching and differential melting. Rock, when encountered, is generally of poor quality and best avoided. As well as the spectacular steep faces, most

Far left *Cerro Fitzroy, in Argentinian Patagonia. This peak was first climbed in 1952.* **Left** *Dawn on Cerro Torre, arguably the most spectacular peak in the world. There is some controversy over when it was first climbed. Cesare Maestri possibly did it with Toni Egger (who lost his life during the descent) in 1959. The first definite climb to the peak was in 1974.* **Right** *Peru's Cordillera Blanca, a magnificent mountain range.*

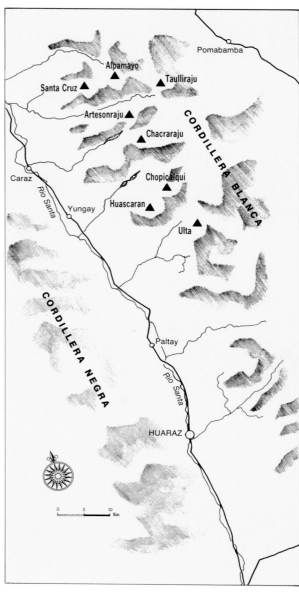

mountains have easier sides which provide simpler snow and glacier routes, similar in difficulty to – although much longer than – the classic snow routes of the Alps. On the easier climbs the equipment required is minimal, but on the harder climbs more specialized snow- and ice-climbing gear (especially ice screws and snow stakes) is mandatory. Climbing can be very insecure on the unconsolidated snow, and belays are often poor, while you have to be wary of avalanches, especially in the surprisingly hot afternoons. Very early starts and night climbing can often make ascents easier and safer.

Slow acclimatization to the high altitude is absolutely essential; impatience to get into the mountains can kill you. Anything above 4,000m (13,000ft) has to be treated with great caution. Force yourself to devote at least your first fortnight in the area to acclimatization.

The highest peak in the Blanca (and in Peru) is Huascaran (6,768m [22,205ft]). The easier north peak was probably first climbed in 1908 by a US woman, Annie Peck, and two Swiss guides, although some dispute the claim. The higher south peak was first climbed in 1932. The first ascent route is a long glacier and snow climb that is the goal of many climbers from all over the world. Huascaran is a complex mountain, and there are many different routes of varying difficulty, the north face of the north peak being particularly steep and difficult.

Among the many other notable mountains in the Blanca are the four peaks of the Huandoy group, rising to 6,395m (20,981ft), Ulta (5,875m [19,275ft]), Chopicalqui (6,345m [20,817ft]), Chacraraju (6,113m [20,055ft]), Artesonraju (6,025m [19,767ft]), Taulliraju (5,830m [19,127ft]), Alpamayo (5,947m [19,511ft]) and Santa Cruz (6,259m [20,535ft]). The nearby Cordillera Huayhuash can be reached by taking a day's drive south (to Chiquian) and then a two-day walk to base. It, too, is well worth a visit – many regard it as even more beautiful than the Blanca, and it has many excellent climbing possibilities.

Anyone who likes the challenge of climbing at high altitude and who is experienced in climbing in an area such as the Alps will find the Blanca ideal.

169

EAST AFRICA

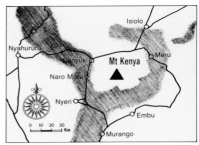

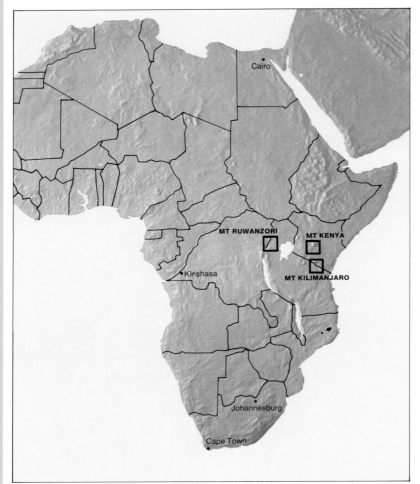

Looking across Hut Tarn to Point John – at 4,883m (16,020ft) one of Mt Kenya's highest and finest summits, with some superb rock climbs. Giant lobelia and groundsel squat in the foreground.

Africa has no range to match the scale of the Andes or Himalayas, but it does boast several isolated massifs, each of which has its own unique atmosphere. There are the High Atlas Mountains of Morocco and, further south in Algeria, the fantastic rock towers of Hoggar, rising out of the Sahara Desert. There are the remote Tibesti Mountains in Chad, the Semien range in Ethiopia, Malawi's forest-clad Mt Malangi and, at the southern tip of the continent, Cape Town's Table Mountain and the Drackensbergs, ringing Lesotho. However, if you are seeking a wide variety of climbing among high peaks in a shortish period (say, a month) you should travel to East Africa – to Kenya, Uganda and Zaire.

Food is very scarce in Uganda, but everything can be bought in Kenya. Try to avoid Ugandan hotels: they are ridiculously expensive. Consult a doctor about inoculations, and check with all three embassies about visas.

MOUNT KENYA

Batian, the highest point of Mt Kenya (5,199m [17,057ft]), was first climbed in 1899 by a team led by Sir Halford Mackinder. It was a remarkable feat for its time: Mackinder's Chimney is still graded IV+, giving many a modern climber an awkward struggle. Nowadays it is usual to follow Shipton's variation, first attaining the slightly lower summit of Nelion (5,188m [17,022ft]) and from there crossing the Gate of the Mists to Batian.

The twin summits crown an eroded volcanic plug. It is a spectacular tower of syenite – a rough rock similar to granite and a joy to climb. Foremost a rock climber's mountain, Mt Kenya has a wealth of excellent routes. The Shipton route on Nelion is the easiest, and is thus the standard descent route; much longer and harder is Shipton's 1930 route *via* the west ridge of Batian. There are numerous face climbs dating from the 1960s and

1970s; they include the Diamond Buttress (grade VI), Eastern Grooves (VI+) and the Scott-Braithwaite route (VI+). Choice of route is affected by the seasons. Mt Kenya lies right on the equator: during the August-September dry season the north side is in summer condition, while the January-February season is best for the rock climbs on the south side.

There are also superb ice climbs on the north side, best climbed during the August-September north-face 'winter'. The Ice Window route has crux moves through an icicle-fringed grotto. The more recent Diamond Couloir is direct, compelling and one of the world's most famous.

Mt Kenya is higher than any European summit. Even its third summit, Lenana, which can be reached by an easy glacier walk, is 4,985m (16,355ft). Acclimatization is essential. The best method is to take time over the approach, exploring the many outlying summits and outcrops and enjoying the mountain vegetation. There are numerous approaches to choose from, the most popular and boggiest being the Naro Moru route, but the eastern Chogoria route probably has the best walking and scenery.

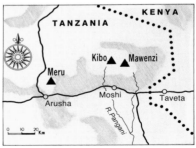

KILIMANJARO

Most mornings during the dry season the summit of Kilimanjaro (5,895m [19,341ft]), the highest mountain in Africa, appears above the clouds as a vast snow-capped dome hanging remote and aloof in the sky. Because no technical skill is required to reach the summit, people often underestimate the mountain's scale. Even the 'normal' route involves rising 4,000m (13,000ft) from the road head if you are to reach Uhuru Peak, the highest point. This route is a very long walk, well equipped with comfortable

Left The Chogoria approach to Mt Kenya. The jagged ridges in the background are typical of Mt Kenya's outlying summits, remains of the original volcanic crater rim. **Right** Kilimanjaro from the Barranco hut: it is still two days' climb to the summit. **Below** McConnell's Prong and Lake Kitandara, Ruwenzori.

the Messner route, which breaks through the Breach Wall by a spectacular giant icicle.

Mandatory fees make climbing on Kilimanjaro expensive. If you want to enjoy the six-day dash up and down the mountain, acclimatize on Mt Kenya, where fees are negligible, before travelling south to Kilimanjaro.

RUWENZORI

In AD150 the geographer Ptolemy wrote of a range he called 'The Mountains of the Moon', a name that conveys perfectly their mysterious atmosphere. The high ridges of Mt Stanley (5,109m [16,763ft]) and Mt Baker (4,843m [15,889ft]) are adorned with weird rime encrustations; walking them is an unforgettable experience. Even during the dry seasons (late December to late February, mid-June to mid-August) intermittent rain is the norm, and the Ruwenzori bogs are famous. Mornings and evenings are usually clear, though, and sometimes the weather remains fine for several days. Be prepared with all the suitable equipment to cope with the weather and you will enjoy your journey through this magical landscape.

The most popular climbs are the normal routes on Mt Stanley's two highest summits, Margherita and Alexandra (5,091m [16,703ft]); the biggest problem might be a whiteout on the Stanley Plateau. The complete traverse of Mt Baker is a more ambitious snow and ice expedition. The steepest ice climbing is on the Zaire side of the range, for which permits are required. No permits are required on the eastern side, but you will probably need a visa to enter Uganda.

huts; the pre-dawn final stage to the summit is very cold. Far more adventurous is the Umbwe route further west, which follows a narrow ridge through dense forest for two days to the dilapidated but scenic Barranco hut. As on Mt Kenya, excellent local porters can be hired, and most will be skilled enough to continue beyond the hut to the Arrow Glacier and Western Breach – a long scramble requiring some proficiency on snow and rock. For something more technical, skirt around east from the hut to one of the long, remote ice routes on the Heim or Kersten glaciers, or to

THE HIMALAYAS

Easily the greatest mountain chain in the world is the Himalayas. They somehow symbolize the loftiest yearnings of the human spirit. It is no accident that many peaks bear the names of Hindu gods or that even more are regarded as sacred by the local peoples. Holiest of all is Mt Kailas (6,714m [22,028ft]) in Tibet, an object of such reverence to Hindu and Buddhist alike that it has never been climbed: one would like to think it never will.

Western climbers, too, give the mountains personalities – but hostile ones, to be assaulted and conquered rather than worshipped. Only recently has a more humble respectful approach become apparent in the writings of climbers such as Doug Scott.

To some mountaineers the figure of 8,000m (26,000ft) has acquired the mystique once accorded to 4,000m (13,000ft) in the Alps. Others prefer the freedom and independence of a small party and the excitement of exploration among the myriad unclimbed lower peaks. Either way, it is now possible – thanks to cut-price international fares and an expanding network of roads built for basically military reasons – to regard a trip to the Himalayas as a climbing holiday rather than a major expedition. Even the élite, interested only in that 8,000m figure, can consider three expeditions a year: two decades ago very few climbers had ascended more than one 8,000m peak, but now at least one man, Reinhold Messner, has climbed all 14, and soon others will equal his feat. In a way, then, the Himalayas have become the new 'Playground of Europe'.

The Himalayas cover a region about 2,500km (1,500 miles) long by 320km (200 miles). The mountains are geologically young, created by the collision of the Indian and Central Asian tectonic plates a mere 50 million years ago. This youth is demonstrated by frequent earth tremors throughout the region, which remind you that this is still a geological frontier zone, and that mountains do not stay the same forever.

Really the Himalayan chain consists of a complex of different ranges. In the west lies the Hindu Kush, spanning the border of Afghanistan and Pakistan; its offshoot, the Pamirs, lies within the USSR. The Hindu Kush culminates in a knot of 7,000m (23,000ft) peaks in the small Pakistan state of Chitral. At its eastern end, north of Gilgit, the Hindu Kush merges imperceptibly into the Karakoram. This great range tails off in the east into the mountains of Ladakh and the high arid plateau of western Tibet. The deep gorge carved by the Indus River, which flows northwest through Tibet and Ladakh before bending south near Gilgit, separates the Karakoram from Kashmir and the main Himalayan chain, which can be said to start with Nanga Parbat (Pakistan), running southeast across northern India – where there are rather lower mountains in Pir Panjal, Kishtwar, Lahul, Spiti and Kulu. Peaks of 7,000m are encountered once more in Garwhal and Kumaon. East again lies Nepal, with many of the world's highest peaks, and beyond that are the little known mountains of Sikkim, Bhutan and Assam.

Much of the Himalayan watershed is also a political boundary between the Chinese provinces of Turkestan and Tibet, to the north, and Pakistan, India and Nepal, to the south. One 8,000m+ peak, Xixabangma (8,046m [26,398ft]) lies entirely within China (or Tibet), and the highest unclimbed peak in the world, Namcha Barwa (7,756m [25,446ft]), is also in Chinese territory. The opening up in recent years of the Chinese side of the watershed has been an exciting development for mountaineers.

SEASONS

Climatically, much of the Himalayan chain is affected by the monsoon rains that sweep up from the Bay of Bengal in early June and continue until late September. They are heaviest and most prolonged in the east, but even in areas like Kashmir and Kulu the rain is persistent enough to render climbing virtually impossible in July and August. An added complication at this time of year is that mountain roads are washed away or blocked by landslides, making access difficult. The ideal is to climb either in April or May, before the monsoon, or in October and November, after it. The latter period offers the better chance of long spells of clear, settled weather, but temperatures are falling and

Trekking in the foothills of the Himalayas can either follow a well beaten path or take in some of the wildest, most far-flung places in the world.

the prevailing strong westerly winds are picking up.

The Hindu Kush is far enough north and west to escape the monsoon, and here the best season for climbing is during July and August. To a lesser extent the same is true of the Karakoram: being both higher and further east, it has a greater chance of being affected by the monsoon. In practice, the weather here is often unsettled, and choosing when to climb is often a matter of taking pot luck. Likewise, regions such as Zanskar, Lahul, Spiti and the north of Garwhal should theoretically, being in a rain-shadow, provide good climbing conditions during the monsoon, but in practice this is often not the case.

All that can really be said is that, as in mountains anywhere, the weather in the Himalayas is rarely good for long. Since success or failure is as often as not determined by the weather, rather than by any human quality, our fortunes lie in the laps of the gods. Perhaps the Hindus are right: one's approach to these mountains should have the nature more of a pilgrimage than of a military expedition.

TREKKING

A recent offshoot of the hill-walking game is trekking. It can be both an exotic and an adventurous pastime. The term really applies to walking in the mountains of the greater ranges without actually climbing the mountains themselves – although some big country can be taken in on a trek. In Pakistan, for instance, a trekking permit allows you to climb peaks up to 6,000m (20,000ft), and there are some fairly ferocious mountains that size in the Karakoram!

The Himalayan nations of Nepal, India and Pakistan are probably the most popular with trekkers; Tibet and Bhutan are also opening up, but are still very expensive. Wherever you are, there are regulations to observe. Generally these restrict the height of peak that may be undertaken on a trekking permit. It is, however, perfectly possible to enjoy fine treks amid stunning scenery without ever setting foot on a summit.

Treks usually follow tracks, paths and trails, although some of these are infrequently trodden and can take the

ardent trekker to some of the most remote places in the world. A good example is the trek to K2 Base Camp at 5,000m (16,500ft), which takes you through the mighty Braldo Gorge and up the Baltoro Glacier – through perhaps the most spectacular mountain scenery on this planet – to Concordia, where mountains crowd on every side, joining the heavens to the earth in dazzling array. Such a trek, which takes the average party about 24 days for the round trip, is a fairly serious and arduous affair, but is becoming increasingly popular.

That is an extreme example – perhaps *the* extreme example. You tailor your trek to match your energy and ambition. A three-day stroll in Kashmir or Nepal can be a most satisfying experience, and the daily distance, at a leisurely stroll, need not be more than about 10km (6 miles). The normal procedure is to hire a porter or two, or in some areas a mule, so that you are relieved of the burden of carrying what you need for a journey lasting several days. The greatly increased enjoyment is usually held to be well worth the extra cost. Some porters will cook for you, too, and if your way lacks inns or resthouses such a luxury will leave you freer still.

Most of the main towns of the Himalayan areas have agencies where you can get information on trekking and the hiring of porters, and they may also be able to sell you suitable equipment. In India or Pakistan, try the nearest office of the Tourism Development Corporation; if in Kathmandu, ask in the tea shops of Ason Tole or try one of the companies that specialize in organized group treks, such as Sherpa Cooperative. If you wish to join an organized group trek you will find plenty advertised in any of the leading outdoor magazines.

Of course, trekking is by no means confined to the Indian subcontinent. There are first-rate treks to be found in most areas of high mountains, especially in South America (Peru in particular), the European Alps, the United States and around African mountains such as Mt Kenya, Kilimanjaro and the High Atlas range.

THE HINDU KUSH

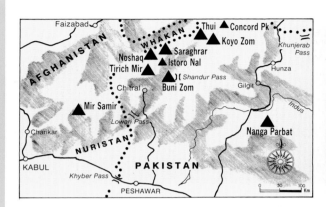

If you fly from Peshawar to Chitral over the Hindu Kush it seems a parched brown wilderness, apparently devoid of life, until, just before you land, the white cone of Tirich Mir (7,700m [25,263ft]) appears floating over the end of the valley. No trees grow here except in a few sheltered *nullahs* and around villages, where they are carefully protected from marauding goats. As in the Karakoram, villages are oases, and life can survive only thanks to extensive irrigation. In the summer there is fresh fruit everywhere. However, for half the year the valleys of the Hindu Kush are snowbound, and there is little for the inhabitants to do but huddle around fires – made from dried dung more often than wood – and indulge in locally produced hashish, opium or mulberry wine.

Access to Chitral from the plains is by air or by a hair-raising jeep-ride; even today, the 110km (70-mile) drive from Dir over the Lowari Pass takes a day. Many of the hairpin bends require even a jeep to make a three-point turn, and it is usual for the driver's mate to jump off and place a stone behind the wheel at each turn, for a brake or clutch failure would prove fatal. Jeeps in the Hindu Kush (and the Karakoram) sometimes carry as many as 20 people, and inclines can be so steep that three or four passengers are deputed to sit on the bonnet to prevent the vehicle performing a back-flip.

On the Afghan side of the border is the Wakhan Corridor, a narrow finger of land some 250km (150 miles) long, diplomatically contrived in the 19th century to prevent the British Raj sharing a common frontier with Russia. Further south lies Nuristan, 'The Land of Light', which gained its name after the forcible conversion to Islam of its Kafir population; only on the Chitrali side of the border have a few Kafir villages survived

Mountaineering in the Hindu Kush started late, when a Norwegian team ascended Tirich Mir in 1950. However, during the 1960s fighting between India and Pakistan put many areas of the Himalayas out of bounds and, with Nepal, too, closed for a while, the Hindu Kush became a

popular goal for small parties of two to four climbers. Air travel was expensive and petrol still relatively cheap, so many took the adventurous overland route. Since the revolution in Iran and the Russian invasion of Afghanistan this has ceased to be a viable option; indeed, Chitral has only just been reopened to climbers after the turmoil caused by the Afghan resistance.

The core of the Hindu Kush lies in a knot of peaks, 7,000m (23,000ft) or more high, in Chitral: Tirich Mir, Saraghrar (7,349m [24,110ft]). Istoro Nal (7,398m [24,271ft]), Noshaq (7,492m [24,581ft]) and the eastern peak of Tirich Mir (7,692m [25,236ft]). Noshaq has the twin distinction of being the venue for the first ski descent of a big peak (by an Austrian expedition in 1970) and of the first Himalayan winter ascent, by a Polish team in 1973, when a temperature of −48°C (−54°F) was recorded on the summit.

Further east is found the Hindu Raj, not really a part of the Hindu Kush but generally considered alongside it. Another area that was discovered late, it contains significant mountains such as Buni Zom (6,551m [21,493ft]), Koyo Zom (6,889m [22,602ft]) and Thui, whose taller peak (6,524m [21,404ft]) was climbed only on the fourth attempt by a British party.

The season for the entire region is July and August.

Left A climber makes his way over the glacier moraine in a typical Hindu Kush valley – dry, dusty and very hot, even at altitudes of 3,000m (10,000ft). This is the dry end of the Himalayan chain.
Right A typically inhospitable campsite in the Hindu Kush, very different from the lush green valleys of Nepal.

KARAKORAM

Below The Karakoram, with the Mustagh Tower at centre. **Right** The huge south face of K2, the second highest mountain on Earth. The ridge on the right is the Abruzzi spur.

The Karakoram is one of the most inhospitable regions on earth. Not only is it the most heavily glaciated region outside the Arctic and Antarctic, its valleys are extremely dry and arid. Gilgit, at the western end of the range, receives a mere 125mm (5 inches) of rain a year, while Leh, at the eastern end, receives still less: 75mm (3 inches). Precipitation is greater at higher altitudes, but on the whole the Karakoram is a mountain desert where little grows naturally.

The name Karakoram, 'Black Stones', comes from the 5,671m (18,606ft) Karakoram Pass, the highest point on what used to be one of the principal trade routes between India and China. It was a notoriously difficult crossing, the final kilometres leading up to its bleak stony summit littered with the skeletons of pack animals that had succumbed to exhaustion, thirst or cold. Even today, approaching the mountains is not easy and sometimes downright dangerous. Villages are few and far between, and there are none of the tea shops and shepherds' encampments that make travel in the main Himalayan chain such a delight. Dehydration is a serious problem, river crossings are perilous, rain can cause catastrophic mud slides, jeep-drivers are fond of pointing out the wreckage of their rivals far below, and some climbers have died through losing their footing on precipitous paths.

Yet the Karakoram exerts a powerful hold on the imaginations of travellers. When the discomfort has been forgotten, memories linger on of the rich glow of reds, ochres and browns in the evening sunlight …

Settlements are usually found on the fertile soil of alluvial fans, and are dependent on water carried from a glacial stream in carefully tended leats – sometimes for miles. Even in the villages, though, beware: as anywhere else in the Himalayas, water cannot be trusted unless it has been boiled or treated, and eating fruit without peeling it or washing it is to ask for trouble.

For walking, a sunhat is essential (some of the locals use umbrellas), and it is wise to wake at dawn and walk only until midday, perhaps moving on in the cool of the evening. Light cotton trousers and a long-sleeved shirt can be useful in case of sunburn, and trainers rather than boots are better for walking until you reach unstable moraine or snow.

Today the Karakoram Pass is well inside China, and so out of bounds, but the Karakoram Highway, built for Pakistan by the Chinese in the 1970s, runs from Rawalpindi up the Indus Valley to Gilgit, and from here through Hunza to the Kunjerab Pass (4,934m [16,188ft]). This road allows easy access to mountains such as Rakaposhi (7,788m [25,551ft]), the Batura group, and formidable, little known peaks like Trivor (7,720m [25,328ft]), Distaghil Sar (7,875m [25,837ft]) and Kinyang Chish (7,852m [25,761ft]), overlooking the Hispar Glacier. Most expeditions prefer to fly to Gilgit and travel from there by jeep, but bad weather can make flight impossible for weeks, so it may prove less frustrating simply to accept an uncomfortable three-day drive in order to reach Gilgit, and you might even opt for the long but interesting approach on foot from Swat or Chitral to the west.

The central portion of the Karakoram contains the enormous Biafo and Saltoro glacier systems as well as, at the head of the Baltoro Glacier, K2 and a collection of other mighty peaks* – Broad Peak (8,047 [26,401ft]) and the Gasherbrum group (up to 8,068m [26,470ft]). K2, also known as Godwin Austen and Qogir Feng, is at 8,611m (28,250ft) the second highest mountain in the world, and is widely regarded by climbers as even more hostile than Everest. The Abruzzi spur on the southeast is the easiest route, and was first ascended by an Italian team in 1954. The northeast ridge was climbed by a US expedition in 1978.

This region is most easily approached by flying to Skardu where, once again, waiting is often the name of the game. It can be reached by jeep from Gilgit; the shorter and more logical route south to Kargil and over the Zoji Pass is now impossible because of the tense territorial dispute between China, Pakistan and India over the area of the Rimo and Saser Kangri groups.

NEPAL

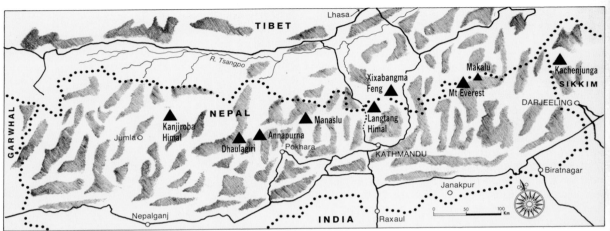

Right The Annapurna Himal, home of numerous excellent peaks, including 11 that exceed 7,000m (23,000ft).

To the general public and to many climbers Nepal *is* the Himalayas. Here are eight of the world's 14 peaks over 8,000m (26,250ft), and a host of others that are not much lower. And, of all the Himalayan nations, it is Nepal that has cashed in most effectively on the tourist boom of the late 20th century: it is as easy to book a package tour to the Everest Base Camp as to book a ski holiday in Switzerland, and not much more expensive. Yet ironically Nepal was the last of the Himalayan countries to open its frontiers to foreign climbers. During the 1920s and 1930s five successive expeditions to Everest had to take the long and circuitous route through Tibet, itself then normally closed to foreigners.

Above Mt Everest, the highest mountain on Earth at 8,848m (29,028ft). Nuptse (7,879m [25,726ft]), rises in the foreground.
Right Steep ice on Jannu (7,902m [25,925ft]).

One of the first expeditions to be allowed in was a French one led by Maurice Herzog, in 1950. The French explored the approaches to Dhaulagiri, but instead eventually climbed Annapurna I (8,078m [26,504ft]), the first 8,000m peak to be climbed – only to be involved in a harrowing descent graphically described by Herzog in one of the classics of mountaineering literature (*Annapurna* [1953]). A flood of expeditions followed, resulting in the so-called 'Golden Age' of Himalayan climbing. By 1960 virtually every major peak in Nepal had been climbed, and soon most obvious ridges had likewise succumbed. Since 1970 – the ascent of Annapurna's south face was a pivotal climb – the trend, as in the Alps 40 years earlier, has been to seek new routes on ever steeper and more formidable faces. Winter ascents, too, are now in vogue. In these developments, climbers from the United States, Japan, Poland, Czechoslovakia and Yugoslavia – all but excluded from the 'Golden Age' – have been playing an important role. Meanwhile, each year a steady stream of expeditions climbs the normal routes on the prestigious 8,000m peaks, while Everest (8,848m [29,028ft]) – called by the Tibetans Chomolungma ('Goddess Mother of the World') – continues to exert a curious and often fatal fascination, booked up by expeditions for 10 years in advance. Recent claims that K2 might in fact be the higher mountain must have caused consternation in Kathmandu!

The ascent of Everest in 1953 by Edmund (later Sir Edmund) Hillary and Sherpa Tenzing Norgay, as part of an expedition led by Colonel John (later Lord) Hunt, was one of the great events of mountaineering history. Well over 100 climbers have since reached the summit, a number travelling solo and a few travelling solo without oxygen equipment; the first woman to reach the summit did so in 1975. The other side of the coin is that at least 50 climbers have died in the attempt – which in percentage terms is not quite as bad as Annapurna, where the number of deaths approximately equals the number of people who have attained the summit, but is nevertheless a gloomy figure.

The great charm of trekking or climbing in Nepal is the country's cultural and geographical diversity. For example, the roadhead for the 7,000m (23,000ft) Langtang peaks is Trisuli Bazar, a mere 450m (1,500ft) above sea level, where bananas grow beside the road and monkeys swing in the trees. As you gain height, different seasons are encountered almost every day. The landscape is marvellously varied, with bewildering numbers of unfamiliar birds and plants in each of the different habitats. However, soil erosion is a major problem in some areas thanks to overcropping of the forests, and so expeditions are required to bring their own fuel.

The climbing seasons are April/May and October/November.

THE INDIAN HIMALAYAS

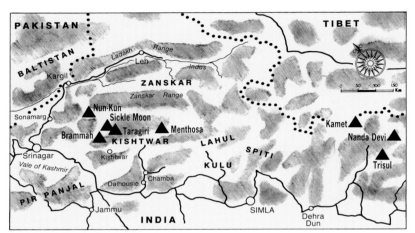

Right *Nanda Devi (7,817m [25,646ft]), the highest mountain in India, seen from the Changabang glacier. The secret of the passage into this great cirque was discovered by Shipton and Tilman in 1934. Recently, environmental damage caused by climbing expeditions has forced the Indian authorities to ban foreigners from the area.*

In some ways the mountains of northern India are the most attractive of all in the Himalayas. Perhaps it is because their pine forests and flowery meadows are reminiscent of the European Alps; perhaps it is because their lower altitude allows you to enjoy climbing among them while you are actually doing so, rather than in retrospect.

With the exception of Nun-Kun (7,135m [23,409ft]) and Pinnacle Peak (6,952m [22,808ft]), the mountains north of the Vale of Kashmir are small: from the turn of the century they were enjoyed for both climbing and skiing by British schoolteachers, missionaries and army officers. Today Gulmarg boasts India's only ski resort, and ski-mountaineering by both Indian and European parties is on the increase.

The more spectacular peaks of Kishtwar, however, were unvisited by mountaineers until 1947, when two Austrians who had been interned in India for the duration of World War II explored and climbed them in an impressively frugal and energetic fashion. After that, the area was virtually ignored until the late 1960s, when a series of expeditions from Cambridge University opened the eyes of other climbers to the potential of the area. Since then a number of hard routes have been climbed and much of the area has been explored. Development concentrated initially on the Brammah peaks (up to 6,416m [21,050ft]) in the west, working gradually eastward towards the Barnaj and Hagshu groups. The highest peak in Kishtwar, Sickle Moon (6,575m [21,572ft]), is a formidable mountain that has been climbed only once, in 1975, by an Indian team.

Like Kashmir, Kulu was a favourite stamping-ground for officers of the Raj looking for a mountaineering holiday rather than an expedition. During the 1960s it was one of the few parts of India to be accessible to foreigners, and a large number of small British parties visited the area. Although some hard climbs have been achieved on peaks of the order of 6,000-6,600m (20,000-21,300ft) in height, eminently suited to alpine-style tactics, the region seems currently to be out of fashion.

Garwhal is the present focus of attention of small parties looking for technically hard climbing. Climbing has a long history here. Trisul (7,120m [23,360ft]) was climbed as early as 1907, when Tom Longstaff with his guides, the brothers Brocherel, went from 4,875m (16,000ft) to 7,000m (23,000ft) and back again in a single day. Kamet (7,756m [25,447ft]) was first attempted in 1910, but succumbed only in 1931. The magnificent cirque of the Nanda Devi Sanctuary (7,817m [25,646ft]) has attracted climbers ever since Shipton and Tilman found a way up the Rishi Ganga in 1934. In recent years, following the discovery of a US satellite-tracking device on Nanda Devi and concern about environmental damage, the Sanctuary has been closed to foreigners, and so instead attention has switched to the sheer granite walls of peaks like Shivling (6,543m [21,467ft]) and the Bhagirathis (up to 6,500m [21,325ft]).

To the north of Kishtwar and Kulu lie Zanskar, Lahul and Spiti, all geographically and culturally Tibetan although politically parts of India. Travelling in these areas gives a glimpse of what Tibet itself must have been like before the Chinese destroyed the monastic system. The mountains here are generally lower than on the other side of the watershed, but there are some fine peaks in remote settings to be enjoyed by small parties travelling light.

East of Nepal, at the wettest end of the Himalayas, lie the

three small states of Sikkim, Bhutan and Assam.

Sikkim used to be well known to climbers. All the early attempts on Kanchengunge (8,600m [28,215ft]) were made from this side, and, even before World War I, A. M. Kellas was making remarkable lightweight ascents of peaks in the height-range 6,500-7,000m (21-23,000ft). Since the Chinese invasion of Tibet in 1950, however, access has been restricted.

Bhutan has never been easy to get to, although over the years a few travellers have been invited in. In 1937, for example, Chomolhari (7,314m [23,996ft]) was climbed by Spencer Chapman. However, determined to learn from Nepal, the Bhutanese have started to allow westerners into the country – but on their own terms. Tourists are allowed to visit Thimphu, the capital, but only in organized groups which must spend a stipulated amount of foreign currency each day. In the last few years, climbing expeditions have been admitted, but their numbers are strictly limited and the price is not low.

Between East Bhutan and Namcha Barwa, in Tibet, lies Assam, one of the most inhospitable and least known mountain areas in the world. The humid, unhealthy forests of Assam have always had a reputation for being wild and lawless, and many early explorers of the Tsangpo River perished at the hands of head-hunting tribes. The Naga tribesmen are still a thorn in the flesh of the Indian authorities; of the even wilder Abors in the far north they seem to have despaired completely! It is not surprising that the Tsangpo Gorge has yet to be fully explored.

The climbing seasons for the Indian Himalayas are April/May and October/November.

GUIDEBOOKS AND MAPS

THE BRITISH ISLES
The North of England
- Series published by the Fell and Rock Climbing Club covering the Lake District: *Great Langdale*; *Buttermere and Eastern Crags*; *Scafell, Dow and Eskdale*; *Borrowdale*; *Great Gable and Pillar Rock*
- *Rock Climbing in the Lake District*, G. Cram (Constable)
- *Winter Climbs in the Lake District*, Bob Bennett and Bill Birkett (Cicerone)
- British Mountaineering Council series covering the Peak District: *Stanage Millstone*; *Chew Valley*; *Staffordshire Area*; *Derwent Gritstone*; *Derwent Valley*; *Limestone (Stoney Middleton Area)*; *Limestone (Chee Dale)*; *Limestone (Matlock, Dove Dale and Manifold)*; *Dark Peak*
- *Bleaklow Area*, Paul Nunn (Climbers' Club)
- *Yorkshire Limestone*, Graham Desroy (Yorkshire Mountaineering Club)
- *Yorkshire Gritstone*, Eddie Lesniak (Yorkshire Mountaineering Club)
- *Rock Climbs in Lancashire and the North West*, Les Ainsworth (Cicerone)
- *Northumberland*, Norman Houghton (Northumbrian Mountaineering Club)
- *Northern England*, Stew Wilson and Ron Kenyon (Cordee)

The best maps for the Lake District are produced by the Ordnance Survey in the 1:25,000 series – 'Outdoor Leisure' maps nos. 4, 5, 6 and 7. Less comprehensive is the 1:50,000 series – 'Landranger' series nos. 89, 90, 96 and 97.

For the Peak District as a whole there is the one-inch Ornance Survey tourist map. The 'Outdoor Leisure' maps 1 (Dark Peak) and 24 (White Peak) are the best. For the Yorkshire Dales there are the 'Outdoor Leisure' maps 2, 10 and 30 and the 'Landranger' maps 98, 99, 103, 104 and 110.

The South of England
- *Swanage*, Gordon Jenkin (Climbers' Club)
- *Wye Valley*, John Wilson, Dave Hope, Matt Ward and Tony Penning (Climbers' Club)
- *Avon and Cheddar*, Richard Broomhead and Martin Crocker (Climbers' Club)
- *South Devon and Dartmoor*, Pat Littlejohn and Pete O'Sullivan (Cordee)
- *Southern Sandstone*, Tim Daniells (Climbers' Club)
- *Cornwall (West Penwith)*, Pete O'Sullivan (Climbers' Club)
- *North Cornwall*, Pete O'Sullivan and Bob Moulton (Climbers' Club)
- *Lundy*, Gary Gibson (Royal Navy Mountaineering Club)
- *North Devon and North Cornwall*, Iain Peters (Climbers' Club)
- *South West Climbs*, Pat Littlejohn (Diadem)

For Swanage use the Ordnance Survey 'Outdoor Leisure' map no. 15 (Purbeck) or the 'Landranger' map no. 195 (Bournemouth and Purbeck). For the South West the 'Outdoor Leisure' map no. 28 of Dartmoor is useful, as are maps 171, 172, 182, 192 and 201 in the 'Landranger' series. The Torbay region is covered by 'Landranger' map no. 202 (Torbay and South Dartmoor) and 'Outdoor Leisure' map no. 20. The 'Landranger' map 180 covers Lundy, while nos. 180, 190 and 200 cover North Devon and North Cornwall.

Scotland
- Scottish Mountaineering Club publications: *Glencoe and Etive*; *Lochaber and Baderoch*; *Skye*; *Arran*; *Ben Nevis*; *Arrochar*; *Northern Highlands Volume 2*; *Creag Dubh and Craig a Barns*; *Climber's Guide to the Cairngorms*; *Northeast Outcrops of Scotland*; *Climber's Guide to Central and Southern Scotland*
- *Scottish Climbs*, Hamish McInnes (Constable)
- *Scottish Winter Climbs*, Hamish McInnes (Constable)
- *Winter Climbs in the Cairngorms*, John Cunningham (revised by Allen Fyffe) (Cicerone)
- *Winter Climbs in Ben Nevis and Glencoe*, Ed Grindley (Cicerone)

The Ordnance Survey's 'Outdoor Leisure' maps nos. 3 and 8 cover, respectively, Aviemore and Cairngorm, and the Cuillin and Torridon Hills. There are tourist maps for Glencoe and Ben Nevis and for Loch Lomond and the Trossachs. Numerous maps in the 'Landranger' series are of use; the best bet is to look at the grid on the back of any one of them and select the map(s) you need for a particular expedition.

Wales
- A series of rock-climbing guidebooks to the area is published by the Climbers' Club: *Clogwyn Du'r Arddu*; *Lliwedd*; *Tremadog*; *Gogarth*; *Llanberis Pass*; *Ogwen*; *Carneddau*
- *Rock Climbing in Wales*, Ron Jones (Constable)
- *Snowdonia Rock Climbs*, Paul Williams (Extreme)

184

- *Dolegellau Area,* John Sumner (West Col)
- *North Wales Limestone,* Andy Pollitt (Dark Peak)
- *Winter Climbs in North Wales,* Rick Newcombe (Cicerone)
- *Gower and Southeast Wales,* Mike Danford and Tony Penning (South Wales Mountaineering Club)
- *Pembroke,* Jon de Montjoye, Mike Harber (Climbers' Club)
- *Lleyn Peninsula,* Trevor Jones (Climbers' Club)
- *Aran and Caderidris,* John Sumner (West Col)
- *Clwyd Limestone,* Stuart Cathcart (Cicerone)
- *Central Wales (Omnibus Guide),* John Sumner (West Col)

The best maps for North Wales are the Ordnance Survey 'Outdoor Leisure' maps nos. 16, 17 and 18. A more general picture is given by the 'Landranger' maps nos. 115, 116, 124 and 125.

For the Gower Peninsula use 'Landranger' map no. 159; for Pembroke 'Landranger' maps nos. 157 and 158; for Anglesey 'Landranger' map no. 114.

Ireland
- FMCI (Federation of Mountaineering Clubs in Ireland) publications: *Mournes; Twelve Bens; Fairhead Antrim Coast; Donegal; Dalkey Quarry; Bray Head; Burren; Wicklow*
- *Rock Climbing in Ireland,* C. Torrans (Constable)

THE ALPS
- *The Alps,* Ronald Clark (Weidenfeld and Nicolson)
- *The Alps from End to End,* Martin Conway (first published 1895)

Any good map of Europe will indicate the chief mountain areas.

MONT BLANC
- *Mont Blanc,* L. Griffin and Robin Collomb (3 vols, West Col)

The IGN 1:25,000 series sheets 231 and 232 are the recommended maps.

THE PENNINE ALPS
Pennine Alps, Robin Collomb (3 vols, West Col)
High Level Route, Eric Roberts (West Col)

Maps from two series are useful. First are the Swiss 1:50,000 ski series (blue covers), with routes marked in

red. The relevant sheets are 282 (Martigny), 283 (Arolla) and 284 (Zermatt). Maps of the Swiss 1:50,000 large-format series are good, too. The sheets are 5,006 (Mont Blanc – Grand Combin) and 5,003 (Matterhorn Mischabel).

THE BERNESE OBERLAND
- *The Bernese Oberland,* Robin Collomb (West Col)

Use either the large-format map 5,004 (Bernese Oberland) or the small-format maps 254 (Interlaken) and 264 (Jungfrau).

SCANDINAVIA
- *Walks and Climbs in Romsdal,* Tony Howard (Cicerone)
- *Mountain Holidays in Norway,* Per Praag (Norway Travel Association)
- *'Ice Climbing in Norway',* Steve Hellmore (*Mountain Magazine,* no. 113)
- *East Jotunheimen* (Jotunheimen Fjeu Club)
- *Rock Climbing in Norway* (Norway Travel Association)
- *Rock Climbing in Lofoten* (Norway Travel Association)

For Sweden use the 1:50,000 and 1:100,000 maps published by Liberkartor in cooperation with the Swedish Touring Club and the National Land Survey of Sweden. Norwegian maps are available from Torsk Tindeklub (Post Boks 1,727, Vika, Oslo 1) or from Der Norsk Turistforening (Post Boks 1,963, Vika, N-0125, Oslo 1).

FRANCE
- *French Rock Climbs,* Pete Livesey (out of print but possibly available from Cordee)

Cordee have several walking guides to France. French guidebooks are usually topo, and can be found in the sports shops in each local area. All are available from Aux Vieux Campeur, 48 rue des Acoles, 75009 Paris.

The IGN 1:25,000, 1:50,000 and 1:100,000 maps are similar in detail to the British Ordnance Survey maps of the same scales.

THE GERMANIES AND CZECHOSLOVAKIA
- *Kletterführer Schwäbische Alb,* vol. 3, A. Pasold and G. Junker
- *Pískovcové Skály V Cechách* (several volumes), Karel Smid (not available in UK)

SPAIN

Spanish guidebooks, often topo, are available in the sports shops of each area. Readers should also refer to issues 112-15 of *Mountain Magazine*.

Spanish maps are stocked by West Col. The Mapas Militares are of similar standard to those of the Ordnance Survey in Britain.

ITALY

There are at present no guidebooks available in Britain. *100 Best Climbs in the Dolomites*, with Italian text and topo diagrams, is available in sports shops (sometimes bookshops) within the Dolomites. Topo guidebooks for all limestone areas are available locally.

UNITED STATES OF AMERICA

The American Alpine Journal, published annually, is a fine source of reference. UK readers can find this at The Alpine Club Library, London, and The Alan Rouse Collection at Sheffield Central Library. It is worth trying other specialist libraries.

The Tetons
● *A Climber's Guide to the Teton Range*, Leigh Ortenburger (published by the author)

Boulder, Colorado
● *The Climber's Guide to North America: Rocky Mountain Rock Climbs*, John Harlin (Chockstone)
● *Lumpy Ridge: Estes Park Rock Climbs*, Scott Kimball (Chockstone)
● *High Peaks*, Richard DuMais (published by the author)
● *Rocky Heights: A Guide to Boulder Free Climbs*, Jim Erickson
● *Boulder Climbs: A Pictorial Guide to Boulder Climbs*, Richard Rossiter (published by the author)

Mount Rainier
● *Cascade Alpine Guide: Columbia River to Stevens Pass*, Fred Beckey (The Mountaineers)
● *Cascade Alpine Guide: Rainy Pass to Fraser River*, Fred Beckey (The Mountaineers)

The Northeast
● *The Climber's Guide to North America: East Coast Rock Climbs*, John Harlin (Chockstone)
● *Shawangunks Rock Climbs*, Richard C. Williams (American Alpine Club)

● *An Ice Climber's Guide to Northern New England*, Rick Wilcox (International Mountain Equipment, Inc.)

Yosemite Valley
● *The Climber's Guide to North America Volume 1: West Coast Rock Climbs*, John Harlin (Chockstone)
● *Yosemite Climbs*, George Meyers and Don Reid (Chockstone)
● *Rock Climbs of Tuolumne Meadows*, Don Reid and Chris Falkenstein (Chockstone)
● *Joshua Tree, A Rock Climbing Guide*, Randy Vogel (Chockstone)

THE CANADIAN ROCKIES
● *Rocky Mountains of Canada, South and North*, Alpine Club of Canada/American Alpine Club
● *The Canadian Rockies Trail Guide*, Brian Patton and Bart Robinson
● *High and Dry, Alpine Huts in the Canadian Rockies*, Murray Toft
● *The Polar Circus*, Summit Publishing, Calgary
● *Mount Robson Park*, British Columbia Provincial Park Service

The Canadian Alpine Club is always worth referring to. It can be found in the usual specialist libraries.

Maps for all areas in Canada are produced by the Department of Energy, Mines and Resources. Copies may be purchased from equipment stores, from Geological Survey Maps and Publications (look under 'Government of Canada' in the Calgary telephone book) and from Carter Mapping in Calgary. Specific map numbers are as follows: Assiniboine, Map 82 J/13; Temple, Map 82 N/8; Athabasca, Map 83 C/3; Andromeda, Map 83 C/3; Edith Cavell, Map 83 D/9; Robson, Maps 83 E/2 and E/3.

ALASKA
● *Mt McKinley Climber's Handbook*, Glenn Randall (Genet Expeditions)

Mt McKinley Map, created by Bradford Washburn, is available from the United States Geological Survey, Western Region, in Menlo Park, California.

GREENLAND
● *Staunings Alps – Greenland* (Gastons, Westcol)
● *Greenland*, Mike Banks (David & Charles)

AUSTRALIA AND NEW ZEALAND
- *Arapiles*, Kim Carrigan (Victoria Climbing Club)
- *Grampians*, Chris Baxter (Victoria Climbing Club)
- *Blue Mountains – Cosmic County*, Andrew Penny (Climbing Club of New South Wales)
- *Blue Mountains – Mount Piddington*, Andrew Penny (Climbing Club of New South Wales)
- *Frenchman's Cap*, Phil Robinson (Climbers' Club of Tasmania)
- *Moonaries*, Tony Barker and Quentin Chester (Climbing Club of South Australia)
- *The Mount Cook Guidebook*, Hugh Logan (NZAC)
- *Whanganui Rock*, Len Gilman (NZAC)

Also recommended are *Classic Climbs of Australia* by Joe Friend, *Land of Mountains* by Peter Radcliffe, and *Wild New Zealand* published by Reader's Digest. Maps of New Zealand are published by the New Zealand Lands and Survey Department.

SOUTH AMERICA
- *Mountaineering in the Andes – A Source Book for Climbers*, Jill Neate (Expedition Advisory Centre, Royal Geographical Society)
- *Yuraq Janka*, John F. Ricker (Cordee)

EAST AFRICA
- *Mountain Club of Kenya Guide to Mt Kenya and Kilimanjaro* (Ian Allan, West Col)
- *East Africa – International Guide*, Andrew Wielochowski (West Col)
- *Guide to the Ruwenzori*, D. Pasteur and H.A. Osmaston (West Col)
- *Mountains of Kenya*, Peter Robson (West Col)
- 'Mount Kenya', Andy Hyslop and Bill Ruthven (*Climber and Rambler*, March 1982)
- 'Kilimanjaro', Graham Donnan (*Climber and Rambler*, April 1985)

Maps are available from West Col. There are five covering Kenya as well as one for Kilimanjaro, one for Mt Elgon and two for Ruwenzori. Also, the map room of the Royal Geographical Society has a good collection of relevant maps.

THE HIMALAYAS
- *The Trekker's Guide to the Himalayas and Karakoram*, Hugh Swift (Hodder and Stoughton)

The best maps are at a 1:50,000 scale. However, all good maps to the Himalayas are, for military reasons, regarded as classified information, and are available only on loan from expedition liaison officers.

INDEX

Page numbers in *italics* indicate the sites of relevant captions.

189

190

ACKNOWLEDGEMENTS

Quarto Publishing would like to thank the following for supplying photographs: J. Allen, John Barry, Kim Carrigan, David Cheesmond, Rob Collister, Jim Curran, Roger Durban, Paul Forrester, Mick Fowler, Simon Fraser, Pete Gomershall, Steve Gorton, Brian Hall, John Harlin III, Karrimor International Ltd, Steve Long, Des Marshall, Roger Mear, Nigel Shepherd, Dick Turnball, Stephen Venables, Peter Weibel, Mike Woolridge.

Diagrams were drawn by Malcolm Campbell (Wind Chill Factor), Roger Durban, Mick Hill and Vana Haggety.

All maps by Malcolm Couch.

USEFUL ADDRESSES

The International Mountaineering
and Climbing Federation (UIAA)
Postfach CH - 3000 Bern 23
Switzerland
Tel: +41 (0)31 3701828

The American Alpine Club
710 Tenth Street, Suite 100
Golden, CO 80401
United States of America
Tel: +1 303 384 0110

Austrian Alpine Club
Wilhelm-Greil-Straße 15
A-6010 Innsbruck
Austria
Tel: +43 (0)512 59547

French Mountaineering Federation
8-10, quai de la Marne
75019 Paris
France
Tel: +33 (0)140 187 550

German Alpine Club
Von-Kahr-Str. 2-4
8097 Munich
Germany
Tel: +49 (0)89 140030

Italian Sport Climbing Federation
Via del Pilastro 8
40127 Bologna
Italy
Tel: +39 (0)51 6333 357

Swiss Alpine Club
Monbijoustrasse 61, Postfach
3000 Bern 23
Switzerland
Tel: +41 (0)31 370 1818

British Mountaineering Council
177-179 Burton Road
Manchester
M20 2BB
UK
Tel: +44 (0)870 010 4878

Expedition Advisory Centre
Royal Geographical Society
1 Kensington Gore
London
UK
SW7 2AR
Tel: +44 (0)20 7591 3030

The Mountaineering
Council of Scotland
The Old Granary
West Mill St
Perth
Scotland
PH1 5QP
Tel: +44 (0)1738 638227

The Alpine Club
55 Charlotte Road
London
UK
EC2A 3QF
Tel: +44 (0)20 7613 0755

Mountaineering Council of Ireland
House of Sport
Longmile Road
Dublin 12
Republic of Ireland
Tel: +353 0001 4507376